THE JOYFUL COOK'S GUIDE TO HEAVENLY GREEK CUISINE

Georget Photos

W. R. PARKS
Hershey, PA

"He prepares the earth for His people and sends them rich harvests of grain.
…He crowns it all with green, lush pastures in the wilderness; hillsides blossom with joy.
The pastures are filled with flocks of sheep, and the valleys are carpeted with grain.
All the world shouts with joy and sings."

Psalm 65

Dedicated To:
The saintly Joyous Cook who
was with me during the preparation,
cooking and presentation of these recipes.

ISBN: 978-0-88493-033-4

Library of Congress Control Number: 2016942618

William R. Parks
Hershey, Pennsylvania
WRParksPublishing@gmail.com
www.WRParks.com

CONTENTS

ACKNOWLEDGMENTS

To my departed parents, James and Carry Kontos, who gave me my rich Greek heritage, a legacy of cooking, a love for learning and creating. To my departed sister, Shirley Kontos, iconographer and artist, for making me aware of my creative cooking talents and directing my goals. To my father and mother–in-law, Fred and Sophie Photos, for your encouragement, assistance and support.

To my husband Fr. Dean Photos, for incorporating the Cooking Schools in the cultural and ethnic outreach of his Parishes to the surrounding communities. The Cooking Schools, via the Greek cuisine, invited the public to enjoy the famous Greek hospitality, offered fellowship among neighbors and cultivated relationships with our neighbors.

To my proofreader, Marialice Quinn, freelance reporter, for her diligent and meticulous efforts of reviewing each recipe, based upon her participation in the Greek Cooking School and Parish Greek Festivals in Florida. To Calvin Knight, former Director of Newspaper photography, for his newspaper and magazine layouts, and endless encouragement for this book.

To those who instructed at the Cooking School classes, who gave freely and generously to see others enjoy Greek cuisine and hospitality. To the students who have attended the classes, for their invaluable recommendations and critique for the preparation and execution of the recipes.

I have counted on two individuals for a number of my ingredients. These individuals have provided great support through their products:

John Varvaresos Sr. and John Jr. have put together a wonderful business in Tarpon Springs, Florida offering the latest Greek foods items. On any given day you may walk into his warehouse area to find anything you need to make your meal a success. I consider their store a definite stop when I am in the area for my class needs and for my Greek Food Festival Bakaliko (Greek Grocery) and even my personal kitchen.

Greek Boys Choice Foods, Inc.
Importers – Distributors of Fine Food & Wine
744 Anclote Road.
Tarpon Springs, FL 34689
Phone: 727-939-8999
Fax: 727-943-9552
E-Mail: **info@gbcfoods.com**   **http://www.gbcfoods.com/**

Mary Edline, of Polk County, Florida of, the sister of Sarah Edline the founder of Sweetriots®, a chocolate manufacturer introduced me to her wonderful chocolate. The dark chocolate, dark chocolate with flax, dark chocolate with coconut and the cocoa nibs and bars of 60%, 70% and 85% cocoa, enhanced many of my recipes that used carob or chocolate. Their chocolate is not "gritty" when added to a recipe. It has added a flavor kick to even the most complete pastry, dessert and cookie recipes. I highly recommend Sweetriots®.

Sweetriots, Inc.
131 Varick St., Suite 930
New York, NY 10013
212.431.RIOT
http://www.sweetriot.com/

I have used many olive oils in my cooking school experiences. The standards for the olive oil I use are simple: an oil produced from a single country and not a combination of olive oils from different countries; an olive oil not blended with various types of oils for example canola, sunflower, etc.; an oil that is pure extra virgin; and an olive oil which is 1st cold press. These are four basic standards that enhance the quality of your cooking, the taste of your food and most of all your meal's nutritional value. I have recently discovered these very qualities in the olive oil produced by Nicholas Flevaris and his Achladokampos Olive Oil Company from Argolidos Greece. The oil has a distinct zesty olive taste; you will taste the olives! Personally, I have found this oil has enhanced these recipes as it will your cooking. This is a new oil in production and for additional information email: info@achlaco.com

INTRODUCTION

In March of 1979, in a small office of the Behavioral Science Building of the University of Illinois, Chicago Campus, I sat with my Academic Counselor, Dr. Edmund Draine. It was during this meeting that Dr. Draine, a Cultural Geographer, made a point that has become the basis for my research and cooking endeavors - to understand someone and their culture, you must learn their cuisine, religious customs and traditions.

Throughout the years the words that Dr. Draine spoke continually rang in my mind. This challenge propelled me forward in my cooking research. My mother, Carry Kontos, was from mainland Greece, while my father, James Kontos, shared a dual lineage from the Dodecanese Island of Symi and Asia Minor. In my cooking, the mild flavors of the mainland met up with the fiery flavors of Asia Minor and the spices of Symi.

Books studied to further my knowledge were selected on their authenticity, region and styles of Greek cuisine. Family recipes were compared to those in various Greek cookbooks. Finally, however, it was a family member who provided the impetus for my research endeavors into Greek Cuisine.

During a Parish Greek festival in Miami, Florida, my sister, Shirley, was introduced to cooking demonstrations. This was a novel idea for the 1980s. After pondering the idea, she found a venue for presenting my vast accumulation of original Greek recipes: a Greek Cooking School to gather people together who were interested in learning about Greek cooking and culture.

The birth of the First Greek Cooking School of Chicago occurred in the mid-1980s at a suburban Chicago Greek Orthodox Parish. Initially, I was the main instructor and prepared the recipes based on the following criteria: first, the recipes were authentically original and did not include processed ingredients; second, secrets were disclosed, which were integral to the success of the recipe; third, to incorporate the cultural customs and traditions in the recipes which are vital to enrich and enhance the experience of Greek cuisine; and fourth, to ultimately enable the students to convey the famous Greek "philoxenia", hospitality to their family and friends.

Subsequently, additional instructors were utilized based on their conformance to the criteria. These instructors offered their expertise in styles of cooking from their particular region of Greece. Thus, teaching the students additional, methods, styles and secrets to broaden their culinary background. Due to facility limitations, the students were not involved in the preparation of the recipes. The students took notes, were allowed to ask questions and sampled what was prepared. At the 10th-week class there was a final exam, at which everyone was asked to prepare and bring a recipe they learned during the classes and sample each other's dishes.

In my role as the Director of the Cooking School, I also offered classes during Parish Greek Festivals, demonstrations for national media conventions, and seasonal articles for the Chicago Tribune and Chicago Suntimes. The popularity of the Greek Cooking School also led to the publication of several of my original family recipes in two Greek cookbooks.

Throughout the several years of the First Greek Cooking School, I became aware of a distinct weakness in the presentations. The students wanted more "hands on" involvement in the preparation and execution of the recipes. To become further proficient in the skills, they wanted to assist the instructors and prepare the recipes at their places. I vowed to incorporate this "innovation" in the instruction.

After my marriage to an Orthodox Clergyman in 1992, we were transferred from the Chicagoland area. The cooking school found new homes in Greek Orthodox Parishes in Rock Island, Illinois and Winter Haven, Florida. These locations provided the perfect venues to implement the "hands-on" method. In addition, there were presentations, lectures and demonstrations in local high schools and universities and numerous articles in regional newspapers and magazines.

"The Joyful Cook's Guide to Heavenly Greek Cuisine" is the outcome of this background. These recipes and techniques are the culmination of those demonstrated throughout the 30 years of the Cooking Schools. The "hands-on" techniques guide the cook from novice to advanced and serve a number of purposes:

❖ For the novice or intimidated cooks – they give simple instruction with professional results, gaining confidence with new abilities;

❖ For the intermediate cooks – they give them the basic techniques of Greek cooking, while allowing them to explore alternative flavors and methods;

❖ For the advanced cooks – they give them ideas and spur creativity in the exploration of their own variations to recipes, through the information provided;

Finally, for someone interested in starting their own Greek Cooking School or for the current instructors, this book, in addition to the techniques, offers versatility in its recipes for the development of unique variations for classroom menus. These recipes have been tried and tested, repeatedly in the various Cooking Schools with equal success. Beginner or intimidated cooks have astonished family and friends with these recipes. Intermediate cooks have gained expertise and confidence to sponsor gatherings at their homes with other students, testing the weekly recipes. Advanced cooks have acquired additional skills and information that has enabled them to further cultivate their techniques and led them to further research and innovations. Many have felt so confident that they have gone on to successfully teach Greek Cuisine in academic venues.

If you enjoy Greek cooking; if you enjoy taking a recipe – learning it, tweaking it and finally making it into a recipe to be enjoyed by family and friends; if you love entertaining and seeing people happy with your accomplishments; this book is for you. These recipes brought "the joy" of original heavenly Greek cooking to my students. They are offered now for your enjoyment with the same secrets, customs and traditions, and advice I offered to my students. May this book guide you in the joys of heavenly Greek Cuisine.

Georget Photos

Chapter 1: Sauces

AVGOLEMONO I
2-3 eggs, separated
Juice of two lemons
1 cup of broth

AVGOLEMONO II
2-3 eggs, separated
Juice of two lemons
10 oz. of wine

AVGOLEMONO III
2-3 eggs, separated
Juice of two lemons
1 cup broth or wine
1 tablespoon flour
2 cups yogurt

AVGOLEMONO IV
2-3 eggs, separated
Juice of two lemons
1 stick butter melted (not burned)

Thoroughly wet bowl and beaters and place in the freezer.

1.   Separate the yolks from the whites and set aside.
2.   Juice lemons and remove the seeds. The pulp is optional.

3. Remove the beaters and bowl from the freezer.
4. First place the whites in the bowl and beat until stiff.
5. Add the yolks and continue beating.
6. Add the additional liquid: broth, wine or butter. Continue to beat.
7. For Avgolemono III: Add the flour to the yogurt until totally combined. Add this to the egg mixture.
8. Place the mixture in the saucepan and heat on medium high heat. **DO NOT STOP STIRRING.** The stirring is important to prevent curdling. Keep heating until the sauce thickens. It takes a few minutes for the thickening process to occur – but keep stirring.

NOTES:
1. If you are using the Avgolemono as a sauce for a vegetable or entrée, heat the egg mixture slowly, stirring continually until it starts to thicken.
2. If you are using this for a soup, pour the egg mixture and stir continually for about two minutes. Remove the soup from the heat and serve.
3. For thicker sauce, add more eggs.
4. The tartness may be adjusted for taste by adding or subtracting lemon juice.
5. I prefer to leave the pulp in. If you wish, you can strain the juice before adding it to the recipe.
6. Reconstituted lemon juice may be used but, be advised, you will taste the difference.
7. Bouillon may be substituted for broth, but you will have a definite taste change with the salt content and natural flavor. This is not recommended for people on a low-salt or salt-free diet.
8. Serve these sauces on all types of vegetables, meats and fish, as well as soups.
9. Adding your favorite herbs such as dill, mint, tarragon, thyme, etc., may enhance these sauces.
10. If you are having more problems with curdling, consider using a high speed blender. Combine the eggs and the lemons together in a high speed blender. Then add the mixture to the liquid warming. Heat on medium until the sauce start thickening.

BÉCHAMEL SAUCE
½ gal milk
1 stick of unsalted butter
½ cup grated Kefalotirie or Parmesan
4 cups flour
4-6 eggs lightly beaten
½ tablespoon nutmeg

1. Beat three eggs lightly, and set aside with the flour and the cheese.
2. Pour milk into a saucepan along with a stick of butter and start raising the heat enough to melt the butter but not scald the milk. The heat should be set at medium high.
3. Add the nutmeg.
4. Using a whisk, add a tablespoon of flour to the milk and continue to stir.
5. Add a little of the eggs to the milk and continue to stir.
6. Add some cheese to the milk and continue to stir.
7. Repeat steps 4 through 6 until all the ingredients are used and the sauce begins to thicken.

8. If the sauce has not thickened, add a little more flour and cheese to the sauce. If it is too thick, add a little more milk.

NOTES:
1. If you wish a richer sauce, substitute two cups of heavy cream for two cups of milk. The cream will also thicken quicker and add a creamier taste to your dish.
2. Start stirring your sauce with a whisk. A whisk will help you eliminate any lumps made by the addition of flour or cheese to the sauce.
3. Switch to a wooden spoon once you detect the sauce thickening to avoid the whisk clumping.
4. Keep a close eye on the sauce once the thickening process begins. You want to avoid the béchamel becoming too thick. Remove the sauce from the heat once the sauce comes to a thin pudding consistency.

BÉCHAMEL SAUCE II

½ gal whole milk
1 or 2 pints cream
1 stick of unsalted butter
1 cup grated Kefalotirie or Parmesan
4 cups flour
4-6 eggs lightly beaten
½ tablespoon nutmeg

1. Beat three eggs lightly and set aside with the flour and the cheese.
2. Place the milk and cream in a saucepan with a stick of butter and start raising the heat enough to melt the butter, but not scald the milk. The heat should be set at medium high.
3. Add the nutmeg.
4. Using a whisk, add a tablespoon of flour to the milk and continue to stir.
5. Add a little of the eggs to the milk and continue to stir.
6. Add some cheese to the milk and continue to stir.
7. Repeat steps 4 through 6 until all the ingredients are used and the sauce begins to thicken.
8. If the sauce has not thickened, add a little more flour and cheese to the sauce. If it is too thick, add a little more milk.

NOTES:
1. This sauce is similar to the other yet it uses four cups cream to support the timpano recipe. Because of the timpano recipe, is an inverted Pastichio a heavier cream is needed to support the weight of dish.
2. You may start stirring your sauce with a whisk. A whisk will help you eliminate any lumps made by the addition of flour or cheese to the sauce.
3. Switch to a wooden spoon once you detect the sauce thickening, to avoid the whisk clumping.

4. Keep a close eye on the sauce once the thickening process happens. You want to avoid the béchamel becoming too thick. Remove the sauce from the heat once the sauce comes to a "thin pudding" consistency.

MODIFIED BROWN BUTTER

1 stick unsalted butter
5 cloves of garlic (optional)
3 onions (optional)
½ teaspoon cumin (optional)

1. Mince the garlic and add it to the skillet.
2. Slice the onions and add it to the skillet.
3. Add the half-teaspoon of cumin.
4. Add and melt the butter in a skillet with the other ingredients.
5. Reduce the heat on the skillet and allow the butter to brown (not burn), while sautéing the onions and garlic.
6. The onions and the garlic must caramelize.

NOTES::
1. Traditional browned butter does not have garlic, onions or cumin in the mixture.
2. The brown butter is traditionally used for spaghetti, orzo, trahana or rice. Add the pasta or rice to the skillet with the sauce and toss to completely distribute the sauce through the pasta or rice.

DAD'S GARLIC GLAZE

10 cloves of garlic
1/2 cup water
1 cup white wine
2 tablespoons of flour or cornstarch for thickening
Sea salt to taste

1. Press the cloves into a sauce pan. Use a knife to scrape the garlic from the press.
2. Add the water and bring the contents to a boil.
3. Reduce the heat to simmer and add the wine.
4. Season with salt.
5. Sift the flour or cornstarch while whisking until the sauce is thickened.

NOTES:
1. This is excellent for all seafood, especially shrimp.
2. This is a simple sauce that can be changed by adding spices, herbs or pepper

YOUVETSI

INGREDIENTS
2 -3 pounds tomatoes, chopped
1 medium onion
1 onion, chopped

1 tablespoon whole cloves
1½ tablespoons whole allspice
2 cups chicken or beef broth
½ cup olive oil
1 cloves of garlic
1 bay leaf
1 cup deep red wine
1 teaspoon sugar
1 cinnamon stick
Salt and pepper to taste
Flour

1. Remove the outer skin and cut the ends off the medium onion.
2. Take each clove and make a design by pushing the cloves into the onion. The design is yours; make circles, rows whatever you want but use all the cloves.
3. Follow Step 2 for allspice.
4. Place the cinnamon stick through the center of the onion or leave it separate; this is your decision.
5. Place the onions and olive oil into a 2-quart pot along with the garlic, rind and bay leaf.
6. Place the medium onion designed with spices, cinnamon stick, sugar and broth into the pot and stew at medium temperature for 15 minutes.
7. Heat the oil and stir with a wooden spoon.
8. Once you start smelling the garlic and bay leaves, add the chopped tomatoes and keep stirring.
9. You want to sauté the ingredients until the tomatoes soften and you find a sauce developing.
10. Stir in the wine and cook for 10 minutes.
11. Salt and pepper to taste.
12. To thicken mix 3 tablespoons of flour with one cup of hot sauce. Dissolve the flour. Add the flour mixture to the sauce. Cook for 10 minutes more.

NOTES:
1. My mother taught me the use of the mosaic onion. I believed that the onion was a form of beauty, and that it was, but it had another job. Unlike a bouquet that you put together in a bag and place in your sauce, stew or soup; the mosaic onion provides a time release of spice flavor. It allows the clove and allspice to be released as the onion stews. That takes away the guessing of how much spice to use and leaves you with just enough flavor. At the end of cooking time, dispose of the onion and bay leaves.
2. This is a mild spicy sauce that may be used with beef, lamb, pork or chicken.
3. This sauce may be used with some vegetables such as cauliflower, broccoli or cabbage.
4. You may use it with rice, pasta or couscous.

5. You may use a toothpick to help make the holes necessary for the spices. If you use the toothpick, just make a slight hole and use the spice to form the total hole. This ensures that the holes will not be too large and that the clove and allspice will not fall out during the stewing time.
6. If you have a juicer, the tomatoes may be juiced and used with the pulp to form the sauce. This is a simple trick to expedite the recipe.
7. If you do not want to use the mosaic onion, you may opt for the lemon half bags. Lemon half bags are the mesh fabric that hold the half or wedge of lemon when used at the dinner table.

KAPAMA I

INGREDIENTS
2 -3 pounds tomatoes, chopped
1 medium onion
3 onions, chopped
1 tablespoon whole cloves
1½ tablespoons whole allspice
2 cups chicken or beef broth
½ cup olive oil
6 cloves of garlic
6 bay leaves
2 cups deep red wine
1/8 teaspoon sugar
½ cup orange or lemon rind
1 cup chopped Kalamata olives
1 cinnamon stick
Salt and pepper to taste
Flour

1. Remove the outer skin and cut the ends off the medium onion.
2. Once the onion is cleaned start with your cloves. Take each clove and make a design by pushing the cloves into the onion. The design is yours; make circles, rows whatever you want but use all the cloves.
3. Follow Step 2 for allspice.
4. Place the cinnamon stick through the center of the onion or leave it separate; this is your decision.
5. Place the onions and olive oil into a two-quart pot along with the garlic, rind, olives and bay leaves.
6. Heat the oil and stir with a wooden spoon.
7. Place the medium onion designed with spices, cinnamon stick, sugar and broth the pot and stew at medium temperature for 15 minutes.
8. Once you start smelling the garlic and bay leaves, add the chopped tomatoes and keep stirring.
9. Sauté the ingredients until the tomatoes soften and you find a sauce developing.
10. Stir in the wine and cook for 10 minutes.
11. Salt and pepper to taste.

12. To thicken mix 3 tablespoons of flour with one cup of hot sauce. Dissolve the flour. Add the flour mixture to the sauce. Cook for 10 minutes more.

NOTES:
1. My mother taught me the use of the mosaic onion. I believed that the onion was a form of beauty, and that it was, but it had another job. Unlike a bouquet that you put together in a bag and place in your sauce, stew or soup, the mosaic onion provides a time release of spice flavor. It allows the clove and allspice to be released as the onion stews. That takes away the guessing of how much spice to use and leaves you with just enough flavor. At the end of cooking time you dispose of the onion and bay leaves.
2. This is a spicy sauce that may be used with beef, lamb, pork or chicken.
3. You may use it with rice, pasta or couscous
4. You may use a toothpick to help make the holes necessary for the spices. If you use the toothpick, just make a slight hole and use the spice to form the total hole. This ensures that the holes will not be too large and that the clove and allspice will not fall out during the stewing time.
5. If you have a juicer, the tomatoes may be juiced and used with the pulp to form the sauce. This is a simple trick to expedite the recipe.
6. If you do not want to use the mosaic onion, you may opt for the lemon half bags. Lemon half bags are the mesh fabric that hold the half or wedge of lemon when used at the dinner table.

TOMATO SAUCE – MEAT

INGREDIENTS
1 pound ground beef
4 pounds tomatoes
Olive oil
2 cloves of garlic
1 tablespoon each basil, parsley, thyme, nutmeg and cinnamon
¼ teaspoon clove
2 cups red wine
2 onions
1 green peppers
2 teaspoons of sugar

1. Place herbs, spices and garlic in a sauce pot.
2. Add olive oil and sauté on medium high heat.
3. Chop the onions and place them in a sauce pot when you begin smelling the herbs.
4. Chop the tomatoes and green peppers, and place them in the sauce pot when you begin smelling the onions.
5. Sauté until the tomatoes have cooked down, about 15 minutes.
6. Add the ground meat and brown. If you need to add olive oil, do so.
7. Continue to stir the ingredients until meat is brown.

8. Add the sugar.
9. Stir the sauce, add wine and reduce the heat to a low medium.
10. Salt and pepper to taste.

NOTES:
1. Purchase the tomatoes based on how much sauce you need. Plum or roma would give you a smaller amount of sauce in comparison to beefsteak tomatoes. You make the selection.
2. The amount of wine might vary. For a small portion of sauce one cup might be sufficient. Do not be afraid to increase the wine. It adds more flavor to your sauce and the alcohol will burn off.
3. The use of sugar is necessary to cut the acidity of the tomato.
4. Sometimes time is of the essence and you need to make a shortcut. I highly recommend jar or carton tomato sauce. It works better for my recipes and has less acidity.
5. Consider adding chopped olives or one teaspoon of olive paste.
6. Consider adding veggie meat instead of real meat for a vegetarian version.

KAPAMA II

INGREDIENTS
2 -3 pounds tomatoes chopped
1 medium onion
3 onions chopped
1 tablespoon whole cloves
1½ tablespoons whole allspice
2 cups chicken or beef broth
½ cup olive oil
2 cloves of garlic
2 bay leaves
1 cup deep red wine
1/8 teaspoon sugar
½ cup lemon rind
1 cinnamon stick
Salt and pepper to taste
Flour

1. Remove the outer skin and cut the ends off the medium onion.
2. Take each clove and make a design by pushing the cloves into the onion. The design is yours: make circles, rows, whatever you want, but use all the cloves.
3. Follow Step 2 for allspice.
4. Place the cinnamon stick through the center of the onion or leave it separate; this is your decision.
5. Place the onions and olive oil into a 2-quart pot along with the garlic, rind and bay leaves.
6. Place the medium onion designed with spices, cinnamon stick, sugar and broth in the pot and stew at medium temperature for 15 minutes.

7. Heat the oil and stir with a wooden spoon.
8. Once you start smelling the garlic and bay leaves add the chopped tomatoes and keep stirring.
9. Sauté the ingredients until the tomatoes soften and you find a sauce developing.
10. Stir in the wine and cook for 10 minutes.
11. Salt and pepper to taste.
12. To thicken mix 3 tablespoons of flour with one cup of hot sauce. Dissolve the flour. Add the flour mixture to the sauce. Cook for 10 minutes more.

NOTES:
1. My mother taught me the use of the "mosaic" onion. I believed that the onion was a form of beauty, and that it was, but it had another job. Unlike a bouquet that you put together in a bag and place in your sauce, stew or soup, the mosaic onion provides a time release of spice flavor. It allows the clove and allspice to be released as the onion stews. That takes away the guessing of how much spice to use and leaves you with just enough flavor. At the end of cooking time, dispose of the onion and bay leaves.
2. This is a moderate spicy sauce that may be used with beef, lamb, pork, or chicken.
3. You may use it with rice, pasta, or couscous
4. You may use a toothpick to help make the holes necessary for the spices. If you use the pick, just make a slight hole and use the spice to form the total hole. This ensures that the holes will not be too large and that the clove and allspice will not fall out during the stewing time.
5. If you have a juicer, the tomatoes may be juiced and used with the pulp to form the sauce. This is a simple trick to expedite the recipe.
6. If you do not want to use the mosaic onion, you may opt for the lemon half bags. Lemon half bags are the mesh fabric that hold the half or wedge of lemon when used at the dinner table.

OLIVE OIL AND LEMON SAUCE

Juice of 1 lemon
Olive oil
1 tablespoon oregano, dill or mint
Salt and pepper to taste

1. Juice the lemon and remove the seeds
2. Add an equal amount of olive oil
3. Add the herb you selected.
4. Salt and pepper to taste.
5. Whisk the sauce until thoroughly combined.

NOTES:
1. Consider for salads and vegetables
2. Great for fish

OLIVE OIL AND VINEGAR

1 cup olive oil
½ cup balsamic vinegar
1 teaspoon each oregano, thyme, and parsley
¼ pound feta (optional)
1/8 teaspoon white pepper
¼ teaspoon sea salt

1. Crumble the feta into a bowl or glass jar with a lid.
2. Combine the ingredients above and add them to the container.
3. Whisk or shake vigorously.

NOTES:
1. Excellent for salads and vegetables
2. Great for fish

POMEGRANATE SAUCE

2 cups Pomegranate Syrup
1 cinnamon stick
3 whole cloves
1 bay leaf
½ cup water

1. Pour the syrup into the saucepan.
2. Add the spices.
3. Add the water and heat.

NOTES:
1. Great sauce for pork, chicken, or seafood.
2. You may give the sauce a kick by adding fresh pomegranate.
3. Make sure if you use fresh pomegranate that you cut the fruit in half first. Place the halves of the pomegranate fruit in a bowl of cold water. Extract the seeds from the fruit under the water.

SKORDALIA

INGREDIENTS
1 to 2 heads of garlic
1 boiled Idaho russet potato, chopped (optional)
2-3 slices of dried bread, (optional)
Olive oil, vegetable oil or walnut oil to taste
2 tablespoons white vinegar or white wine
1 cup walnuts or almonds (optional)
Juice of 1 lemon
Salt and pepper to taste

1. Peel all the garlic you intend on using. The more garlic used, the better the sauce.
2. Boil your potato until done and then chop.
3. Lightly toast the bread before using. The bread should be light in color.
4. Ground the nuts you wish to use.
5. Place all the cloves of garlic in the processor with 2 tablespoons of oil, and puree.
6. Slowly add the oil, nuts, bread, vinegar or wine, lemon juice and potato, at different intervals during the puree mode.
7. Use the spatula to scrape the sides of blender or processor, and continue to blend until you obtain a mashed potato texture.

NOTES:
1. Depending on the region of Greece you are from, bread, potatoes or both are used for this sauce.

   The combination of bread and potatoes is acceptable. The sauce is made according to preference of texture and thinness of the sauce.
2. The use of nuts is again an option. The nuts were used to take the bite from the garlic sauce. The nuts may be omitted without jeopardizing the sauce itself.
3. Garlic may be increased or decreased to taste.
4. You may also add the garlic chopped instead of pressed into the sauce. Some people enjoy chewing on the garlic chunks in their Skordalia.
5. The sauce is traditionally used on fish. It may also be used on fried vegetables or as an appetizer.

DAD'S SKORDOSTUBE

2 cups white vinegar
1 teaspoon dill (optional)
10 cloves of garlic
1 glass jar
Sea salt and pepper to taste

1. Mince the garlic and place it in a saucepan.
2. Add the dill to the saucepan.
3. Add the vinegar and bring the saucepan to a boil.
4. Turn off the heat let the liquid cool.
5. Salt and pepper to taste.
6. Pour the garlic, dill and vinegar into the jar.
7. Cool and refrigerate.

NOTES:
1. My father made this both ways. The heating of the vinegar is optional. The heating process actually intensifies the taste of the sauce for soups and seafood.
2. This garlic vinaigrette is used on some seafood and in soups.
3. You may increase or decrease the garlic to taste. Dad liked his vinaigrette strong.
4. Parsley or tarragon may be substituted for dill.
5. Dad sometimes added Turkish red pepper to spice things up.

SPINACH VINAIGRETTE

1 bunch of spinach
2 green onions
½ teaspoon coriander
¼ cup balsamic vinegar
¾ cup of olive oil
¼ teaspoon salt
1/8 teaspoon pepper

1. Chop the green onions and place them in the skillet with the spinach.
2. Sauté the spinach and green onions until cooked.
3. Puree the spinach and the green onions and place in a bowl.
4. Combine the vinegar with coriander, salt and pepper.
5. Combine the vinegar mixture in the bowl with the spinach and mix thoroughly.

NOTES:
1. Great for vegetable, seafood, and pasta use.
2. Optional herbs are dill, mint, tarragon or parsley.

TOMATO HERB SAUCE

INGREDIENTS
4 large tomatoes
Olive oil
1 tablespoon each oregano, thyme, parsley and fennel
1 sweet onion (Vidalia)
½ teaspoon red pepper
1 cup red sweet wine or port
1 tablespoon sugar (optional)
Salt and pepper to taste

1. Heat the olive oil in a skillet with the herbs and red pepper.
2. Chop the tomatoes and onions.
3. When the herbs become a bright green and are fragrant, add the onion.
4. Sauté the onion with the herbs until glossy.
5. Add the tomatoes.
6. If necessary add more oil, sauté until tomatoes breakdown to a sauce, about 15 minutes.
7. Add the sugar, 1 cup of water and wine.
8. Stew until sauce.
9. Salt and pepper to taste.

NOTES:
1. Garlic may be added according to your taste.
2. This sauce is primarily for pasta, but may be used on meats, poultry and vegetables.
3. If you want a stronger wine taste, substitute water with wine.

TOMATO SAUCE – MEATLESS

<u>INGREDIENTS</u>
2 – 4 pounds of tomatoes
2 onions
½ cup olive oil
1 cup red wine
1 bunch each fresh herbs - parsley, oregano, thyme
Salt and pepper to taste
1 teaspoon granulated sugar

1. Chop the herbs and place them in a sauce pot.
2. Add olive oil and sauté on medium high heat.
3. Chop the onions and place them in the sauce pot when you begin smelling the herbs.
4. Chop the tomatoes and place them in the sauce pot when you begin smelling the onions.
5. Stir continually until sauce is made, about 15 minutes. Add wine and continue to sauté.
6. Salt and pepper to taste.

NOTES:
1. Purchase the tomatoes based on how much sauce you need. Plum or roma would give you a smaller amount of sauce in comparison to beefsteak tomatoes. You make the selection.
2. The amount of wine might vary. For a small portion of sauce one cup might be sufficient. Do not be afraid to increase the wine. It adds more flavor to your sauce and the alcohol will burn off.
3. The use of sugar is necessary to cut the acidity of the tomato.
4. Sometimes time is of the essence, and you need to make a shortcut. I highly recommend jar or carton tomato sauce. It works better for my recipes and has less acidity.
5. Consider adding chopped olives or one teaspoon of olive paste.

TOMATO SAUCE – SAUSAGE

<u>INGREDIENTS</u>
1 pound ground pork
4 pounds tomatoes
Olive oil
2 cloves of garlic
1 tablespoon each cumin, fennel, nutmeg and cinnamon
¼ teaspoon clove
2 cups white wine
Zest of one orange
2 onions
1 green pepper
2 teaspoons of sugar

1. Place herbs, spices and garlic in a sauce pot.
2. Add olive oil and sauté on medium high heat.
3. Chop the onions and place them in the sauce pot when you begin smelling the herbs.
4. Chop the tomatoes and green peppers. Place them in the sauce pot when you begin smelling the onions.
5. Sauté until the tomatoes have cooked down, about 15 minutes.
6. Add the ground pork and brown. If you need to add olive oil, do so.
7. Continue to stir the ingredients until meat is brown.
8. Add the sugar and orange rind.
9. Stir the sauce, add wine and reduce the heat to a low medium.
10. Salt and pepper to taste.

NOTES:
1. Purchase the tomatoes based on how much sauce you need. Plum or roma would give you a smaller amount of sauce in comparison to beefsteak tomatoes. You make the selection
2. The amount of wine might vary. For a small portion of sauce one cup might be sufficient. Do not be afraid to increase the wine. It adds more flavor to your sauce and the alcohol will burn off.
3. The use of sugar is necessary to cut the acidity of the tomato.
4. Sometimes time is of the essence and you need to make a shortcut. I highly recommend jar or carton tomato sauce. It works better for my recipes and has less acidity.
5. Consider adding veggie meat instead of real meat for a vegetarian version.

TOMATO SAUCE – SPICY

INGREDIENTS
4 pounds of tomatoes
Olive oil
4 cloves of garlic
1 tablespoon Turkish pepper or ½ teaspoon cayenne pepper
1 tablespoon each allspice, nutmeg and cinnamon
¼ teaspoon each clove, cardamom
1 carrot shaved
2 cups red wine
2 onions
1 bay leaf
2 teaspoons of sugar
Salt and pepper to taste

1. Place carrot, spices and garlic in a sauce pot.
2. Add olive oil and sauté on medium high heat.

3. Chop the onions and place them in the sauce pot when you begin smelling the herbs.
4. Chop the tomatoes and green peppers. Place them in the sauce pot when you begin smelling the onions.
5. Sauté until the tomatoes have cooked down, about 15 minutes.
6. Add the sugar.
7. Stir the sauce, add wine and reduce the heat to a low medium.
8. Salt and pepper to taste.

NOTES:
1. Purchase the tomatoes based on how much sauce you need. Plum or roma would give you a smaller amount of sauce in comparison to beefsteak tomatoes. You make the selection
2. The amount of wine might vary. For a small portion of sauce one cup might be sufficient. Do not be afraid to increase the wine. It adds more flavor to your sauce and the alcohol will burn off.
3. The use of sugar is necessary to cut the acidity of the tomato.
4. Sometimes time is of the essence and you need to make a shortcut. I highly recommend jar or carton tomato sauce. It works better for my recipes and has less acidity.
5. Consider adding chopped olives or one teaspoon of olive paste.

TSATZIKI

1 quarts yogurt
3-10 cloves of garlic
1 cucumber
½ bunch mint or dill
1 bunch parsley
Olive oil
1 teaspoon lemon juice

1. Place the yogurt in a bowl.
2. Use a garlic press or mortar and pestle to mash the garlic cloves. Set the garlic in the bowl.
3. Prepare the cucumber by scoring the exterior of the cucumber with a fork.
4. Grate the cucumber into the bowl.
5. Mince the parsley and mint and add it to the bowl.
6. Add lemon juice and olive oil to the yogurt mixture, and combine all the ingredients.
7. Allow the mixture to sit in the refrigerator for an hour to set the taste.

NOTES:
1. Prior to placing the cucumber into the bowl, you have the option of removing some of the water by using a flour sack cloth. Place the grated cucumber onto the center of the cloth. Bring the ends of the cloth together and twist over a sink or bowl, removing the fluid from the cucumber. Then place the pressed cucumber into the bowl.

2. Mint or dill is preferred, but some tastes believe basil makes a better sauce.
3. This sauce has been used for a condiment on Gyros sandwich, but it may be used as for an appetizer, on vegetables, seafood, chicken, turkey, beef and pork. Be adventurous and try it on some different dishes you wish to perk up.

SPICY YOGURT SAUCE

3 cups yogurt
1 tablespoon dill
¼ pound feta cheese
1 teaspoon Turkish red pepper (Optional)

1. Place the yogurt into a bowl.
2. Add the dill.
3. Crumble the feta into the yogurt.
4. Add the red pepper and combine.
5. Place the yogurt in the refrigerator for at least an hour to set.

NOTES:
1. This sauce is simple, but can also be used as an appetizer.
2. Cayenne pepper may be used instead of Turkish pepper.
3. Mint may be substituted for dill.

Chapter 2: Appetizers

VEGETABLE SAGANAKI

<u>INGREDIENTS</u>
4 squares of Kasseri, Kefalotirie, Parmesan or Asiago cheese
Olive oil
1 lemon halved
1 shot of either Cognac or Scotch
1 green pepper, zucchini, capers, onion, tomato, mushrooms or eggplant
¼ teaspoon each parsley and oregano
1 clove of garlic
Pepper to taste

1. Press the garlic into the skillet.
2. Place some oil in the skillet, add the herbs and pepper and heat.
3. Add the vegetables you selected and sauté.
4. Place the sautéed mixture in a bowl.
5. Reheat the skillet.
6. Cut the cheese into squares that fit the skillet and set on a plate.
7. If your skillet is large enough it might hold all the squares. If not, consider using a shot of liquor for each slice of cheese.
8. Heat the oil until it sizzles.
9. Add the cheese.
10. Turn the cheese so that both sides are glazed with oil.
11. Add the sautéed vegetables onto the cheese.
12. Add liquor and flame with a match or igniter until brown and crispy
13. Extinguish with fresh squeezed lemon juice.

NOTES:

1. The vegetables that you use should be easily sautéed. You are not restricted to those mentioned. You may even add hot peppers
2. Serve with crusty bread.
3. Some claim that wine works very well for the recipe, but this is not a traditional recipe.
4. When working on more than one piece, the skillet must be hot for each piece you are making.
5. Keeping the skillet in the oven is one way of keeping it warm.
6. Cast iron skillet is the best utensil for the recipe.
7. Use the half bag lemon covers for the lemons that extinguish the flame

FRIED VEGETABLES

INGREDIENTS

1 eggplant, zucchini (any kind)
Olive oil
Flour
2 eggs
1 tablespoon dill or mint
1 tablespoon parsley
Salt and pepper to taste

1. Cut the selected vegetables into slices; circles or long slices are fun, about ½" in thickness.
2. Place the eggs in a bowl and beat with a fork. Set the mixture aside.
3. Depending on the amount of slices you have, place 1 to 2 cups of flour into a plastic bag with the selected herbs, salt and pepper.
4. Seal the bag and shake making sure the herbs are completely combined.
5. Dip the slices in the egg mixture.
6. Remove the slices from the egg mixture and place them in the flour bag and shake, making sure the slices are covered.
7. Repeat Steps 5 and 6 until all the slices have been coated.
8. Place enough oil in a skillet to cover the bottom and heat.
9. Drop the slices into the oil and fry until golden.
10. As the slices have reached the appropriate color, use a tong, slotted spoon or slotted flipper to remove the vegetables from the oil and place on a plate covered with two layers of paper towels.
11. Repeat Steps 9 and 10 until all vegetable slices have been fried.
12. Serve hot as an appetizer or side dish.

NOTES:

1. People are sometimes sensitive to dill. Mint is a common alternative. You may also substitute tarragon, oregano or thyme.
2. Other oils such as walnut, peanut, soy bean, corn or sunflower may be used. Be cautious. For those who have a nut sensitivity, do not use those oils.
3. Fried vegetables may be served with Ladolemono (Oil and Lemon Sauce), Skordalia, Sweet Potato Skordalia or Tzaziki sauce.

4. You may try other vegetables if you like

GREEK STYLE PICKLED GREEN TOMATOES

INGREDIENTS
2-4 pounds green tomatoes
1 green pepper (optional)
1 white onion (optional)
12 sprigs of dill
½ teaspoon oregano, parsley, rosemary and/or thyme
4 or more cloves of garlic
3 cups white or balsamic vinegar
1 bay leaf
¼ cup sea salt
Sliced Kalamata olives
1 tablespoon olive oil
½ tablespoon Turkish pepper (optional)
5 cups water
¼ cup capers

1. Cut the tomatoes into wedges and set to the side.
2. Slice the green pepper and onion into wedges and set to the side.
3. Slice the garlic and the olives and set aside.
4. Take the Mason jar and arrange the wedges of tomatoes, onions, green peppers, garlic, capers and dill. It is best to layer and/or stack.
5. Distribute the sliced olives around the jar.
6. Bring the vinegar, water, oil, spices and salt to a boil.
7. Immediately pour the heated liquid, with the spices, over the tomatoes, onions and pepper in the jar.
8. Try to bring the liquid as close to the top of the jar as possible.
9. Let the liquid cool and cover with the cap, then refrigerate.

NOTES:
1. The pickled tomatoes should remain good for months.
2. This is a simple recipe. The tomatoes may be added to salads, soups, appetizers or used as a side dish.

GREAT GRANDMA IRENE'S GREEK TOAST

Basic Olive Oil Bread Recipe or French bread
Olive oil
Pressed garlic or garlic powder
1 cup sweet or dry red wine

1. Cut your loaf of bread into thick slices about ½" to 1" thick.
2. Grease or place baking paper on a cookie sheet.
3. Dip one side of your bread in olive oil.
4. Turn the slice so that the soaked side faces upward on the prepared cookie sheet.

5. Using a basting brush, coat the oiled bread with wine.
6. Sprinkle with garlic powder or pressed garlic. Use the amount of garlic that you would like. Remember the more cloves you use the more intense the flavor.
7. Bake at 325°F until golden and toasted.

NOTES:
1. My Great-Grandmother Irene was an awesome cook. This recipe is one of her best. My dad used to tell me how in the morning she would grill her bread dipped in olive oil and wine. My father at the age of eight tried that recipe. He found himself waking up at night after one slice.
2. This modified recipe may be used as an appetizer, to prepare bread for a sandwich or even for dinner.
3. You may add oregano, thyme and parsley.

DADDY'S HUMMUS

3 cans or jars* of chickpeas
1 teaspoon each coriander, turmeric, allspice, cumin and ginger
½ teaspoon each oregano and thyme (optional)
½ cup tahini or ground sesame seed
1 cup olive oil
½ cup lemon juice
½ red onion
3 cloves garlic (more if your taste buds can handle it)

1. If you are using sesame seeds, grind them in the grinder and set aside. If you are using Tahini, skip this step.
2. In a blender combine Tahini or ground sesame seed, 1 can of chickpeas, the herbs, spices, garlic, onion, lemon juice and a little oil.
3. Blend on high speed in pulses until combined.
4. Use a spatula to test the blender contents. If the texture is still lumpy, add a little more oil and lemon juice. Water may even be added a little at a time.
5. Thoroughly blend again.

NOTES:
1. The classes taught require fresh ingredients. There are some instances when a short cut might be a necessity. This is one of those cases. This recipe is my dad's and though the recipe calls for a can or jar chickpeas, you may want to use your own boiled chickpeas. The use of the can or jar version of the bean makes no difference to the recipe.
2. Dad also liked garlic. Though three cloves are mentioned above, he was known to put as much as a half of a head to a whole head of garlic in his hummus. I must say it was very good.
3. Ground sesame seed is Tahini. The difference is when bought in a store the jar contains sesame seed oil and it resembles a paste consistency. By grinding your own sesame seed, you do not have the same amount of oil. You may use olive oil or sesame seed oil for the grinding. This will not change the recipe. In either method the flavor will remain the same.
4. The cumin and ginger, though not always seen, was Dad's secret.

DOLMA

1 bunch fig, mulberry, hazelnut or grape leaves blanched
1 cup whole milk
¼ teaspoon salt (optional if feta is too salty)
4 ounces figs, chopped
4 ounces currents
1 cup walnuts, pine nuts or pecans
2 tablespoons honey
½ teaspoon cinnamon
½ cup rice
2 eggs
½ cup feta
1 stick unsalted butter
1 orange

DIPPING SAUCE

I cup Greek yogurt
2 tablespoons honey
½ teaspoon cinnamon

1. Blanch the leaves you are using by dipping them in boiling water for 5 seconds and laying them on a baking sheet to dry. If you are using jar leaves, the leaves need only be rinsed prior to using.
2. Sauté the rice in melted butter, cinnamon and 1 tablespoon honey.
3. Add the milk and allow the rice to simmer.
4. In a bowl add the figs, currents, nuts and crumbled feta.
5. When the rice has absorbed the entire fluid, remove the skillet from the heat and add the contents to the bowl and combine.
6. Place one teaspoon of the mixture just above the leaf stem.
7. Bring the outer leaves inward to cover the dough, and then roll upward toward the tip.
8. Slice the orange into circles and lay them at the bottom of the pot.
9. Lay the dolmathes atop the orange slices, against the sides of the pot going in a circular formation working inward.
10. Continue Steps 4, 5, and 7 until all the leaves are stuffed and in the pot.
11. Mix the remaining honey in 1 cup of water and add it to the pot.
12. Place the plate over the finished dolmathes.
13. Simmer for 30-40 minutes.
14. Combine the yogurt, honey and cinnamon in a bowl for dipping.

NOTES:

1. This is one of the most entertaining recipes I have ever used. They look like a dolma, but they have a very sweet taste that will surprise your guests.
2. Though modified, they were initially used during Great Lent in a lesser role to provide a nutritious alternative.

Rice Dolmathes

1 jar of grape leaves or 1 bunch fresh grape leaves
1 ½ cup rice
1 tablespoon mint or dill
1 tablespoon parsley
2 onions, chopped
½ cup white wine
Carrots halved lengthwise or celery stalks
1 lemon

Leaves

1. Blanch the leaves you are using by dipping them in boiling water for 5 seconds and laying them on a baking sheet to dry. If you are using jar leaves, the leaves need only be rinsed prior to using.
2. Lay three to five leaves on your work space, with the vein side up.
3. Snip off the stem with a kitchen shears.

Filling

4. In a large skillet, sauté the onions and herbs.
5. Add the rice and continue to sauté.
6. Add 1 cup water and ½ cup wine when you see the rice turn white, and cook until the fluid has been absorbed.

Assembly

7. Line the bottom of your pot with either celery or carrots.
8. Place 1 teaspoon of the filling at the stem bottom.
9. Bring the two lower side leaves to the center covering the filling slightly.
10. Pick up the stem end and roll forward, forming an eggroll shape.
11. Place the finished dolma on top of the bedding in the pot. Lay the dolma up against the side of the pan and continue laying the dolmathes side by side working inward, until the first layer is finished.
12. Repeat the same distribution on the second layer and so forth until the leaves and filling is used.
13. Place a plate over the finished dolmathes.
14. Add 2 cups water with the juice of one lemon.
15. Simmer for 30 minutes.

NOTES:

1. Leaves used are usually grape. Geranium leaves, leaves from fruit trees such as mulberry, orange, etc., and leaves from nut trees such as walnuts, pecans or almonds have been used. Remember that you try the basic leaf of grape vine first to understand the taste. Then experiment with other types of leaves. When in doubt regarding the use of another leaf type, investigate the leaf origins and its nature; is it edible? What are, if any, their side effects once ingested? For example, I have used mulberry leaves and found a wonderful variation of the recipe. Yet, I experienced a blood sugar drop. Further research provided that Mulberry leaves are beneficial to a diabetic diet. You might want to check the leaf you are considering at this site **http://www.permies.com/t/3350/plants/Trees-shrubs-edible-leaves**.

2. Wrapping the rice in the leaves is similar to rolling eggrolls.
3. A "pot the size needed" refers to the amount of dolmathes you are making. Depending on the size of each roll, you might need a larger pot than anticipated.
4. The celery or carrots at the bottom of the pot serves two purposes. First, it stops the scorching of the dolma in the event your pot runs dry from fluid. Second, it seasons the water and subsequently the rice as it is cooking.
5. The addition of the plate keeps the rolls together while they are cooking.

SAGANAKI

INGREDIENTS
4 squares of Kasseri, Kefalotirie, Parmesan or Asiago cheese
Olive oil
1 lemon halved
1 shot of either Cognac or Scotch

1. Cut the cheese into squares that fit the skillet and set on a plate.
2. If your skillet is large enough, it might hold all the squares. If not, consider using a shot of liquor for each slice of cheese.
3. Place oil in the skillet, about two tablespoons for each piece of cheese.
4. Heat the oil until it sizzles.
5. Add the cheese.
6. Turn the cheese so that both sides are glazed with oil.
7. Add liquor and flame with a match or igniter.
8. Flame until brown and crispy.
9. Extinguish with fresh squeezed lemon juice.

NOTES:
1. Serve with crusty bread.
2. Some claim that wine works very well for the recipe, but this is not a traditional recipe.
3. When working on more than one piece, the skillet must be hot for each piece you are making.
4. Keeping the skillet in the oven is one way of keeping it warm.
5. Cast iron skillet is the best utensil for the recipe.
6. Use half bag lemon covers for the lemons that extinguish the flame

SHRIMP SAGANAKI
INGREDIENTS
4 squares of Kasseri, Kefalotirie, Parmesan or Asiago cheese
Olive oil
1 cup popcorn shrimp
1 lemon halved
¼ pound feta cheese
1 tomato, diced
1 onion, diced
¼ teaspoon red pepper
1 teaspoon each mint and parsley
1 shot of either Cognac or Scotch

1. Place oil in your skillet with the shrimp, red pepper, tomato, onion, mint and parsley and sauté thoroughly.
2. Crumble the feta into a bowl.
3. Add the sautéed mixture to the bowl and combine.
4. Cut the cheese into squares that fit the skillet and set on a plate.
5. If your skillet is large enough it might hold all the squares. If not consider using a shot of liquor for each slice of cheese.
6. Place more oil in the skillet, about two tablespoons for each piece of cheese.
7. Heat the oil until it sizzles.
8. Add the cheese.
9. Turn the cheese so that both sides are glazed with oil.
10. Spread the shrimp mixture over the cheese in the skillet.
11. Add liquor and flame with a match or igniter until brown and crispy.
12. Extinguish with fresh squeezed lemon juice.

NOTES:
1. Serve with crusty bread.
2. This is a great version for a light lunch.
3. Some claim that wine works very well for the recipe, but this is not a traditional recipe.
4. When working on more than one piece, the skillet must be hot for each piece you are making.
5. Keeping the skillet in the oven is one way of keeping it warm.
6. Cast iron skillet is the best utensil for the recipe.
7. Use half bag lemon covers for the lemons that extinguish the flame

DADDY'S SKORDALIA

INGREDIENTS
1 head of garlic
Olive oil
3 slices dried bread
1 tablespoon parsley
2 boiled red potatoes
1 cup almonds, pecans or walnuts
½ cup white vinegar
Salt and pepper to taste

1. Peel the garlic and place the cloves to the side.
2. In a bowl soak the dried bread with vinegar.
3. Mince the parsley and set aside.
4. Skin and chop the potatoes.
5. In a food processor start with olive oil. Place about ½ cup in the food processor along with the garlic and nuts. Process until almost smooth.
6. Add the parsley, potatoes and dried bread, and process until smooth.
7. Add more olive oil and vinegar according to taste.
8. Salt and pepper to taste.
9. Blend until smooth.

NOTES:
1. This is a traditional appetizer that may be used also as a seafood and vegetable sauce.
2. The amount of garlic may be lessened according to your taste. My dad loved it strong.
3. If you are serving this as an appetizer, make sure that everyone partakes. If everyone has the spread, no one will be able to smell the sauce on anyone else.
4. A food processor is great for this recipe, but a mortar and pestle may also be used.
5. Garlic press may help.
6. Elephant garlic will give a milder effect.
7. The nuts and parsley take the bite out of the garlic and help digest the garlic.
8. This is great for high blood pressure.
9. If you wish a different oil try walnut, corn, avocado or sunflower oil.
10. For a variation on vinegar, try balsamic or wine.

SPICY FETA DIP
1 pound of feta cheese
1 whole roasted red pepper
Minced garlic¾ cup yogurt
Dash of cayenne pepper or Turkish red pepper
1 teaspoon olive oil

1. Crumble the feta into a bowl.
2. Finely chop the roasted red pepper.
3. Add minced garlic, yogurt, pepper and olive oil.
4. Stir and allow the mixture to chill in the refrigerator for at least 24 hours.
5. Serve with vegetables, crackers or toasted bread.

NOTES:
1. This is a failsafe recipe. Even if you extremely alter the recipe by using sour cream and garlic powder, someone will always lick the bowl.
2. Turkish red pepper is oven-toasted cayenne peppers glazed in olive oil.
3. Garlic may be either pressed or minced depending on the intensity of flavor you wish.

SWEET POTATO SKORDALIA
2 medium size sweet potatoes
1/3 cup walnuts or almonds (optional)
10 cloves of garlic to one head of garlic
1 cup olive
¼ cup balsamic vinegar
¼ teaspoon salt
Dash of Turkish pepper

1. Boil the sweet potatoes until soft.
2. Remove the sweet potatoes from the water, when cooked, and allow them to cool.
3. Gently remove the skin with your fingers under cold running water.

4. Mash the sweet potatoes in a bowl.
5. Pulverize the nuts and add them to the bowl.
6. Puree the garlic with the olive oil and add it to the bowl.
7. Add the vinegar, salt and pepper and combine the bowl ingredients thoroughly.

NOTES:
1. You have a wonderful choice of boiling your potato using the conventional method or using a potato bag, which is placed in the microwave for at least 10 minutes.
2. The old style of mashing the potato or placing it in a mortar and pressing it can be easily substituted with a food processor. Any of these three work well for this recipe. The introduction of the food processor makes the job tremendously simpler by adding all the ingredients together and blending thoroughly.
3. Some traditions of Greece use white stale, dried or toasted bread with this recipe instead of potatoes.
4. Depending on the region of Greece, a thicker spread is more appealing.
5. The use of nuts is optional and may be omitted if someone has allergies. The use of nuts assists in cutting the sharp taste of the garlic.
6. If you do use a food processor, chop the potato into cubes prior to adding.
7. Garlic press or chopped garlic is up to you. Pressed garlic will give you a milder taste while chopped garlic will have a more intense flavor. You may increase the garlic cloves or decrease as your taste demands, but it must have a recognized garlic flavor.
8. Fresh garlic may be used only, you cannot substitute garlic cloves with minced jar cloves, powders or salts.
9. Traditionally this may either be used as an appetizer spread on bread or pita or it may be a condiment for seafood.

TARAMOUSALATA

4 ounces or more of fish roe
1 large potato
1 small onion
3 tablespoons lemon juice
½ cup mayonnaise (optional)
Olive oil
½ teaspoon ground coriander

1. Boil the potato until tender.
2. Gently work off the skin of the potato by rubbing the spud under cold water.
3. Mash the potato with about 2 tablespoons of olive oil to start, then add coriander and lemon juice
4. Mince the onion and add it to the potato.
5. Add the fish roe and mayonnaise and combine thoroughly. If more oil is need to come to the consistency you like, add it slowly.

1. You have a wonderful choice of boiling your potato using the conventional method or using a potato bag which is placed in the microwave for at least ten minutes.
2. The old style of mashing the potato or placing it in a mortar and pressing it can be easily substituted with a food processor. Any of these three work well for this recipe. The introduction of the food processor makes the job tremendously simpler by adding all the ingredients together and blending thoroughly.
3. If you do use a food processor, chop the potato into cubes prior to adding.
4. The addition of mayonnaise makes the spread fluffy and light. Homemade mayonnaise that is not sweetened is preferred.
5. Add the olive oil carefully. The olive oil and the mayonnaise cut the saltiness of the roe you are using. Too much olive oil might make the spread too runny and greasy. You may remedy this by adding one more small potato.

TSATZIKI

1 quart Greek yogurt – freshly made preferred
3-6 cloves of garlic (more or less if you'd like)
1 cucumber
½ bunch mint or dill
½ bunch parsley
Olive oil
1 teaspoon lemon juice

1. Place the yogurt in a bowl.
2. Mince the garlic and add to the bowl. Placing the garlic in a press is acceptable.
3. Using a fork, grate the cucumber from the top of to the bottom, making sure you have lines of green throughout.
4. Using your grater, grate the cucumber into the bowl.
5. Mince the parsley and mint and add to the bowl.
6. Add lemon juice and olive oil to the yogurt in the bowl. Mix all the ingredients together.
7. Allow the mixture to sit in the refrigerator for an hour to set the taste.

NOTES:
1. If you wish to thicken your yogurt, place the yogurt you are using in the flour sack cloth and hang it for at least one to two hours. The cloth will absorb most of the moisture of the yogurt and leave you with a thicker consistency. Then add the yogurt to the bowl. Thick Greek yogurt is preferred for this recipe.
2. Chopped garlic vs. pressed garlic is up to your taste. Chopped garlic will give you a strong flavor and is ultimately better for you. Yet pressed garlic is appreciated at gatherings where this may be served.
3. Some people prefer to place the grated cucumber directly into the flour sack cloth and drain of fluid. You would place the grated cucumber into the center of the cloth, bring up all the sides, leaving the grated mass to hang. Then by twisting the cloth, you wringing out the liquid. This step will give a thicker sauce.
4. There are many people who have sensitivity to dill. Know what your guests' sensitivities are.

Chapter 3: Soups

The Greek kitchen has a variety of soups. Based on religious traditions the soups vary to with dietary requirements for that particular season. During times of Great Lent, the Greek kitchen becomes totally vegan even eliminating olive oil. For the purposes of this book, alternatives will be supplied for people who wish to follow a vegan diet.

Your soup pot should determine the amount of soup you wish to make. Leftovers, even with Egg Lemon Soup, have been successfully frozen and reheated. I really prefer that meals be made fresh, but in the bustling society we live in that sometimes is not attainable. At the sake of sparing freshness to make sure you or your family has a nutritional option.

Vegan Instructions:

1. For the sake of these recipes, use two quarts of water
2. Salt and pepper a soup only in the last 10 minutes of cooking. This helps you give just enough flavor and not over-salt.
3. Replace olive oil or butter with grapeseed oil, walnut oil, coconut oil, flax seed oil or shortening you prefer. Remember the type of shortening you use directly influences the taste of your soup. The alternatives I suggest have a high nutritional value for the diet you wish to maintain.
4. Tahini may be substituted for eggs in any of the soups described. It must be the final ingredient added before serving to make a thick and flavorful soup.
5. Read the labels of the margarines you intend to use. Some contain olive oil or butter.
6. I have not experimented with the use of soy milk to replace creams, so I cannot recommend the substitute.

TOMATO HERB SOUP

1 tablespoon each of oregano, thyme, savory, basil, marjoram, mint and parsley (for fresh herbs use 2 to 3 sprigs)
6 cloves of garlic, chopped
4 plum or roma tomatoes, chopped
1 teaspoon Turkish red pepper or ½ teaspoon cayenne pepper
1 cinnamon stick
5 pieces of whole clove
5 piece of allspice
2 tablespoons of orange rind
3 tablespoons of honey
1 leek chopped
4 sundried tomatoes
2 medium onions sliced
2 quarts water
Olive oil
Salt and pepper to taste
1 pint yogurt
2 tablespoons flour

1. Cut a small piece of cheesecloth about 3" square or purchase a cheese cloth bag, similar to the bag you place lemons when using wedges for juice at a dinner.
2. Place your spices in the bag, bringing the ends together. Seal the bouquet with a piece of floral wire or twist tie that has had the paper striped.
3. Place enough olive oil to cover the bottom of the skillet.
4. Add the onions, garlic, Turkish pepper, bouquet of spices and herbs to the oil and sauté until the onions are well cooked.
5. Chop the tomatoes, and add them to the skillet with the sundried tomatoes and leeks.
6. Add the sautéed herbs to a soup pot along with enough water to fill the soup pot.
7. Add the orange rind and honey and allow the ingredients to come to a boil.
8. Reduce the heat and simmer for one hour.
9. Remove the bouquet from the soup.
10. Just before you are ready to serve the soup, place the yogurt in a bowl. Add the flour and combine thoroughly.
11. Add a cup of hot broth to the yogurt mixture and stir vigorously.
12. Pour the yogurt into the pot and continue stirring until fully combined.
13. Salt and pepper to taste.

NOTES:
1. This is a vegetarian soup, but if you wish to use chicken broth to enhance the flavor, you may.
2. Fresh herbs are preferred for this recipe, but you may use dried.
3. Tupelo honey may be used for diabetics.
4. Tahini may be substituted for yogurt.

5. Whisk the yogurt and flour until totally combined to avoid lumps before adding the hot broth.
6. Add the yogurt mixture right before serving and remove from the heat.
7. The use of a crockpot will intensify the vegetarian flavor.

TAHINI SOUP

6 cloves of garlic
½ bunch green onions
½ bunch parsley
1/3 cup rice
Rind of one lemon
2 quarts water, approximately
2 tablespoons saffron
1 cup Tahini
½ cup of watercress or roucketta, chopped
 1 tablespoon each of oregano, thyme, savory, basil, marjoram, mint and parsley (for fresh herbs use 2 to 3 sprigs)
6 cloves of garlic, chopped
4 plum or roma tomatoes, chopped
1 teaspoon Turkish red pepper or ½ teaspoon cayenne pepper
1 cinnamon stick
5 pieces whole clove
5 pieces allspice
2 tablespoons of orange rind
3 tablespoons of honey
1 leek, chopped
4 sundried tomatoes
2 medium onions, sliced
Olive oil
Salt and pepper to taste

1. Cut a piece of cheesecloth about 3" square or purchase a cheese cloth bag similar to the bag you place lemons when using wedges for juice at a dinner.
2. Place your spices in the bag, bring the ends together and seal the bouquet with a piece of floral wire or twist tie that has had the paper striped.
3. Place enough oil to cover the bottom of the skillet you are using.
4. Add the onions, garlic, Turkish pepper, bouquet of spices and herbs to the oil and sauté until the onions are well cooked.
5. Chop the tomatoes and add them to the skillet with the sundried tomatoes and leeks.
6. Add the sautéed herbs to the soup pot along with enough water to fill the soup pot.
7. Add the orange rind and honey and allow the ingredients to come to a boil.
8. Reduce the heat and simmer for one hour.
9. Remove the bouquet from the soup and add the rice.
10. Salt and pepper to taste.
11. Zest one lemon.

12. Simmer the saffron, lemon rind and 2 slices of lemon in one cup of water on low heat.
13. The water must change color and have the lemon scent.
14. Remove the lemon slices from the saffron water.
15. In a bowl place 1 cup of Tahini and add the scented water and combine.
16. Pour this into the soup pot and stir.
17. Serve with chopped watercress

NOTES:
1. This is a vegan soup.
2. Tupelo honey may be used for diabetics.
3. The flavor may be enhanced by using a meat base stock.

SPLIT PEA

INGREDIENTS
1 cup of green split peas
1 onion, chopped
1 Bay leaf
½ cup olive oil
2 cloves of garlic
2 quarts of water

Condiments:
Olive oil and vinegar
Or
Skordostube

1. Chop the garlic and onion.
2. Place them in a skillet with olive oil and bay leaf and caramelize.
3. Place them in a soup pot with 2 cups of water for 2 hours on medium high heat or a crock pot 4 hours on low.
4. Remove the bay leaf and salt and pepper to taste.

NOTES:
1. You may add more water if the soup is too thick, but bring the soup to a boil for a few minutes in order that the flavors meld.
2. The soup may be placed in a blender to form a puree.
3. Fried onions have also been used as a condiment.

SPICY CHICKEN TRAHANA SOUP

INGREDIENTS
1 quartered chicken
2 tomatoes, chopped
1 cup spicy trahana
1 onion, chopped
1 bay leaf
½ cup unsalted butter
1 cinnamon stick

½ bunch parsley, chopped
¼ teaspoon Turkish pepper
8 ounces red wine
Water
Salt to taste

1. Melt the butter in a skillet.
2. Sauté the bay leaf, pepper, parsley, cinnamon stick, onions and tomatoes.
3. Add the trahana and continue to sauté.
4. Lay the chicken quarters onto the sautéed mixture.
5. Add the red wine and ½ cup of water, cover and stew for 1 hour on a low medium heat.
6. Check the skillet halfway through cooking time to add water if necessary.

NOTES:
1. Olive oil may be substituted.
2. Slow cookers can be used, set on low for three hours.
3. Trahana is homemade sourdough pasta that can be made as a cereal if sweetened or in soups, as pasta and stews if made as a plain sourdough or peppery when made with a special trahana horto or trahana weed. This is the spicier version of the pasta and, personally, I feel tastier.

ROUMELI STYLE LEEK SOUP

2 leeks, sliced in half and chopped
1 potato, peeled and diced
¼ pound button mushrooms
1 stick unsalted butter
2 quarts water or broth
Chicken, beef, lamb or pork (optional)
1 egg
2 tablespoons whipping cream
Salt and pepper

1. Wash the leeks, mushrooms and potato.
2. Place them in a skillet with the melted butter, selected meat. Salt and pepper and sauté. This makes a great vegetarian base.
3. Add water, beef, lamb, pork or chicken stock and boil, or place the skillet ingredients into a crock pot and turn on low for 5 hours or place in a soup pot and cook on medium heat for 1 ½ hours.
4. Right before serving, whisk one egg with 2 tablespoons of whipping cream and add it to the soup and continue stirring for a few minutes.
5. Turn off heat and serve.

NOTES:
1. This soup may be made either as a meat base soup or as a vegetarian soup.
2. When whisking the egg and whipping cream, add ½ cup of the steaming broth to temper the egg. Then pour the egg mixture into the pot, stir slightly and remove from heat source.
3. Season the soup with lemon juice for additional flavor.

VEGETABLE SOUP

INGREDIENTS
2 cup of white wine
2 carrots, chopped
1 medium onion, chopped
1 cup celery, chopped
Celery leaves from the stalks chopped
1 green or yellow zucchini, chopped
¼ cup green peas
1 chopped russet potato
1 tomato, chopped
1 cup mushrooms
½ cup chopped green beans
1 cup chopped green pepper
2 cup shredded green leafy vegetables: Dandelions, Swiss chard, spinach or beet greens
3 cloves of garlic, chopped
1 red cayenne pepper, chopped (optional)
½ bunch green onions, chopped
½ cup olive oil
1 tablespoon each dried savory, dill and parsley
Salt and pepper
2 quarts water
Slices of Grandma's Toast sprinkled with kefalotirie or parmesan cheese

1. Heat the olive oil in a soup pot.
2. Add onion, celery leaves, tomato, mushrooms, green pepper, leafy vegetables, garlic, cayenne pepper, green onions, savory, dill and parsley and sauté until you have cooked down your tomato and the greens are cooked.
3. Add water and the remaining chopped vegetables.
4. Bring the water to a boil, reduce and cook at a medium heat for 40 minutes
5. Add the wine and salt and pepper.
6. Prepare Grandma's toast made with cheese.
7. Place soup in bowls and top with a piece of Grandma's Toast.

NOTES:
1. You do not need to use all the vegetables. You may adjust the recipe by adding or removing ingredients.
2. Pasta or rice may be added.
3. Chicken stock may be used.
4. Grandma's Toast could be made with garlic and cheese.

BEEF TRAHANA SOUP

INGREDIENTS

2 pounds beef soup bones, beef stew meat
4 cloves of garlic
½ cup trahana (sour dough pasta)
½ bunch each parsley and mint
2 quarts water
1 tomato
Olive oil
Salt and pepper

1. Chop the onions tomato, garlic and herbs.
2. Place it in a skillet with several tablespoons of olive oil and sauté until the onions are caramelized.
3. Add the meat and brown.
4. Place the skillet mixture into the soup pot.
5. Add the water, pasta, and bring the water to a boil.
6. Reduce the heat to medium and stew for 1 ½ hours.
7. Salt and pepper to taste.

NOTES:

1. This soup may be made with chicken or lamb.
2. You may spice up the soup with Turkish red pepper.
3. Trahana is homemade sourdough pasta that can be made as a cereal if sweetened or in soups, as pasta and stews if made as a plain sourdough or peppery when made with a special trahana horto or trahana weed. This is the sourdough version of the pasta, which has a mild flavor and texture.

AVGOLEMONO SOUP

2-4 pieces of chicken (thighs, leg quarters, breasts)
4 stalks of celery, chopped
2-3 yellow onions, chopped
2 quarts water
Salt and pepper
¼ cup rice or orzo
Avgolemono Sauce Recipe

1. Inspect the chicken for fat around the neck area and remove whatever you find.
2. Wash the pieces of chicken, and place on a dry towel.
3. Fill ¾ of the pot with water.
4. The chicken may be quartered or placed whole in the pot. Bring the water to a boil.
5. As the water comes to a boil, spot check the pot for scum or froth that emanates from the boiling chicken. Skim this froth from the broth and dispose. Reduce the heat to medium flame and continue simmering.
6. While the chicken is simmering, chop the celery and the onions and add them to the pot.
7. Remove the chicken from the pot and chop. Remove and dispose of the bones.

8. Return the chopped chicken to the pot.
9. Add the rice or orzo.
10. Once the rice is cooked, salt and pepper to taste. Then prepare the Avgolemono Sauce.

NOTES:
1. The broth base may be made with beef or lamb as well as chicken.
2. I have never attempted to make this soup with "meat-less" chicken. If you wish to try this substitution, it might be fun.
3. Variations to the above recipe involve sautéing parsley, rosemary and/or thyme in a skillet with one tablespoon of olive oil. Add this to the soup after skimming if you are using the soup pot" method. If you are using the crock pot method, you may add the ingredients at the start of simmering.
4. Chopped carrots may be added to the soup after skimming if you are using the soup pot method. If you are using the crock pot method, you may add the ingredients at the start of simmering.
5. If you are using a crock pot, cook the chicken on high for no more than four to five hours. DO NOT EXCEED THIS TIME. Exceeding the time limit will produce a bitter soup. A crock pot extracts flavors that exist in the chicken bones, overcooking starts breaking down the bones. The five hour time will give you an aspic type of broth.
6. The egg lemon sauce is added right before serving. The heat from the soup cooks the egg mixture. Be careful that you remove the soup from heat before you add the egg mixture and you continue to stir the soup until the egg has combined with the soup.

CHICKPEA SOUP

INGREDIENTS
1 pound chickpeas, dried
1 tomato
3 onions
1 bay leaf
2 teaspoons sea salt
Ground pepper to taste
½ cup olive oil

Olive oil and vinegar dressing
Or
Skordostube

1. Chop the tomato and onion into slices and add to a skillet with the bay leaf and olive oil.
2. Sauté until onions are caramelized.
3. Add to the soup pot with 2 quarts water and bring it to a boil or cook in a crock pot for 4-5 hours on low.
4. Add the salt and pepper to taste.

NOTES:
1. This soup is extremely easy to make. But don't make the mistake of adding the salt too soon. Add the salt slowly and only what is needed.
2. You may use either dressing as a condiment listed above for the soup.
3. The soup will be quite thick. You may either add more water and bring the soup to a boil or place it through a blender and puree. In either case the soup is very tasty.
4. Another condiment is fried onions

FASOLADA

INGREDIENTS
1 cup dry navy beans
3 carrots
2 white onions
1 tomato, chopped
½ bunch each parsley and thyme
4 stalks of celery
Salt and pepper
½ cup olive oil
2 quarts water
1 bay leaf

Condiments:
Olive oil and vinegar
Skordostube
1. Caramelize onions with the bay leaf, herbs and tomato in olive oil.
2. Deposit the sautéed onion mixture into a soup pot or crock pot with the beans, celery, carrots and water.
3. If you are using a soup pot, cook the mixture for 2 hours at low medium heat. If you are using a crock pot, cook the soup for 4 hours on low.
4. When the beans are tender, remove the bay leaf and salt and pepper to taste.

NOTES:
1. Use one tablespoon each of the herbs if dry.
2. Rice or orzo may be added.

FAVA

INGREDIENTS
1 cup of yellow peas
1 onion chopped
1 bay leaf
½ cup olive oil
2 cloves of garlic
2 quarts water
Condiments:
Olive oil and vinegar
Or
Skordostube

1. Chop the garlic and onion.
2. Place them in a skillet with olive oil and bay leaf and caramelize.
3. Place them in a soup pot with water for 2 hours on medium high heat or a crock pot 4 hours on low.
4. Remove the bay leaf and salt and pepper to taste.

NOTES:
1. You may add more water if the soup is too thick, but bring the soup to a boil for a few minutes in order that the flavors meld.
2. The soup may be placed in a blender to form a puree.
3. Fried onions have also been used as a condiment.

FISH SOUP – PSAROSOUPA

INGREDIENTS
1 whole red snapper or any other fatty fish
2 tablespoons olive oil
½ bunch parsley
2 sprigs dill, chopped or 1 tablespoon dill weed
2 cloves of garlic
4 stalks of celery
2 carrots
2 tomatoes
1 green pepper seeded
2 onions
2 potatoes
½ cup rice
Salt AND pepper
3 tablespoons olive oil
Avgolemono Recipe

1. Chop the garlic, herbs, onions and tomatoes and place them in a skillet with olive oil.
2. Heat the oil on a high heat and sauté the content until the tomatoes have created a sauce and the onions have become glossy, about 10 minutes.
3. Chop the remaining vegetables and set them aside in a bowl.
4. Wrap your fish in a cheesecloth tying the ends, to ensure that fish bones do not escape.
5. Place the fish in the soup pot with 2 quarts of water.
6. Add the sautéed ingredients, rice and the chopped vegetables to the soup pot.
7. Bring the mixture to a boil.
8. Reduce the heat to medium and continue to cook until the vegetables are soft and rice is cooked.
9. Remove the cheesecloth and scrape the meat from the fish bones. Take the meat from the fish and place that back into the soup pot. Dispose of the bones.
10. Allow the soup to simmer. Salt and pepper to taste.
11. Add the avgolemono sauce you wish and serve.

1. You may use fish fillets but the secret to this soup is the use of the fish bones to create a perfect broth. The fish bones provide the flavor for the soup.
2. Fish heads are equally as important when making the soup. Do not dispose of the bones or the heads until after they are boiled.
3. I remember that even my father would not dispose of the fish head. He enjoyed that the most.
4. This is a very rich soup. Serve with crusty bread.

GARLIC SOUP

INGREDIENTS
2-4 heads of garlic
5 full sprigs of fresh thyme
2 bay leaves
10 black peppercorns
2 quarts of water
¼ pound feta cheese, crumbled
1 cup yogurt or sour cream
2 tablespoons flour
2 large eggs
Olive oil
Salt
½ cup of watercress, chopped

1. Freeze your metal bowl and beaters.
2. Peel all the cloves of the garlic you intend on using.
3. Place the garlic, thyme, bay leaves, salt and peppercorns into a skillet with olive oil and sauté.
4. Place the sautéed items into the slow cooker and cook on high for four hours. If you need to make this immediately, use a large pot, a little more water than you would need and slow boil on medium heat for 40 minutes.
5. Separate 2 eggs, whites from yolks.
6. Combine the flour and the sour cream with a fork or small whisk and set aside. Make sure the flour is entirely combined with the cream to avoid lumps.
7. Reduce the heat of the soup to low or simmer.
8. Remove the bowl and beaters from the freezer and assemble the mixer.
9. Beat the egg whites first in the bowl on a fast setting.
10. Add the yolks and continue to beat.
11. Add the yogurt mixture and continue to beat.
12. Add 2 ladles of stock and continue to beat.
13. Add the egg mixture to the soup and turn off the heat. Continue stirring.
14. Serve with a sprinkle of watercress and/or feta on top.

NOTES:
1. This soup is not as garlic tasting as you might think. It is mild, but very tasty.
2. For the vegan variation of this soup see the Tahini Soup recipe.
3. The flavor may be enhanced by using a meat-base stock.
4. Freezing of the beaters promotes quicker and thicker egg whites and will give you a great egg lemon base.

5. After tempering the egg mixture, combine it with the soup and continue stirring. Do not forget to turn off the pot or remove the pot from heat so the eggs do not curdle.
6. Consider using black garlic, for an interesting change.

LAMB SOUP 1
ORIGINAL MAGERITSA

INGREDIENTS
Lamb heart, lungs, intestines and tripe
1 Lamb shank
1 bunch each dill, mint, parsley and fennel
3 cloves garlic
5 stalks of celery
1 bunch green onions
1 white onion
½ cup rice
Olive oil
1 jug white vinegar
¼ cup baking soda
Salt and pepper
Avgolemono Sauce

1. Clean the lamb intestines, heart, tripe and lung by washing them in warm water. Today's butchers have power washers that clean the intestines and tripe very well. This is important to avoid bacteria problems.
2. Place the lamb organs in a large bowl of white vinegar, baking soda and water, while you prepare the remainder of the soup.
3. Chop the garlic, onions and herbs and place them in a skillet with the rice.
4. Sauté the herb mixture in olive oil until the rice becomes white and the onions are glossy.
5. Chop the celery.
6. Add the lamb shank.
7. Fill a soup pot with 3 quarts of water, and bring the water to a boil.
8. Remove the organs from the vinegar bath and rinse them thoroughly.
9. Place the organs in the heating water.
10. Allow the water to come to a boil and skim the froth that appears.
11. Reduce the heat to medium high and cook the organs, skimming the broth at the appearance of froth.
12. Repeat this step until there is no more froth.
13. Remove the organs from the broth and chop them into small pieces.
14. Return the organ pieces into the broth. Add the rice and the skillet ingredients.
15. Cook for 1 hour or until the rice is cooked.
16. Salt and pepper to taste and use a simple Avgolemono sauce for the recipe.

NOTES:
1. This soup is traditional eaten on Easter Sunday at probably 2 or 3 a.m. This soup has to use every portion of the lamb, traditionally the spleen and liver are to be used as well, but those organs make the soup bitter and therefore are used elsewhere in another recipe.
2. The use of the lamb shank is a secret. The use of the shank provides the meat and the marrow flavor, giving the soup an intense flavor.
3. Scrubbing the tripe and intestines are important if they have not been professionally cleaned, to remove bacteria and digested material.
4. The bath in vinegar and baking soda is important. Whatever the scrubbing does not remove the vinegar kills the bacteria and the baking soda removes that awful smell.
5. Finally, the boiling and skimming removes the impurities that could possibly remain. The skimming clarifies the broth and makes the soup more appetizing.
6. You really do need a strong constitution in order to make this soup, but the end result is really worth the trouble. After my mother's passing, I was treated royally to render this soup. The preparation did not bother me, if I kept on cleaning up, but the look on my guest's faces was worth the work it is a delicious soup.

LAMB SOUP 2
MODIFIED MAGERITSA

INGREDIENTS
2 lamb shanks
1 bunch each dill, mint, parsley and fennel
3 clove garlic
5 stalks of celery
1 bunch green onions
1 white onion
½ cup rice
Olive oil
1 jug white vinegar
¼ cup baking soda
Salt and pepper
Avgolemono Sauce

1. Chop the garlic, onions and herbs and place them in a skillet with the rice.
2. Sauté the herb mixture in olive oil until the rice becomes white and the onions are glossy.
3. Chop the celery.
4. Fill a soup pot with 3 quarts of water, and bring to a boil.
5. Skim the froth that appears.
6. Reduce the heat to medium high and continue cooking the lamb.
7. Skim the froth floating on the top of the broth again.
8. Repeat this step until there is no more froth.
9. Remove the lamb from the broth and chop into small pieces.
10. Return the lamb pieces to the broth. Add the rice and the skillet ingredients.
11. Cook for 1 hour or until the rice is cooked.

12. Salt and pepper to taste and use a simple Avgolemono sauce.

NOTES:
1. This recipe for lamb soup gives you a similar taste to the original mageritsa soup, without the organ meat. For those who are "faint of heart" this is your soup.
2. This is a more user-friendly soup to prepare with less preparation work.

LENTIL SOUP

<u>INGREDIENTS</u>
1 cup of brown or red lentils
2 cloves garlic
1 bay leaf
1 onion
Olive oil

Olive oil and vinegar
Or
Skordostube

1. Chop the garlic and onion.
2. Place them in a skillet with olive oil and bay leaf and caramelize.
3. Place them in a soup pot for 2 hours on medium high heat or a crock pot 4 hours on low.
4. Remove the bay leaf and salt and pepper to taste.

NOTES:
1. Other versions include adding ½ cup orzo, sautéed spinach and chopped carrots to the cooking process.
2. Fried onions have also been used as a condiment.

PAPOU GEORGE'S KAKAVIA

<u>INGREDIENTS</u>
All shell fish, any kind, any amount and any selection (NO FISH)
  Including octopus, lobster, clams, oysters, crab legs, crawfish, mussels, abalone, cuttlefish
 conches, squid, crab, cuttlefish, shrimp
2 cloves of garlic
1 bunch of parsley
2 large tomato
2 medium onion
½ teaspoon cayenne pepper
6 strands to 1 tablespoon saffron
2 bay leaves
2 quarts of water

3 tablespoons flour
1 cup rich white wine
¼ cup crumbled feta cheese (optional)
Olive oil
Salt and pepper to taste
Avgolemono Sauce

1. Heat enough oil to cover the bottom of the pot.
2. Chop the garlic, onions, herbs, spices and vegetables, and sauté them in a soup pot with the saffron until glazed.
3. Add the flour to the spice mixture and stir.
4. If the paste is too thick add a little water.
5. Add the soft seafood first and sauté.
6. Add the remaining seafood with the shells and fill the kettle with water.
7. Bring the soup to a boil, reduce the heat to medium and cook for 1 hour.
8. Add the wine and simmer.
9. Salt and pepper to taste.
10. Sprinkle with crumbled feta cheese and serve with crusty bread.

NOTES:
1. This soup originated in Marseilles, which was a Greek province. The original recipe did not call for fish, only shellfish. Fish were too important of a money maker to be used by fisherman in a soup, so they sold their catch. The shellfish and other catch were brought home and made into this stew.
2. My Great-Grandfather George had sponge diving boats on the island of Symi. My father would tell me that this was one of his favorite soups, but there was a crazy secret.
3. Major Secret: All shellfish must be accompanied by their shells in the soup. That included couch, shrimp, clams, oysters, sea fingers, etc. The shells may be rinsed but not scrubbed.
4. The above might be crazy but it makes all the difference in the recipe. It makes a beautiful soup bowl.
5. Serve with Grandma's Toast.
6. Every time I made this soup, the main complaint was that the pot was not large enough. If made correctly the room wafts with the scent of a seashore.

PATSAS

INGREDIENTS
2 pounds tripe beef, veal or lamb
½ bunch fresh dill or 2 tablespoons dry
2 sprigs mint or 1 teaspoon dry
2 sprigs parsley or 1 teaspoon dry
½ bunch green onions
4 stalks celery
2 tablespoons olive oil
2 quarts water

1. In a skillet, heat the olive oil with the herbs and green onions. Sauté until the content of the pot has a bright color and is fragrant.
2. In a soup pot, bring 2 quarts of water and the tripe to a boil.
3. Reduce the heat to medium high heat and skim the froth from above the water.
4. Repeat the skimming at least two more times until the broth is clear.
5. Remove the tripe from the soup pot and cut it into small squares. Return the squares to the soup pot.
6. Pour the content of the skillet into the soup pot.
7. Bring the soup pot to boil once more.
8. Reduce the heat and simmer for ½ hour.

NOTES:
1. This is a fatty soup. The condiment is definitely needed.
2. This skimming is an important part of the recipe. The froth is impurities that could make your soup bitter and smelly.
3.   Skordostube is a favorite condiment for this soup.
4. When considering the type of Avgolemono for your soup consider the use of the condiment. If you opt for egg lemon with wine, you might want to rethink the need for Skordostube.

Chapter 4: Salad & Vegetables

VILLAGE SALAD

<u>INGREDIENTS</u>
1 sharp white onion
1 beefsteak tomato
1 cucumber
½ pound olives, green or black
2 tablespoons capers
7 Pepperoncini
¼ pound feta cheese
1 teaspoon each oregano and thyme

Dressings: Olive Oil and Lemon or Olive Oil and Vinegar

1. Slice the onion into ringlets and place on a plate.
2. Slice the tomato into circular slices and arrange on the dish slightly over the onions
3. Using a fork, scrape the green peel of the cucumber from one end to the other, and continue this around the entire cucumber.
4. Slice the cucumber in circular slices, wedges or triangular pieces. Spread the pieces on the plate.
5. Sprinkle the olives, Pepperoncini, feta cheese and capers.
6. Sprinkle the herbs.
7. Add the salad dressing

<u>NOTES:</u>:
1. Though the familiar "Greek Salad" with the lettuce is considered common, the Village Salad is extremely common.
2. This is a refreshing salad that is made during the summer.

ARTICHOKE MOUSSAKA

INGREDIENTS
4 large artichoke flowers
1 pound ground beef or lamb OR
    ½ cup of rice
2 tomatoes diced
1 pint white mushrooms, sliced
2 zucchinis, sliced in circles
1 bag frozen artichokes
Juice of one lemon
½ teaspoon allspice, cinnamon and nutmeg
2 onions chopped
2 tablespoons olive paste or ½ cup chopped olives

Prepare other Artichoke Flowers
1. Cut the stems off the artichoke flowers
2. Remove about 15 stems from the bottom of the artichoke, around the stem. You should see a lighter green around the area.
3. Place the flowers into a pot of water to boil for about 10 to 15 minutes. **Try not to over boil.**
4. Remove the flowers from the hot water, and let them cool on a plate.
5. Take the plate over to the kitchen sink, and hold one flower at a time under cool running water.
6. The flower will open as a blossom. With your thumb and two fingers, grab the center of the flower, twist and pull out. Place the thorny petals in a bowl and carefully place the flower back on the dish.
7. Follow Steps 5 and 6 until you have taken out the centers of all the flowers.
8. Take the centers you have pulled from the flower and cut off the thorny portion of the leaf. Place the trimmed leaf into the bowl.

Prepare other Veggies
9. Thaw the frozen artichoke hearts, or drain the jar of artichoke hearts.
10. Slice the zucchinis into small circles and place them on a cookie sheet, brush with olive oil, lightly sprinkle the zucchini with cumin, salt and pepper. Bake until limp at 300°F.

Rice
11. Place the diced tomatoes, onion, olives and spices into a skillet and cook them down.
12. If you wish to add meat and/or rice, you may do so here. If you are using rice, allow it to absorb the liquid in the skillet. Otherwise, use a slotted spoon to remove the mixture during construction.
13. Take the open flower and arrange layers of the prepared vegetables: zucchinis, tomato, artichoke and mushroom. Repeat the layers until you reach ½" of the top of the flower. Repeat the layers for the remaining flowers.
14. Place a heaping layer of béchamel sauce at the opening of the flower.

15. Place the flower in a semi-deep baking pan. When you have placed all the flowers in the pan, add 1 cup of water with lemon juice.
16. Bake at 330°F for about 45 minutes or until the béchamel is golden.

NOTES:
1. **Béchamel Sauce Recipe of your selection**
2. This recipe may be prepared meatless by substituting the rice for meat.
3. This recipe may also be prepared without the artichoke flower by using a baking pan and frozen artichoke hearts. The difference would be the layers you would normally arrange in the artichoke flower would be layered in a pie or baking pan.
4. Other vegetables or greens may also be used. The moussaka is a layered terrine. Remember that the base layer should be something that provides a good base for cutting squares and absorbing juices such as a potato.
5. Panko bread crumbs, which are thicker than most bread crumbs may be added as an optional topping to the Béchamel. Baste with broth while baking.

ARTICHOKES

INGREDIENTS
4 artichoke flowers or frozen artichokes
Olive oil
Lemon juice

1. Take the flower in hand and hold it upside down so that the stem is exposed.
2. Remove the bottom leaves until you begin to see a lighter color green closer to the stem.
3. Cut the stem close to the base of the flower.
4. Chop approximately 1 ½" from the top. If correctly cut, you will see the thicker portion of the flower exposed.
5. You may boil the flower whole or you may cut the flower in half and steam.
6. Remove the flower from the water or steamer and drain in a colander.
7. If the flower is whole, stand it on its base.
8. Mix the olive oil with the lemon juice and herbs or prepare the Avgolemono sauce that you prefer.
9. For the flower, you want to drop the sauce into the center of the flower and extend outward through the layers. This is especially true with the olive oil and lemon juice.
10. If the flower is halved, lay the halves with the cut side up, drizzle the appropriate sauce throughout the cut portion of the flower.
11. Have an extra portion of the sauce available for leaf dipping and an extra plate for the chewed leaves.

NOTES:
1. Egg lemon sauce is a must; your choice of recipe.
2. Frozen artichokes are preferred over canned.
3. Olive oil and lemon juice is also a great dressing.
4. Dill, rosemary, tarragon or mint may be used as a seasoning.

5. For frozen or canned vegetables, heat the artichoke hearts and then use the selected sauce.

BAKED OKRA

<u>INGREDIENTS</u>

Olive oil
1 layer onions, cut in thin slices
1 green pepper, sliced
1 pound of fresh or frozen okra
½ bunch fresh parsley or 1 tablespoon dried
½ bunch fresh dill weed or 1 tablespoon dried
2 tomatoes, diced
White vinegar
Balsamic vinegar
1 cup red wine
Salt and pepper
Garlic sliced to taste

1. If you are using fresh okra, be careful not to cut into the pod itself. Trim the top crown off, and place it in a liquid mixture of 2 parts white vinegar and one-part water for at least one hour. The liquid must cover the okra. This procedure helps remove the slime.
2. Lightly cover bottom of skillet with olive oil and heat to medium high.
3. Sprinkle sliced onions and green peppers over bottom of pan and sauté.
4. Add the garlic and herbs, and continue to sauté.
5. Add the tomato and sauté until sauce.
6. Place okra in a roasting pan and add sautéed ingredients over the okra.
7. Sprinkle with balsamic vinegar, wine and bake covered at 350° F for 1½ hours.
8. Uncover and bake for 15 minutes to thicken if necessary.

NOTES:
1. This recipe may be made in a crockpot. Deposit the skillet ingredients over the okra with the wine and vinegar and cook on low for 3 hours.
2. Water may replace wine for a simpler taste.
3. Walnut oil may replace olive oil.

DAD'S BEAN SALAD

<u>INGREDIENTS</u>

16 ounces' white beans, kidney beans or chickpeas
1 large white onion
Oregano
Thyme
2 cloves garlic
Dressing: Olive oil and Vinegar

1. You may either mix 16 ounces total of the beans listed above or use one type.
2. Slice the onion into wedges.
3. Rub and sprinkle oregano and thyme to taste.
4. Press the cloves of garlic.
5. Add the dressing and stir.

NOTES:
1. This has to be the simplest of all the salads and the best tasting. As a child I could not wait for my dad to make this particular salad. I did not care which beans he used, just that it was this recipe. When presented in a cooking class, the initial remarks from some of the participants was – yuk; until they sampled.
2. Garlic is optional if you wish to use, either pressed or powdered.
3. Balsamic vinegar can be used in the salad. Change your vinegars to obtain variations on the flavor.
4. Rubbing the herbs before you use them increases the fragrance and taste.

BRIAM – ASIA MINOR VEGETABLE STEW

INGREDIENTS
Olive oil
2 large onions, chopped
2 potatoes Yukon Gold, chopped
2 carrots, chopped
2 zucchinis (yellow and green), chopped
4 tomatoes, chopped
1 each green, red, yellow and orange peppers
2 large green peppers, chopped and seeded
3 cloves garlic, chopped
5 stalks celery, chopped
½ pound okra
1 bag frozen artichokes
1 eggplant, chopped
¼ pound green beans
Sweet Wine (red or white – Port, Muscat or Mavrodaphnie)
1 bunch each tarragon, oregano, dill, thyme and rosemary, chopped (dry herbs may also be used)
Salt and pepper

1. Chop the tomatoes and add them to the skillet with ¼ cup of olive oil and garlic.
2. Add chopped herbs to the skillet, and salt and pepper to taste.
3. Stew the tomatoes and herbs until a sauce forms and you can distinctly smell the herbs.
4. Combine all the vegetables in a roasting pan.
5. Pour the skillet ingredients over the vegetables.
6. Add olive oil and wine.
7. Bake at 350°F for 1 ½ hours to 2 hours covered.
8. Serve as a side dish or over rice.

NOTES:
1. This is a treasured vegetable stew. The beauty of this recipe is that you are not limited to the vegetables that are shown.
2. The more texture and color that is added the more people cannot resist.
3. It is very difficult to limit the portion size to your family and guests, but consider not going over three cups per person.
4. Consider adding different types of mushrooms and Turkish or cayenne pepper to the skillet.
5. Frozen vegetables may be used for convenience, if necessary. Fresh is preferred.
6. Frozen okra and artichokes may be used if you wish to simplify this recipe. The frozen artichokes also provide more hearts than having to prepare a fresh artichoke.
7. If you do not have sweet wine, add ½ cup of sugar to the sauce recipe.

CABBAGE

INGREDIENTS
1 cabbage
Olive oil
1 lemon
Salt and pepper

1. Take the fresh head of cabbage and remove the exterior leaves and quarter
2. Place the quarters in a pot of water and let it come to a boil.
3. Reduce the heat to medium high and let it cook until soft and completely done, about 30 to 40 minutes.
4. Cut the cabbage into quarters and season with olive oil, salt and pepper to taste.

CABBAGE II

INGREDIENTS
1 cabbage
2 tomatoes
2 white or yellow onions
2 cloves of garlic
Olive oil
Salt and pepper

1. Take the fresh head of cabbage and remove the exterior leaves
2. Cut the cabbage in slices
3. Slice the onions and sauté them in a pot with olive oil.
4. Add the chopped tomatoes and continue sautéing.
5. Add the slice cabbage. Sauté until glossy.
6. Salt and pepper to taste.

CAULIFLOWER

INGREDIENTS
1 cauliflower

Olive oil
1 lemon
Salt and pepper

1. Take the fresh head of cauliflower and remove the exterior leaves and quarter
2. Place the quarters in a pot of water and let it come to a boil.
3. Reduce the heat to medium high and let it cook until soft and completely done, about 30 to 40 minutes.
4. Cut the cauliflower into quarters and season with olive oil, salt and pepper to taste.

CAULIFLOWER II

INGREDIENTS
1 cauliflower
2 tomatoes
2 white or yellow onions
2 cloves of garlic
Olive oil
Salt and pepper

1. Take the fresh head of cauliflower and remove the exterior leaves
2. Cut the cauliflower in slices
3. Slice the onions and sauté them in a pot with olive oil.
4. Add the chopped tomatoes and continue sautéing.
5. Add the slices of cauliflower. Cook until cooked thoroughly.
6. Salt and pepper to taste.

DOMATOKEFTEDES
(Tomato Fritters)

INGREDIENTS
6 large tomatoes or 10 Roma, peeled and chopped
1 large yellow onion, minced
1 teaspoon sugar
1 egg
2 tablespoons fresh mint or 1 tablespoon dry mint
½ cup each parmesan and feta
2 cups all purpose flour (for dredging)
Fresh ground sea salt and pepper
Olive oil for frying
½ lemon (optional) for serving

1. Combine the peeled and chopped tomatoes in a bowl with the onion, sugar, mint and cheese.
2. After combining the ingredients well, cover the bowl with plastic and refrigerate for 30 minutes.
3. Place enough oil in the skillet to cover the bottom and heat.

4. While the oil is heating, remove the bowl from the refrigerator and form the cooled mixture into balls.
5. Cover with flour and fry for 5 minutes on each side or until golden brown.
6. Place on paper towel to absorb excess oil before setting on plate.
7. Serve warm with a squeeze of lemon on the side.

NOTES:
1. This is a Greek veggie burger
2. Mashed potato may be substituted for the egg
3. If your patties are too moist you might want to add some flour or potato to the mixture prior to forming the patties.

EGGPLANT SALAD

INGREDIENTS
2 large eggplant
2 Roma tomatoes
2 tablespoons dried parsley
1 tablespoon dried oregano
1 onion
3 cloves garlic
½ cup olive oil
2 teaspoon lemon juice
Olives for garnish

1. Cut your eggplants in half and place them on a cookie sheet.
2. Brush with olive oil and bake at 375°F for 45 minutes. The eggplant skin must be dried and easily removed and the meat soft.
3. When the eggplant is removed from the oven, allow to cool. Remove the skin from the eggplant and add it and the meat of the eggplant to the food processor, blender or mortar.
4. Slice the onion and tomatoes sautéing slightly with the herbs and pressed garlic in olive oil until limp.
5. Once limp and the herbs and garlic become fragrant, add the garlic mixture to the eggplant.
6. Beat the eggplant adding the remainder of the olive oil when needed.
7. The salad should be a whipped consistency. Chop or purée the olives as a garnish.

NOTES:
1. The sautéing of the onion, tomatoes, herbs and garlic blends the flavors and adds a natural sweetness.
2. The food processor or blender is your best bet for blending these vegetables.
3. The addition of olive oil helps blend the vegetables.

BYZANTINE EGGPLANT OR EGGPLANT TERRINE

1 eggplant, cut in ½"-thick slices
¼ cup olive oil
Salt and pepper
1 cup kefalotirie or parmesan cheese

Sauce
2 tomatoes, diced
1 teaspoon oregano
1 diced onion
¼ cup olive oil
Chopped olive
1 cup yogurt

1. Arrange the eggplant slices on a cookie sheet, baste with olive oil and salt and pepper.
2. Bake for 15 minutes at 300°F or until limp. After baking, set the eggplant aside to cool.
3. Sauté the tomatoes, oregano, onion and olives in the olive oil until the tomatoes form a sauce.
4. Add the yogurt, reduce heat, stir until thick and remove from heat.
5. Using a well-greased meatloaf container or pie plate, place the first layer of eggplant.
6. Place a layer of sauce.
7. Place a layer of cheese.
8. Repeat Steps 4 through 6 until all the ingredients are used.
9. Finish with a layer of cheese.
10. Bake the eggplant at 300°F for 30 minutes or until cheese is melted and eggplant is done.
11. Slice and serve hot.

NOTES:
1. Mashed potatoes may be substituted for the cheese.
2. Grapeseed oil may be substituted for olive oil.
3. Sliced olives may be added to the sauce.
4. 1 tablespoon of flour may take the place of the yogurt in the sauce.

KOLOKITHOKEFTEDES FRITTERS (ZUCCHINI FRITTERS)
INGREDIENTS
1 ½ pounds zucchini, trimmed and grated
2 bunches green onions, minced
6 ounces feta cheese, crumbled
½ cup parmesan cheese
2 eggs beaten
4 tablespoons fresh dill and mint or 1 tablespoon dry dill and mint
2 cups all purpose flour (for dredging)
¼ teaspoon cayenne pepper and/or garlic powder
Fresh ground sea salt and pepper
Olive oil for frying
½ lemon (optional) for serving

1. Mix the zucchini, green onions, feta, parmesan, eggs, herbs, salt and pepper.
2. After combining the ingredients well, cover the bowl with plastic and refrigerate for 30 minutes.
3. Place enough oil in the skillet to cover the bottom and heat.
4. While the oil is heating, remove the bowl from the refrigerator and form the cooled mixture into balls.
5. Optional: add cayenne pepper or garlic powder to the flour.
6. Cover with flour and fry for 5 minutes on each side or until golden brown.
7. Place on paper towel to absorb excess oil before setting on plate.
8. Serve warm with a squeeze of lemon on the side.

NOTES:
1. This is the Greek version of veggie burgers
2. Mashed potatoes may be substituted for eggs as a binder
3. If your patties are too moist, you might want to add some flour to the mixture prior to forming.
4. You may season your flour with onion powder or other spices
5. Grapeseed oil may be substituted for olive oil.

GREEK GRANDMA POTATOES

INGREDIENTS
4 or 5 potatoes
2 or 3 cloves garlic or garlic powder
1 onion
Juice of one lemon
½ tablespoon each dried oregano and thyme
Olive oil
Salt and pepper

1. Traditionally all Greeks peel their potatoes. This is an optional step. It has been found that the majority of the nutrients of vegetables are in the actual skin. If you do not peel the skin, wash the exterior of the potato with a vegetable brush.
2. Slice the onion into wedges.
3. Place the potatoes and onions into a roasting pan.
4. If you wish to use the zest of the lemon, you may. That always adds flavor. Juice one lemon and add that to a cup.
5. Add the herbs to the lemon juice.
6. Grate the fresh cloves in a garlic grater or press them into the cup.
7. Add 2 parts olive oil to the lemon juice mixture in the cup.
8. Add salt and pepper to the mixture.
9. Beat the contents of the cup until everything is thoroughly combined.
10. Sprinkle the lemon mixture over the potatoes and onions.
11. Bake at 350°F until golden brown.

NOTES:

1. Yukon Gold potatoes work wonderfully for this recipe.
2. Garlic powder can be used.
3. Fresh herbs maybe used in this recipe.
4. Juice from lemon is preferred, but you may use concentrated lemon juice.

GREEK SALAD

INGREDIENTS

One stalk romaine lettuce
1 beefsteak tomato
1 semi-peeled cucumber
½ pound pitted Kalamata olives
8 Pepperoncini peppers
4 ounces feta cheese, sliced or crumbled
1 green bell pepper
1 medium onion, sliced in rings
1 tablespoon each dried oregano, thyme, dill and parsley
6 anchovies (optional)

Dressings: Olive Oil and Lemon or Olive Oil and Vinegar

1. Shred the lettuce by hand into a bowl.
2. Hold the cucumber in your hand. Take the fork and scrape lines from one end to the other.
3. Slice the cucumber into circles maintaining the green and scraped peel. Place the slices into the bowl.
4. Slice the tomato wedges and place them in the bowl with the lettuce.
5. Cut the green pepper in half and remove the seeds. Slice the pepper in thin slices and add them to the bowl.
6. Peel the onion. Then proceed to either cut circle "onion ring" pattern or into wedges and add them to the bowl.
7. Add the olives and Pepperoncini to the bowl.
8. Add the feta cheese, either crumbled or in slices, to the bowl.
9. Sprinkle the dried herbs.
10. Give a preliminary toss of the salad using your hands.
11. Add the dressing and toss. Enjoy.

NOTES:
1. This is a wonderful salad for lunch or as a side dish.
2. Radish, beets or boiled potatoes may be added.
3. Traditionally in Tarpon Springs, Florida a ½ cup of potato salad is placed under the tossed salad.
4. Anchovies added at the very end is a definite tradition.

GREEK SEAFOOD SALAD

INGREDIENTS

One stalk romaine lettuce
1 beefsteak tomato
1 semi-peeled cucumber
½ pound pitted Kalamata olives
8 Pepperoncini peppers
4 ounces feta cheese, sliced or crumbled
1 green bell pepper
1 medium-sized onion, sliced in rings
1 tablespoon each dried oregano, thyme, dill and parsley
6 anchovies
1 cup "popcorn" shrimp
1 cup steamed seafood mix (mussels, clams, octopus, etc)

1. Shred the lettuce by hand into a bowl.
2. Hold the cucumber in your hand. Take the fork and scrape lines from one end to the other.
3. Slice the cucumber into circles maintaining the green and scraped peel. Place the slices into the bowl.
4. Slice the tomato wedges and place them in the bowl with the lettuce.
5. Cut the green pepper in half and remove the seeds. Slice the pepper in thin slices, and add them to the bowl.
6. Peel the onion. Then proceed to either cut circle "onion ring" pattern or into wedges, and add them to the bowl.
7. Add the olives and Pepperoncini to the bowl.
8. Add the feta cheese either crumbled or sliced to the bowl.
9. Sprinkle in the dried herbs.
10. Give a preliminary toss of the salad using your hands.
11. Add the pickled or steamed seafood mix.
12. Add the dressing and toss. Enjoy.
13. Top with anchovies.

NOTES:
1. Dressings: olive oil and lemon or olive oil and vinegar
2. This is a wonderful salad for a meal or as a side dish.
3. Radish, beets or boiled potatoes may be added.
4. The seafood department of any grocery store has a mixed seafood bag that can either be pickled or steamed for use in this recipe.
5. Anchovies added at the very end is a definite tradition.

GREEK STYLE PICKLED GREEN TOMATOES

INGREDIENTS

2-4 pounds green tomatoes
1 green pepper (optional)
1 white onion (optional)
12 sprigs of dill
½ teaspoon oregano, parsley, rosemary and/or thyme

4 or more cloves of garlic
3 cups white or balsamic vinegar
1 bay leaf
¼ cup sea salt
Sliced Kalamata olives
1 tablespoon olive oil
½ tablespoon Turkish pepper (optional)
5 cups water
¼ cup capers

1. Cut the tomatoes into wedges and set aside.
2. Slice the green pepper and onion into wedges and set aside.
3. Slice the garlic and the olives and set aside.
4. Arrange the wedges of tomatoes, onions, green peppers, garlic, capers and dill in the Mason Jar. It is best to layer and/or stack.
5. Distribute the sliced olives around the jar.
6. Bring the vinegar, water, oil, spices and salt to a boil.
7. Immediately pour the heated liquid, with the spices, over the tomatoes, onions and pepper in the jar.
8. Try to bring the liquid as close to the top of the jar as possible.
9. Let the liquid cool and cover with the cap, then refrigerate.

NOTES:
1. Don't forget to sterilize the jars, boil them for 15 minutes, dry them opening side down on lint-free cloth.
2. Do not forget to boil the tops.
3. The pickles should remain good for months.
4. White vinegar is traditional, but balsamic gives you better flavor.
5. Try different types of vinegars - cider, wine, etc.

GREEN BEANS

INGREDIENTS
1 pound green beans
2 large red potatoes, peeled and chopped
1 large onion, chopped
1 tomato, chopped
1 garlic clove, chopped (optional)
Olive oil
½ bunch chopped fresh parsley or ½ bunch chopped fresh dill or 1 teaspoon of either dried
Salt and pepper to taste

1. Place enough oil in a medium to large size pot to cover its bottom.
2. Heat the oil slowly, adding the onion, tomato, garlic and parsley or dill. Stir occasionally.
3. Add the potatoes and a cup of water.
4. Wash the green beans in water, and place them in a strainer to drain.

5. Snip off the ends of the green beans with your fingers or a knife, and, if necessary, cut them in half and place in a bowl.
6. If you are adding meat, this is the time you would be adding the portion to the pot.
7. Add the cleaned green beans to the pot, and raise the temperature to a medium heat. Stir and allow the beans to cook for 15-20 minutes, until the beans and potatoes are soft. If necessary add a little more water to the pot (1/2 cup).

NOTES:
1. Fresh tomatoes are the best. Sometimes that's not possible. The recipes are better when jar tomato sauce or carton sauce is used. People with stomach problems found these alternatives worked when they were in a bind.
2. Fresh green beans and vegetables bring the best flavor and nutrition. If fresh is not possible, the next best is frozen. Thaw the vegetables you are using. Use the above recipe but cook for 15 minutes.
3. Meat is an optional addition, about 1 pound (lamb, beef, pork or goat).

KOLOKITHOKEFTEDES FRITTERS (ZUCCHINI FRITTERS)

INGREDIENTS
1 ½ pounds zucchini, trimmed and grated
2 bunches green onions, minced
6 ounces' feta cheese, crumbled
½ cup parmesan cheese
2 eggs, beaten
4 tablespoons fresh dill and mint or   1 tablespoon dried
2 cups all-purpose flour (for dredging)
¼ teaspoon cayenne pepper and/or garlic powder
Fresh ground sea salt and pepper
Olive oil for frying
½ lemon (optional) for serving

1. Mix the zucchini, green onions, feta, parmesan, eggs, herbs, salt and pepper.
2. After combining the ingredients well, cover the bowl with plastic and refrigerate for 30 minutes.
3. Place enough oil in the skillet to cover the bottom and heat.
4. While the oil is heating, remove the bowl from the refrigerator and form the cooled mixture into balls.
5. Optional: add cayenne pepper or garlic powder to the flour.
6. Cover with flour and fry for 5 minutes on each side or until golden brown.
7. Place on paper towel before setting in plate to absorb excess oil.
8. Serve warm with a squeeze of lemon on the side.

NOTES:
1. This is the Greek version of veggie burgers.
2. Mashed potatoes may be substituted for eggs as a binder
3. If your patties are too moist, add some flour to the mixture prior to forming.
4. You may season your flour with onion powder or other spices.

5. Grapeseed oil may be substituted for olive oil.

FRIED OKRA

INGREDIENTS
1 pound okra
1 onion
Olive oil
1 lemon
Salt and Pepper

1. Carefully handle the okra so as not to break the skin.
2. Heat the olive oil in a skillet with the sliced onion.
3. When the onion is caramelized, add the okra and fry until brown.
4. Remove the okra from the oil with the onions and place on a paper towel to dry.
5. Place the okra and onions in a bowl, salt and pepper and sprinkle with lemon juice.

NOTES:
1. Okra is not popular because of its mucus traits. Lemon juice, vinegar and wine can cut this effect.
2. Turkish red pepper spices the taste.
3. Tzaziki is a great sauce to use.

QUINCE – A NEW POTATO

INGREDIENTS
2-4 quince
¼ cup olive oil
½ teaspoon each brown sugar or honey, cinnamon and nutmeg
1 pinch or 1/8 teaspoon of powdered vanilla
½ teaspoon of sugar
1 Vidalia onion
Juice of 1 lemon
Salt and Pepper

1. Parboil the quince for 10 minutes.
2. Quarter the fruit and remove the seeds and core. Slice the quince into thinner wedges. Place the wedges into a bowl of water.
3. Heat some olive oil in a skillet.
4. Slice the onion and add it to the skillet along with the lemon juice, spices, sugar and vanilla.
5. Remove the quince from the water and lay them on baking parchment.
6. Coat the quince with the oil mixture, laying the onions over the slices.
7. Bake the slices at 350°F until golden.

NOTES:
1. Butter or margarine may be substituted for olive oil.
2. Brown sugar or honey may be used instead of honey.

REVITHOKEFTEDES FRITTERS
(CHICKPEA FRITTERS)

INGREDIENTS
2 ¾ cup of chickpeas*
1 large yellow onion, minced
1 large boiled red potato, mashed
1 egg
2 tablespoons fresh parsley or 1 tablespoon dried
½ -1 teaspoon cumin
2 cups all-purpose flour (for dredging)
2 cloves garlic, grated
Fresh ground sea salt and pepper
Olive oil for frying
½ lemon cut in wedges (optional) for serving

1. Use two cans chickpeas. Rinse and add to a bowl.
2. Mash your chickpeas. If you want to use a food processor, that is great.
3. Add the mashed potato, onion, egg, parsley, cumin and garlic.
4. Combine the mixture thoroughly.
5. After combining the ingredients well, cover the bowl with plastic and refrigerate for 30 minutes.
6. Place enough oil in the skillet to cover the bottom and heat.
7. While the oil is heating, remove the bowl from the refrigerator and form the cooled mixture into balls.
8. Cover with flour and fry for 5 minutes on each side or until golden brown.
9. Place on paper towel to absorb excess oil before setting in plate.
10. Serve warm with a squeeze of lemon on the side.

NOTES:
1. Greek version of veggie burger
2. You may use fresh chickpeas. You must then soak them overnight with 1 tablespoon baking soda, and then boil them until tender. This is the only time canned chickpeas may be more appealing.
3. If your patties are too moist, you might want to add some flour to the mixture prior to forming the patties.
4. ½ to 1 teaspoon of garlic powder may be used instead of fresh garlic.
5. In place of the egg you may use an additional potato.
6. Cumin is an interesting spice in this recipe; it enhances the flavor of the chickpeas.
7. About ½ cup of sautéed, minced mushrooms may also be added to enhance the flavor.

SAUTÉED MUSHROOMS

INGREDIENTS
1 pint mushrooms

½ stick of butter or olive oil
1 teaspoon dill or tarragon
Salt and pepper to taste

1. Wash and strain your mushrooms.
2. Slice the mushrooms.
3. Heat the butter in a skillet with the herbs you selected.
4. Add the mushrooms and sauté.
5. Salt and pepper to taste.

NOTES:
1. White mushrooms are great, but this recipe gets interesting when you mix the types of mushrooms.
2. Add about ½ cup white or red wine for a variation of flavor.
3. This is a great side dish, but may also be used to enhance rice or pasta.
4. This recipe may also be used as a sauce.

GREENS

INGREDIENTS
1 bunch dandelions, turnips, kale, beet greens with beets or any type of greens
Lemon
Olive oil
Eggs (optional)

1. Boil or steam the selected greens.
2. Remove the cooked greens and use the appropriate sauce.

NOTES:
1. Greens are very important to a Greek diet. My Godfather use to tell me to eat greens daily for my health.
2. Egg Lemon Sauce is common for dandelions, turnips and kale.
3. Olive Oil and Lemon Juice is common for all greens.
4. Olive Oil and Vinegar is common for all greens.
5. Sadly, beet greens are commonly thrown away in many markets. The greens from the beet plant along with the beets themselves are very tasty.
6. Skordalia is common for beet greens and beets.

VEGETARIAN MOUSSAKA

INGREDIENTS
1 each of any of the following: cauliflower, eggplant, zucchini, artichokes, potatoes, wild greens, turnips, carrots, celery or any other vegetable you would like
1 pint mushrooms
2-3 tomatoes
2 onions
½ teaspoon each allspice, cinnamon, nutmeg and clove
1 cup olives or olive paste
Olive oil

Béchamel Sauce (This is optional)
3 eggs
2 cups milk
1 stick unsalted butter
Grated kefalotiri or parmesan cheese
1 cup of flour

1. Chop the tomatoes, onions, olives, mushrooms and add them to a skillet with olive oil and the spices.
2. Cook the tomatoes to a sauce and the onions become glossy, stirring continually. When finished, set aside to cool.
3. If you are using eggplant, zucchinis, turnips, potatoes, carrots or celery, thinly slice these vegetables lengthwise.
4. In the case of the eggplant, zucchini or turnips you should place them on a greased cookie sheet and bake the slices for 10 to 15 minutes in the oven at 300°F.
5. The potatoes, carrots and celery should be place in cold water.
6. The artichokes, if fresh, must be boiled to extract the heart. If frozen or in a jar, make sure there are no other oils or spices that might change the taste of your dish.
7. The cauliflower should be stripped of the greens, quartered on the flower side and sliced. The broken parts of the flower should be added later to fill spaces.
8. Once the baked vegetables are limp, remove them from the oven and allow them to cool.
9. Grease a roasting pan with olive oil and start arranging your vegetables. Remember, you need a firm base so start with either a potato or turnip.
10. Once you have finished one layer, start another vegetable of your choice.
11. The next layer should be your sauce, and the sauce should always follow a layer of vegetables.
12. Follow the pattern of vegetables in layers you selected with every two layers being your sauce until everything is used.
13. Bake at 330°F for about 1 hour or until the béchamel is golden brown.
14. Remove it from the oven and allow it to set for about 10 minutes before cutting.

NOTES:
1. Select the Béchamel Sauce you'd like to use. The recipe above is an option.
2. An optional method is to top with additional tomato olive sauce and bake at 330°F for about 40 minutes
3. The layering of vegetables is important. Make sure the selected vegetable covers the entire layer.

Chapter 5: Breakfast

ANDROS POTATO AND SAUSAGE OMELET

<u>INGREDIENTS</u>
Butter or olive oil
2-4 eggs
½ pound pork sausage
3 stalks fresh chopped or 2 tablespoons mint or basil
2-3 potatoes
¼ cup feta cheese

1. Slice your potatoes thin, almost like chips. Place them into a bowl of cool water until ready to fry.
2. Heat the butter or olive oil in the skillet with the mint or basil.
3. When the oil starts to sizzle, add the potatoes, reduce the heat and let the potatoes cook and absorb the herbs.
4. Brown your sausage in the scented oil.
5. Beat your eggs.
6. Add the eggs to the skillet, cover and cook.
7. Remove the cover and flip your omelet.
8. Add your feta and cook a little while longer.
9. Fold over the egg encasing the feta.

:
1. This awesome omelet doubles as an appetizer if you use a small muffin pan. If you do opt for the wonderful mini quiches you would need a mini quiche muffin pan and olive oil spray. Generously spray the pan.
2. Prepare the potatoes as above, but once they are cooked place a slice of potato in each muffin port, followed by ¼ teaspoon of the sausage and feta. Beat the eggs and fill each port with the beaten egg. Bake the mini quiches for 20 – 30 minutes at 325°F. They must be raised, golden and firm.
3. Remove the quiches and place them in small metal foils. Hot or cold they are wonderful!

CRETE JAILED EGGS

INGREDIENTS
4 tomatoes or 2 green peppers
4 eggs
1 green pepper, minced or shaved
1 tomato, chopped
½ bunch green onion
½ bunch fresh parsley
1 teaspoon olive paste
¼ cup of feta cheese
Olive oil
Cracked pepper

1. Take each tomato, cut off the top and set aside. If you are using green peppers, slice the stem from the top making sure that you don't leave an opening from the top to the interior of the vegetable. Then cut the green pepper in half and remove the seeds.
2. Scoop out the inside of the tomatoes and place in a bowl.
3. Dice the thick portion of the tomato and return the diced pieces to the bowl.
4. Finely chop or grate the green pepper and add this to the bowl.
5. Chop the tomato.
6. Mince the onions and place them with tomato in the bowl.
7. In a skillet place about 2 tablespoons of olive oil with the olive paste and heat.
8. Add the tomatoes, onions, parsley and green peppers and sauté until tender.
9. Remove the sautéed vegetables from the heat.
10. Add feta cheese to the sautéed vegetables and mix.
11. Scramble your eggs by first beating your whites vigorously, then adding the whites.
12. Place the tomato or green peppers shells into a baking dish.
13. Using a tablespoon, equally distribute the sautéed mixture with the cheese to the four shells. Leave space for the egg.
14. Distribute the scrambled egg with a ladle.
15. Sprinkle with cracked pepper and cover with the tomato tops.
16. Preheat the oven to 375°F.
17. Place the eggs into the oven and bake for 30 - 40 minutes or until done.

NOTES:
1. This awesome omelet doubles as an appetizer if you use a small muffin pan. If you do opt for the wonderful mini quiches, you would need a mini quiche muffin pan and olive oil spray. Generously spray the pan.
2. For the appetizer use Roma tomatoes. You need to estimate how many quiches you will be making. Then slice about two or three tomatoes placing a slice in each muffin port.
3. Follow Step 4 through to Step 10 and place the mixture over the tomatoes.
4. Beat your eggs and ladle the beaten egg over the vegetables in each port. Fill the ports ¾ of the way up. Place them in the oven at 325°F for 20 – 30 minutes, until golden, raised and firm.
5. Remove the quiches and place them in small metal foils. Hot or cold they are wonderful!

FETA CHEESE OMELET

INGREDIENTS
Butter or olive oil
2-4 eggs
½ pound feta cheese

1. Heat the butter or olive oil in the skillet.
2. Beat your eggs.
3. Add the eggs to the skillet when the oil starts to sizzle.
4. Drop in the feta cheese, cover and cook.
5. Remove the cover and flip your omelet.

NOTES:
1. This awesome omelet doubles as an appetizer if you use a small muffin pan. If you do opt for the wonderful mini quiches, you would need a mini quiche muffin pan and olive oil spray. Generously spray the pan.
2. Remove the quiches and place them in small metal foils. Hot or cold they are wonderful!

FRAPPÉ

Half glass of Ice
1 full teaspoon Nescafe Classic
Sugar or non-sugar sweetener
Creamer or non-dairy creamer
Water

Shaker or blender

1. In a shaker container or blender place ice, coffee, sweetener and creamer.
2. Blend vigorously.
3. Add ice to a glass.
4. Pour the contents of the blender or shaker over ice.
5. Add cold water and enjoy.

NOTES:
1. Creamers sweeten the coffee without the need of adding syrups.
2. According to Greek natives, the use of Nescafe Classic is imperative for a perfect frappe.
3. Using a blender or milk shake blender will also render a great frappe.
4. Sugar blends such as Greek Coffee stand for frappe.

CONTINENTAL BRANDIED ORANGE PEEL FRENCH TOAST

INGREDIENTS
Whole grain bread sliced
1 egg for every 2 slices of bread
¼ teaspoon each cinnamon, nutmeg and allspice
Rum, Brandy, Orange water or brandy/rum flavoring
Butter
Peels from 1 or 2 oranges cut into slices
Honey
Cinnamon for sprinkling

1. Combine the eggs with the spices in a bowl and set it aside for the flavor to set.
2. Slice the orange rind, thinly and place the slices in a sauce pot.
3. For every ½ cup of water, use two cups of honey. Place the liquid into the pot with the orange slices and bring it to a boil.
4. Add about ½ cup of brandy or rum (more or less to taste, but should not exceed a 1:2) to the pot.
5. Reduce the heat and allow the syrup to reduce and thicken.
6. Place one slice of bread into the egg mixture. Allow the slice to saturate on both sides.
7. Place 1 tablespoon of butter in a skillet and melt.
8. Place the slice onto the skillet and fry the first side of the bread.
9. Once the side is golden, flip the slice over.
10. When done, place the slice onto the plate.
11. Using a fork place an orange rind from the syrup onto the slice of bread.
12. Using a spoon, drizzle the syrup over the toast.
13. Sprinkle with cinnamon and enjoy.

NOTES:
1. Try adding feta or manouri cheeses with fruit between two slices of the bread making the French toast stuffed.
2. Whipped cream cheese or ricotta with honey also works for this recipe.
3. Fresh ground spices enhance the flavor.

GREEK STYLE BREAKFAST POTATOES

INGREDIENTS
2 cups cold mashed potatoes
2 green onions, finely chopped
¼ cup parmesan or feta cheese
1 or 2 sprigs of parsley, minced finely
2 eggs
Flour
Butter for greasing the pan

1. Combine the mashed potatoes, green onions, cheese, eggs and parsley in a bowel.
2. Grease the pan with butter.
3. Form the potato mixture into patties and place them on a greased baking pan.
4. Bake at 450° F for 15 minutes or until golden.

NOTES:
1. Hash brown or grated potatoes may be used.
2. Turkish red pepper will spice up the potato if you like.
3. Frying using olive oil is preferred.

GREAT-GRANDMA'S GREEK TOAST

INGREDIENTS
Basic olive oil bread recipe or French bread
Olive oil
1 cup sweet or dry red wine

1. Cut your loaf of bread in thick slices about ½" to 1" thick.
2. Grease or place baking paper on a cookie sheet.
3. Dip one side of your bread in olive oil.
4. Turn the slice so that the soaked side faces upward on the prepared cookie sheet.
5. Using a basting brush coat the oiled bread with wine.
6. Bake at 325°F until golden.

NOTES:
1. My father first tried this recipe after seeing his grandmother eat it every morning for breakfast. He was eight years old. After one slice of bread, he was asleep all day, and no one could understand what was wrong with him.
2. This was my great-grandmother's favorite breakfast. But you might enjoy it for lunch or dinner.
3. Wine may be omitted for the breakfast, olive oil on the toasted bread is awesome.

GREEK COFFEE

INGREDIENTS
1 demitasse cup of water
1 teaspoon sugar or non-sugar sweetener
1 teaspoon Greek coffee
1 Brikie (Greek Coffee Pot)

1. Place 1 demitasse cup of water into the pot.
2. Add the sweetener and coffee to the water.
3. Bring the water to a boil.
4. When the water starts to rise, lift it from the range, allow the water to recede and continue to heat.
5. Repeat Step 4 a total of three times.
6. To serve, take a teaspoon and skim the froth from the top of the coffee pot and place that in the demitasse cup you are using.
7. Now pour the content of the pot with the grounds into the cup.
8. Enjoy hot! Drink as far down to the grounds as possible.

NOTES:
1. If you do not have a "breki" Greek Coffee Pot, use a butter melting pot.
2. The coffee comes in three types: No sugar or bitter; 1 sugar or moderate sweet; or 2 or more sugars which is very sweet.

POTATO CAKES

INGREDIENTS
3 cups mashed potatoes
½ cup whipping cream
3 green onions, chopped fine
1 white onion, chopped fine
1 teaspoon of parsley
2 eggs
3 teaspoons of flour
¼ cup feta cheese and kefalotirie or parmesan cheeses combined
¼ cup butter

1. Peel, cube and boil your potatoes.
2. When cooked, mash the potatoes with the whipping cream
3. Finely chop the onion and green onion and place them in the bowl.
4. Crumble your feta, and add it to the bowl containing the onions.
5. Grate your kefalotirie, and add it to the bowl containing the onions.
6. Add the eggs and mix.
7. Melt the butter in a skillet
8. Make small potatoes patties from the mixture in the bowl.
9. Fry the patties until golden brown or you may bake them at 450°F for 10 to 15 minutes.

NOTES:
1. Half & Half may be used instead of whipping cream.
2. Olive oil may be used instead of butter.

Chapter 6: Bread

Greek Village Bread

Ingredients
2 cups milk
1 teaspoon salt
1 teaspoon sugar
Olive oil
3 eggs + 1 yolk
5 pounds' flour
Sesame seeds (optional)
3 packages active yeast

1. Proof the yeast with a teaspoon of sugar and salt.
2. Pour the yeast into the flour.
3. Gradually add the flour with your hand and start to knead the dough.
4. Alternate the olive oil, beaten eggs and milk until all the flour is used.
5. Continue add flour until the dough is moist, but no longer sticks to your hands or the bowl.
6. Cover the dough with a clean, lint-free cloth and allow the dough to rise until it doubles in size.
7. Separate the yolk from one egg and beat.
8. Glaze the bread with egg yolk, sprinkle with sesame seeds, and bake at 325°F until golden. The larger your bread the longer you bake. You will know that your bread is done when it pulls away from the pan and is light.

NOTES:

1. **IF USING a convection oven:** Convection baking will take 35 minutes if using dark coated cake pans. If the convection fan has both high and low settings, set it to low so the bread bakes evenly.
2. Coatings placed on bread directly affect the color of the bread.
3. Place the dough in a draft-free area.
4. The addition of oil, milk and eggs provide richer dough. Emphasis of one or more of these ingredients change the texture and taste of the bread. This is something you need to experiment with by either omitting or changing the balance. Keep careful notes on the texture, taste and scent of the bread in relation to your preference.
5. Scent is very important. The way a food smells increases your craving and love for that food.

ARTO

INGREDIENTS
3 packages active yeast
1 teaspoon sugar
1 teaspoon salt
1 cup orange juice
3 pounds cake flour
2 pounds unbleached flour
Vegetable oil
3 eggs
1 cup sugar
1 tablespoon each cinnamon, nutmeg and allspice
1 tablespoon vanilla

1. Proof the yeast with a teaspoon of sugar and salt.
2. Combine the flours together.
3. Beat the 3 eggs and set this aside.
4. Start beating the oil and the sugar together.
5. When the yeast is proofed add this to the oil.
6. Add some flour.
7. Gradually alternate the eggs, sugar, oil, spices and orange juice while kneading the bread.
8. Continue adding the flour and the ingredients until the dough is moist, and no longer sticks to your hands or the bowl.
9. Cover the dough with a clean, lint-free cloth and allow the dough to rise until it doubles in size.
10. Form the dough into circular loaves.
11. Bake at 325°F until golden. The larger your bread, the longer you bake.

NOTES:
1. **IF using a convection oven:** Convection baking will take 35 minutes if using dark coated cake pans. If the convection fan has both high and low settings, set it to low so the bread bakes evenly.

2. Coatings placed on bread directly affect the color of the bread.
3. Fresh juices are best, but if you need to buy the juice, use not-from-concentrate with high pulp.

BASIC BREAD RECIPE

INGREDIENTS
2 packages active yeast
1 teaspoon sugar
1 teaspoon salt
5 pounds of flour
Water
Olive oil

1. Activate the yeast by placing the two packages of yeast into a bowl of hot water with a teaspoon each of sugar and salt.
2. Work the yeast with your fingers until it is dissolved in the water.
3. Set the bowl to the side and allow the yeast to froth.
4. Sift the flour into a large mixing bowl.
5. Make a well in the center of the flour.
6. When the yeast has frothed, pour the activated yeast into the center of the well.
7. Work the flour with your hands into the yeast.
8. Add about 1/3 cup olive oil and continue to knead.
9. Add water and continue to knead, work as much of the flour into the mixture as needed.
10. Leave about 2 cups of flour to the side.
11. Continue alternating olive oil with water until all the flour is used.
12. Knead the flour adding some of the residual flour to the dough.
13. Continue the process until the dough comes off your hands.
14. Continue kneading until the dough begins to blister.
15. Cover the dough ball with a towel and place it in a warm place away from drafts so that it may rise. Steps 12 and 13 may be repeated up to three times.
16. Knead one more time then shape in a braid or stuff with the mixtures on the additional pages.
17. Place the loaf on a greased cookie sheet and bake at 325°F until golden brown and the loaf moves freely on the cookie sheet.

NOTES:
4. **IF USING a convection oven:** Convection baking will take 35 minutes if using dark coated cake pans. If the convection fan has both high and low settings, set it to low so the bread bakes evenly.
5. Coatings placed on bread directly affect the color of the bread.
6. The amount of oil or water you add to the flour is directly related to the altitude you are making the bread. That is why a specific amount of oil and water cannot be gauged.
7. You may gauge the amount of oil and water you might want to use in the recipe. I prefer more oil than water in order that I have richer dough.
8. The more water you use the lighter the flavor of oil in the dough.

THESSALY KLEPHTIC BEEF IN BREAD

INGREDIENTS
1 pound lean ground beef
1 teaspoon each oregano, thyme, parsley and rosemary
1 tomato, diced
1 onion, minced
Olive oil
Olive Oil Bread Recipe

1. Follow the olive oil bread recipe. When you reach Step 14:
2. Dice the tomato, mince the onion and add it to the olive oil along with the herbs.
3. Sauté the tomato until a sauce starts forming.
4. Add the meat to the sauce and brown the meat. When the meat is browned remove the skillet from the heat.
5. Using a rolling pin, roll out the dough so that you form a rectangle.
6. Place the meat mixture in the center of the dough lengthwise. Keep it one inch from the ends of the bread.
7. Roll the closest end of the dough away from you, folding it over the meat mixture.
8. Repeat Step 7 with the farthest end of the dough.
9. At both of the short ends pinch the dough to seal in the meat and the sauce.
10. Place the loaf on a greased cookie sheet and bake at 325°F until golden brown and the loaf moves freely on the cookie sheet. This may be up to 1 hour, depending on the size of the bread.

NOTES:
1. **IF USING a convection oven:** Convection baking will take 35 minutes if using dark coated cake pans. If the convection fan has both high and low settings, set it to low so the bread bakes evenly.
2. Coatings placed on bread directly affect the color of the bread.
3. You can substitute cinnamon, nutmeg, allspice and cardamom for the herbs, but add about one tablespoon of sugar.

BYZANTINE SPICE BREAD

INGREDIENTS
3 envelopes of yeast
5 pounds each white or wheat flour
2 cups white onions, minced
2 tablespoon minced oregano, basil, thyme and parsley
3 egg yolks + 1 whole egg
1 cup poppy seeds (optional)
1 cup each of dried kasseri cheese, or romano and parmesan
1 teaspoon salt and sugar
1 cup olive oil or as needed
1 cup milk
Water – room temperature

1. Proof the yeast with warm water, 1 teaspoon of sugar and salt.
2. Keep your milk out so that it reaches room temperature at the time you need it.
3. Take one tablespoon of each of the dried herbs and combine them, crumbling them together into a medium bowl.
4. Add the poppy seeds, 4 tablespoons of olive oil, cheese and egg yolks and whole egg to the herbs. Combine and allow them to sit until needed.
5. Place the flour in a large bowl and add the yeast once it has foamed.
6. Add the minced onions and the remaining herbs.
7. Alternate the addition of milk and oil until all the flour is used.
8. Continue to knead adding milk and olive oil or add room temperature water until all the flour is absorbed and your bowl is clean.
9. Remove the dough from the bowl and knead. If the dough is too sticky, add flour. If it is too dry, add olive oil.
10. When you have finished kneading, coat the dough with olive oil.
11. Cover the dough and let rise.
12. Take the dough, once it has doubled in size, knead it once more and place it in a circular pan.
13. Using a spatula or your hands apply the topping generously. You need a thick coating on the top of the bread. If the topping is difficult to work with, add more olive oil to loosen the mixture.
14. Spread the mixture evenly. Place in an oven at 350°F for 40 minutes or until golden.
15. The aroma will be intoxicating! Do not continue opening the oven. This will delay the baking of the bread and will ruin your results. Check the bread once at 30 minutes and once at 40 minutes.
16. You will know that your bread is ready when it is light in feeling and it moves from the sides of the pan. Enjoy this bread with cheese and olive oil or serve with lunch and/or dinner.

NOTES:
1. **IF USING a convection oven:** Convection baking will take 35 minutes if using dark coated cake pans. If the convection fan has both high and low settings, set it to low so the bread bakes evenly.
2. This is a lunch or dinner bread. The coating is specific. Poppy seeds may be omitted from the bread. The cheese coating though is a must.
3. Bake this bread with a pan of water on another level to increase the moisture during the baking processes.
4. This recipe was introduced to my sister and myself by Mrs. Ortho Cherpas of Akron, Ohio. At the time we tried the bread both of us were overwhelmed by the rich flavor.

CHRISTOPSOMO – CHRISTMAS BREAD FROM SYMI (DODECANESE ISLANDS)

INGREDIENTS
3 packages dry yeast
1 cup lukewarm water
¼ teaspoon salt
1 teaspoon sugar

5 pounds flour
2 eggs
1 quart lukewarm milk
1½ cups honey
1½ tablespoons fresh ground cinnamon
2 teaspoons allspice
½ cup chopped walnuts and pecans
¼ cup each chopped figs, chopped dates, dark raisins, light raisins, chopped oranges and/or chopped lemons
1 stick unsalted butter *or* 1 egg and 1 tablespoon orange juice for egg wash
Walnut halves for decoration (amount determined by desired decoration)
½ cup sesame seeds

1. Proof the yeast by combining the package of yeast with sugar, salt, and 1 cup of lukewarm water.
2. While waiting for the yeast mixture to proof, place the flour into a large mixing bowl.
3. With an electric mixer, beat eggs, honey and milk for 2–3 minutes on low speed until combined.
4. Add cinnamon and allspice and mix for 2–3 minutes until blended.
5. Add in the chopped walnuts and chopped pecans.
6. Finally, gently stir in figs, dates, raisins, oranges and lemons.
7. Once the yeast is proofed, add it to the flour.
8. Add the egg mixture.
9. Continue to knead until all the flour is used. Add milk or water if the dough is too dry.
10. Knead the dough. This can be done in one of three ways:
    a. Method A: Place on a lightly floured flat surface and knead until smooth and elastic, about 8–10 minutes.
    b. Method B: Transfer to a stand mixer with a dough hook. Knead until smooth and elastic and until dough does not stick to the sides of the bowl. If the dough is sticky, add 1 tablespoon of flour at a time until desired texture is attained.
    c. Method C: Transfer to a food processor with a plastic blade. If your machine cannot handle the entire 6 cups of flour, divide the dough in half and work with each half separately. Process by adding 1 tablespoon of flour at a time until a soft, elastic ball has been formed that pulls away from the sides of the bowl. When this consistency has been reached, continue to process for only 1 minute.
11. Place the dough in the large bowl. Cover the bowl with plastic wrap. Place a bath towel over the bowl for extra warmth. Allow this to rise about 1½ hours until doubled in bulk. The rising time will depend on the room temperature. (Bread will rise quickly in warm, humid air and may take longer in winter months if room temperature is on the cool side.)
12. Grease a large cake pan.
13. Remove a handful of dough to use for decoration.
14. On a flat surface, form the dough into a ball.
15. Place the loaf into the greased cake pan wrinkled side down.
16. Make a desired decoration for your loaf and lay it on top of the bread.
17. Cover the bread with a large white lint-free kitchen towel. Let rise until double in bulk.
18. Preheat oven to 350°F degrees.

19. While waiting for oven to heat, melt ½–1 stick of butter. With a pastry brush, gently coat the top of the loaf with the melted butter or with an egg wash made with 1 egg and 1 tablespoon of orange juice.
20. Sprinkle the bread with sesame seeds (optional) and adorn with walnut halves.
21. Bake 45 minutes or until the bread is golden in color on top and sides and the sides have pulled away from the pan. Time may vary according to type of cake pan or oven.
22. If you are using a convection oven: Convection baking will take 35 at the most 50 minutes if using dark coated cake pans. If the convection fan has both high and low settings, be sure to set it to low so the inside and outside of the bread bake evenly.
23. Within a few minutes of taking the bread out of the oven, remove the loaf from the cake pans. They fall out easily when baked properly. Place on racks to cool.

NOTES:
1. **IF USING a convection oven:** Convection baking will take 35 minutes if using dark coated cake pans. If the convection fan has both high and low settings, set it to low so the bread bakes evenly.
2. Coatings placed on bread directly affect the color of the bread.

HALOUMI CHEESE BREAD

INGREDIENTS
1 brick or ½ pound Haloumi cheese
1 medium onion, sliced
1 tablespoon each of mint and parsley
Olive oil

Recipe for Olive oil Bread

1. Follow the olive oil bread recipe. When you reach Step 14.
2. Sauté the sliced onion in olive oil with the herbs until translucent.
3. Thickly grate the haloumi cheese.
4. Mixed the cooled sautéed mixture with the cheese. Make sure that the cheese is combined totally with the onions and set aside.
5. Using a rolling pin, roll out the dough so that you form a rectangle.
6. Place the cheese mixture in the center of the dough lengthwise. Keep it one inch from the ends of the bread.
7. Roll the closest end of the dough away from you, folding it over the cheese mixture.
8. Repeat Step 7 with the farthest end of the dough.
9. At both of the short ends pinch the dough to seal in the cheese and oil.
10. Place the loaf on a greased cookie sheet and bake at 325°F until golden brown and the loaf moves freely on the cookie sheet. This may be up to 1 hour, depending on the size of the bread.

NOTES:
1. **IF USING a convection oven:** Convection baking will take 35 minutes if using dark coated cake pans. If the convection fan has both high and low settings, set it to low so the bread bakes evenly.
2. Coatings placed on bread directly affect the color of the bread.
3. After forming the loaf, make sure you pinch the ends to keep the filling from escaping.
4. Haloumi cheese is Cypriot in nature. If you do not have an international grocer nearby, substitute mozzarella and mint mixture (½ pound mozzarella and 1 tablespoon of mint). This mixture is the closest to the haloumi taste.

OLIVE BREAD

INGREDIENTS
Kalamata olives pitted and sliced, at least 1 cup
1 onion, sliced
1 tablespoon olive paste
1 teaspoon each oregano, thyme, parsley and mint
Olive oil

Olive oil bread Recipe

1. Follow the olive oil bread recipe. When you reach Step 14.
2. Sauté the sliced onion, olives, herbs and olive paste in olive oil with the herbs until translucent.
3. Using a rolling pin, roll out the dough so that you form a rectangle.
4. Place the olive mixture in the center of the dough lengthwise. Keep it one inch from the ends of the bread.
5. Roll the closest end of the dough away from you, folding it over the olive mixture.
6. Repeat Step 7 with the farthest end of the dough.
7. At both of the short ends, pinch the dough to seal in the olives, onions and oil.
8. Place the loaf on a greased cookie sheet and bake at 325°F until golden brown and the loaf moves freely on the cookie sheet. This may be up to 1 hour, depending on the size of the bread.
9. Rub the outside of the dough with the remainder of the olive oil and herbs. This will give the bread a red glow and unbelievable scent.

NOTES:
1. **IF USING a convection oven:** Convection baking will take 35 minutes if using dark coated cake pans. If the convection fan has both high and low settings, set it to low so the bread bakes evenly.
2. Coatings placed on bread directly affect the color of the bread.
3. Make sure you pinch the ends of the loaf, so that the filling does not escape.
4. The use of additional olives may replace olive paste.
5. Olive paste basically is olives pulverized with olive oil to paste consistency. Use about 1/8 of a cup of olives to make the paste. If you have a grinder and are willing to do the extra work, this is worth the time and effort.
6. Add garlic to the paste mixture for an extra zip.

TSOUREKI

INGREDIENTS
3 envelopes of yeast
4 cups flour
¼ pound unsalted butter
1 cup + 1 teaspoon sugar
1 teaspoon salt
3 eggs + 1 yolk beaten
¾ cup milk
2 teaspoons either or both mahlepi and/or orange rind
Juice of one orange

1. Proof the yeast with a teaspoon of sugar and salt.
2. Heat the butter, sugar and the milk until the butter is melted and the ingredients are combined. Do not scald the milk.
3. When the yeast is proofed, add it to 2 cups of flour in a bowl.
4. Beat the 3 eggs.
5. Alternate the eggs, mahlepi, milk and orange rind while kneading the bread.
6. Gradually add the flour.
7. Continue to add flour and the ingredients until the dough is moist, but no longer sticks to your hands or the bowl.
8. Cover the dough with a clean, lint-free cloth and allow the dough to rise until it doubles in size.
9. Divide the dough into three parts.
10. Form each of the parts into a long loaf-like form.
11. Join the loaves together at one end, by pinching the three ends together. At this point start to braid by placing one of the outer loaves over the middle loaf. Alternate the sides being used. When you have reached the end of the braid, join the 3 ends together by pinching them as you did in the beginning. If you have the traditional Easter egg you would add it into the braid either in the beginning or end.
12. Glaze the bread with egg yolk and bake at 325°F until golden. The larger your bread, the longer you bake.

NOTES:
1. **IF USING a convection oven:** Convection baking will take 35 minutes if using dark coated cake pans. If the convection fan has both high and low settings, set it to low so the bread bakes evenly.
2. Coatings placed on bread directly affect the color of the bread.
3. Use a juicer or blender to extract the orange juice. Add the pulp to the dough for added flavor.

VASILOPITA BREAD RECIPE

INGREDIENTS
3 packages dry yeast
1 cup lukewarm water
¼ teaspoon salt
1 teaspoon sugar
5 pounds of flour

½ teaspoon each cinnamon and anise seed
Rind from 1 orange and lemon
½ pound unsalted butter
1 cup ouzo or 1 tablespoon of ground anise or anisette flavor
4-5 eggs
2 cups honey
5 cups lukewarm milk - have more milk on hand in case it's needed
¼ cup sesame seeds
Honey
Cloves (whole)
Reserve 1 small piece of dough to make the year
1 coin covered in aluminum foil

1. Proof the yeast by combining the package of yeast with sugar, salt and 1 cup of warm water.
2. While waiting for the yeast mixture to proof, place 5 pounds of flour into a large mixing bowl.
3. Using your fingers to make a well in the center of the flour mound. Set this aside.
4. Combine the spices and rinds together into a different bowl.
5. By this time, the yeast mixture should have completed proofing. Add it to the well of the flour.
6. Combine the flour and yeast mixture with a large mixing spoon or your hands.
7. Add the spices and rind and knead.
8. Add the butter and knead.
9. Add the ouzo. Continue to knead.
10. Add the eggs and honey. Continue to knead.
11. Add the milk slowly, making sure you incorporate all of the flour in the bowl.
12. Add more flour if necessary.
13. Knead the dough in one of three ways:
a. **Method A:** Place on a lightly floured flat surface and knead until smooth and elastic, about 8–10 minutes.

b. **Method B:** Transfer to a stand mixer with a dough hook. Knead until smooth and elastic and until dough does not stick to the sides of the bowl. If the dough is sticky, add 1 tablespoon of flour at a time until desired texture is attained.

c. **Method C:** Transfer to a food processor with a plastic blade. If your machine cannot handle the entire 5 pounds of flour (about 18 cups), divide the dough in half and work with each half separately. Process by adding 1 tablespoon of flour at a time until a soft, elastic ball has been formed that pulls away from the sides of the bowl. When this consistency has been reached, continue to process for only 1 minute.

14. Place the dough in the large bowl. Cover the bowl with plastic wrap. Place a bath towel over the bowl for extra warmth. Allow this to rise about 1½ hours until doubled in bulk. The rising time will depend on the room temperature. (Bread will rise quickly in warm, humid air and may take longer in winter months if room temperature is on the cool side.)

15. Vasilopita can be topped with a cross, the year or a double-headed eagle.
16. Grease a spring form pan, cake pan or other circular shape pan.
17. Remove a handful of dough to use for your decoration.
18. On a flat surface, form the large section of dough into a ball.
19. Place the loaf into a cake pan, wrinkled side down.
20. Cover the bread with a white kitchen towel (not terry cloth) and let it rise until it doubles in bulk.
21. Wrap a coin in aluminum foil. Place a coin in the center of the loaf. Use your finger to press the coin down into the dough. Smooth the dough to hide the indentation.
22. Make sure to conceal the location from those in attendance.
23. Preheat oven to 350°F degrees.
24. Make the desired decoration for your loaf and lay it on top of the bread. With a pastry brush, gently coat the top of each loaf with honey.
25. Sprinkle the bread with sesame seeds (optional).
26. Bake 30–35 minutes or until the bread is golden in color on top and sides and the sides have pulled away from the pan. Time may vary according to type of cake pan or oven.
27. Within a few minutes of taking the bread out of the oven, remove the loaves from the cake pans. It will fall out easily when baked properly. Place on racks to cool.

NOTES:
1. **IF USING a convection oven:** Convection baking will take 35 minutes if using dark coated cake pans. If the convection fan has both high and low settings, set it to low so the bread bakes evenly.
2. Coatings placed on bread directly affect the color of the bread.

Chapter 7: Rice & Pastas

TRAHANA SPICY

INGREDIENTS
1 cup spicy trahana
1 pound lamb, beef or chicken
1 tomato
1 onion, sliced
1 green pepper, sliced
2 cloves of garlic, chopped
1 cup red wine
1 bay leaf
Olive oil

1. Chop the onions, tomato, green peppers and garlic.
2. Sauté the onions, peppers, bay leaf and garlic in a skillet with olive oil.
3. Add the tomato and trahana and sauté.
4. Add the meat and continue to sauté.
5. Add 1 cup of wine.
6. Stew until meat is cooked.

NOTES:
1. Trahana comes in three forms: spicy, sourdough or sweet for cereals. For the purposes of this book we will only concentrate on the first two forms. The spicy trahana has a tomato and red pepper base, whereas the sourdough is plain with milk as a base.

2. Trahana can only be found in Greek or international stores. The pasta itself can be made from scratch. Those recipes will be submitted at a later date.
3. The smaller you cut the chunks, the quicker the meat will cook.
4. The great deal with trahana is that you can make this either a stew or soup. If you make it into a soup, you might want to consider using a slow cooker.

YOGURT RICE (ASIA MINOR STYLE)

INGREDIENTS
2 cups rice
4 cups chicken, lamb or beef broth or 1 bay leaf in 4 cups water
2 cups yogurt or sour cream
3 garlic cloves, minced
3 tablespoons extra virgin olive oil
2 tablespoons mint
4 ounces pine nuts
Salt and pepper to taste

1. Boil your rice with a touch of salt and bay leaf until done.
2. Strain the rice when totally cooked. Remove the bay leaf if you used this option.
3. Heat the olive oil with the pine nuts, garlic, and mint until the scents all come together. You want to lightly sauté, not brown, the garlic. Just slightly heat the mixture until you smell the garlic cooking.
4. Combine the sautéed ingredients with the yogurt.
5. While the rice is still warm, stir in the yogurt mixture.
6. Serve warm.

NOTES:
1. Non-sauté method: Prepare the yogurt mixture ahead of time for a stronger garlic flavor. Add the pine nuts, garlic and mint directly to the yogurt with a touch of olive oil (about 1 tablespoon) and mix, then refrigerate. The earlier this is done the stronger the garlic taste. When the rice is cooked, add the yogurt mixture from the refrigerator, mix and serve.
2. This is very heart-healthy rice. Instead of adding calorie-infused sauces or butter to the rice, yogurt is a substitute.
3. The introduction of a bay leaf also helps in naturally flavoring the rice.
4. A rice steamer may be used. You might want to use two bay leaves, and place them in with the raw rice at the start of steaming.

CABBAGE DOLMATHES

INGREDIENTS
¼ cup olive oil
1½ lbs. lean ground beef, lamb or pork
½ cup white rice
1 tomato, finely chopped
1 large onion, finely chopped

1 garlic clove, pressed
1 tablespoon each parsley, dill and mint, chopped (save stalks)
1 teaspoon cumin
4 stalks celery, carrots, beef bones or lamb bones (bones must lay flat)
Salt and pepper
1 cabbage, steamed whole

PREPARE CABBAGE
1. Take a sharp knife and remove the core of the cabbage at the stem. Try not to cut the cabbage in half.
2. Steam or partially boil the whole cabbage. If you are steaming, cut the head of cabbage in half. You might lose some leaves, but the head will steam easier. Steam the cabbage about 10-15 minutes; if you are boiling, about 10 minutes. Try not to overcook the cabbage leaves.
3. Remove the cabbage and place it to the side to cool. Remove the cooked leaves.
4. Place the remainder of the raw cabbage raw back in the pot to continue to cook.

MAKING THE FILING
1. Place the herbs (if fresh remove the herb from the stalks, place the stalks to the side), cumin, garlic, with the oil in a skillet and sauté until the onions have cooked down and are clear.
2. Add the chopped tomato and onion and rice to the skillet.
3. Continue to sauté until the rice becomes white.
4. Place the stalks from the herbs in the pot you will use to stew your cabbage dolmas. Add the bones, celery or carrots the same pot. Whatever you select, place it side by side so that it creates a grate effect, much like steamer.
5. In a mixing bowl combine the ground meat and the rice mixture and knead until everything is combined totally.
6. Salt and pepper the meat mixture, knead slightly more and set aside.
7. Take the cooled cabbage and remove the cooked leaves. The remaining raw leaves should be placed back into their pots to continue to cook.
8. Lay the leaf with the curved side down. This makes a sort of cup.
9. Spoon 1 tablespoon of the mixture to the center of the leaf closer to the bottom by the stem.
10. Lift the two sides, the right and left parts, of the leaf and bring them toward the mixture.
11. Holding the sides inward, lift the part of the leaf closest to you (the stem) and role it forward toward the top of the leaf, as if rolling an eggroll.
12. Place the rolled dolma in the pot with the tip of the open end facing downward.
13. Continue with Steps 8 through 12 until you have used the entire filling.
14. Once you have finished, place a dish that fits comfortably over the stuffed cabbage leaves and cover.
15. Add enough water to cover the grated bottom, about 3-4 cups.
16. Bring the broth to a boil, reduce the heat to simmer and steam the dolmathes for at least 40 minutes or until the rice is cooked.

NOTES:
1. Sautéing the rice until white, not only seasons the grain, but expedites the cooking process.
2. It is simpler to boil the cabbage, because you do not damage the leaves. Yet, if you cut the head in half and allow the halves to steam, you will prepare the head faster than the first method. The choice is yours.

3. The egg lemon recipe you wish to use is up to you. Other choices for topping is olive oil and lemon juice or yogurt and garlic sauce.
4. The use of a dish, during the cooking process helps keep the dolmathes in place and not unravel.

CHERRY PILAF

<u>INGREDIENTS</u>
2 cups long grain rice
Olive oil
1 medium onion, chopped
4 stalks celery, chopped with the greens
½ cup parsley, chopped
½ pound fresh cherries or 1 cup pomegranate seeds or 1 jar sour cherries or pomegranate
8 ounces cherry juice or pomegranate juice
½ cup walnuts or pecans, chopped
Olive oil
Salt and pepper to taste

1. Using a deep skillet, sauté the chopped onions, celery leaves and parsley until translucent.
2. Add a little more oil, add the celery, rice and walnut and continue to sauté.
3. When the rice becomes white, about 2 minutes, add the fruit, 1 cup of water and juice.
4. Cover and simmer for 20 minutes or until done.

<u>NOTES:</u>
1. This is an awesome rice to serve with poultry or game.
2. To enhance the flavor of the rice you may use the sour cherry or pomegranate syrup. Both of these syrups enhance the flavor of the rice without sweetening the side dish.
3. The use of fresh fruit and nuts is a must, unless you have sensitivity. If you have sensitivity to nuts, use the fruit alone. There is nothing to say that you can't increase the fruit or combine the two types of fruit.
4. Pomegranates store quite well. You may buy them in season during September and place them in your refrigerator. I toss them on the door shelf to use whenever I need them. In the refrigerator they will keep for up to one year.
5. If you do not wish to have your pomegranates in your refrigerator for a year, fill a bowl with cold water. Cut the fruit in half. Place both halves in the water and remove the seeds from the pod. This helps your fingers from being stained. Dispose of the pod and drain the water through a colander to capture the seeds. Place your seeds in a plastic sealable lunch bag and place them in the freezer. The pod does not keep well in the freezer; the seeds become damaged unless they are extracted from the pod.

YOGURT RICE FROM CRETE

INGREDIENTS
2 cups rice
1 ½ cups plain yogurt or sour cream
1 bay leaf
3 tablespoons extra virgin olive oil
1 teaspoon saffron
Salt

1. Boil your rice with the salt and bay leaf until done.
2. Remove the bay leaf and strain the rice.
3. Using a fork, mix the saffron strands with the yogurt and oil.
4. While the rice is still warm, stir in the yogurt mixture.
5. Serve warm.

NOTES:
1. This is very heart-healthy rice. Instead of adding calorie-infused sauces or butter to the rice, yogurt is a substitute.
2. The introduction of a bay leaf also helps in naturally flavoring the rice.
3. The use of saffron for the taste and color is awesome. Spanish saffron works as well as Turkish or Asia Minor saffron; without having to pay an exorbitant amount and can be found easily in Latin American grocers.
4. If you cannot find saffron as easily, you may cheat by using turmeric. Turmeric is easily found in the spice area of your grocer. It does not have quite the same taste as saffron, but it does have the coloring factor that you are looking for in the side dish.
5. A rice steamer may be used. You might want to use two bay leaves, and place them in with the raw rice at the start of steaming.

DOLMATHES

INGREDIENTS
¼ cup olive oil
1½ pounds lean ground beef, lamb or pork
½ cup white rice
1 tomato, finely chopped
1 large onion, finely chopped
1 garlic clove, pressed
1 tablespoon each parsley, dill and mint, chopped (save stalks)
1 teaspoon cumin
4 stalks celery or carrots, or beef bones or lamb bones
Salt and pepper
1 jar of grape leaves or fresh grape leaves

Select your Egg Lemon Sauce

PREPARE GRAPE LEAVES
FROM THE JAR

1. If you are using the jar leaves, remove the leaves from the jar and place them in a colander and rinse with cold water.

2. The jar leaves have been blanched and will be further cooked when stuffed, additional blanching is unnecessary.
3. Placed the rinsed leaves in water with lemon to remove the brine taste from the jar, optional.

FROM THE VINE
1. If you have wild grapevines or grow grapes, you may use their fresh leaves.
2. Select the leaves that are medium in size and not too small. You may use the larger leaves, but you will need to blanch them a little longer.
3. Boil water in a sauce pan.
4. Dip each leaf in for about 30 seconds to 1 minute. The tendons on the leaf should become limp. If that is not reached, re-dip the leaf for 30 more seconds.
5. Place the leaves on a paper towel or wax paper to cool and dry.

MAKING THE FILING
1. Place the herbs (if fresh, remove the herb from the stalks, place the stalks to the side), cumin, garlic, with the oil in a skillet and sauté until the onions have cooked down and are clear.
2. Add the chopped tomato and onion and rice to the skillet.
3. Continue to sauté until the rice becomes white.
4. Place the stalks from the herbs in the pot you will use to stew your dolmathes. Add the bones, celery or carrots to the same pot – whatever you select place it side by side so that it creates a grate effect much like steamer.
5. In a mixing bowl combine the ground meat and the rice mixture and knead until everything is combined totally.
6. Salt and pepper the meat mixture, knead slightly more and set aside.
7. Take the cooled leaves and remove the cooked leaves. The remaining raw leaves should be placed back into their pots to continue to cook.
8. Lay the leaf with the vein side up.
9. Spoon 1 tablespoon of the mixture to the center of the leaf closer to the bottom by the stem.
10. Lift the two sides, the right and left parts, of the leaf and bring them toward the mixture.
11. Holding the sides inward, lift the part of the leaf closest to you (the stem) and role it forward toward the top of the leaf, as if rolling an eggroll.
12. Place the rolled dolma in the pot with the tip of the open end facing downward.
13. Continue with Steps 8 through 12 until you have used the entire filling.
14. Once you have finished, place a dish that fits comfortably over the stuffed cabbage leaves and cover.
15. Add enough water to cover the grated bottom, about 3-4 cups.
16. Bring the broth to a boil, reduce the heat to simmer and steam the dolmathes for at least 40 minutes or until the rice is cooked.

NOTES:
1. Sautéing the rice until white not only seasons the grain, but expedites the cooking process.
2. The egg lemon recipe you wish to use is up to you. Other choices for topping are olive oil and lemon juice, yogurt and Tzaziki sauce.
3. The use of a dish, during the cooking process helps keep the dolmathes in place and not unravel.

MANESTRA

INGREDIENTS
1 pound lean ground meat, stew meat or lamb

1 pound orzo
3 garlic cloves, chopped
1 onion, chopped
1 bay leaf
4 whole peppercorns
5 each of allspice and cloves
1 cinnamon stick
At least 2 cups red wine
1 large tomato, chopped
1 cup of water
½ cup olive oil
Salt to taste
Parmesan

1. Heat oil, garlic, bay leaf, spices and onions in a wok or deep skillet until glazed.
2. Add peppercorns.
3. Take the chopped tomato and add to the heating mixture.
4. Sauté the mixture until tomato is cooked down to a sauce; about 10-15 minutes.
5. Add the meat and brown.
6. Add the orzo and wine.
7. Add 1 cup of water, combine and cover.
8. Allowed the mixture in the skillet to simmer until the pasta has cooked and absorbed all the fluid.
9. Sprinkle with parmesan and enjoy.

NOTES:
1. Optional Cooking Methods – Crockpot or clay pot in the oven
2. Olives may be added.
3. Turkish red pepper would give this a kick.
4. Keep with the fresh tomato.
5. If you want a more intense garlic taste, use a garlic press.
6. Cardamom may be added.
7. Chop the meat into small pieces in order to ensure fast cooking.

SYMIAKA NOODLES

INGREDIENTS
Pasta, #2 macaroni is preferred
3 medium onions, grated finely
2 cloves of garlic
Grated parmesan
Olive oil
Pinch of cumin
Salt and pepper

1. Tradition used #2 macaroni because of the taste and texture. Boil the pasta until it is al dente.
2. In a skillet heat the olive oil with cumin, garlic and onions. Do not burn the oil, but slowly sauté the items until caramelized.
3. Strain the pasta in a colander and place it in a bowl. Salt and pepper to taste.
4. Add the caramelized content of the skillet to the bowl and combine thoroughly.

5. Add the cheese and continue combining.
6. Serve warm with crusty bread.

NOTES:
1. Any type of pasta is fine, orzo, spaghetti, etc., for this recipe.
2. Sliced cabbage may also be added to the sautéing. The cabbage is cooked down with the onions and garlic, but provides a different spin on this dish. The use of cabbage, Haluski, was introduced by a Barbara Fetchenko showing her tradition to this dish. It is amazing to see the variations of one recipe.
3. Oils can be changed to grapeseed, vegetable, walnut or corn.

PASTA WITH BROWN BUTTER

INGREDIENTS
1 pound pasta, any type
1 stick unsalted butter
Salt and pepper
Olive oil
Kefalotirie, mezethra, or parmesan grated cheese

1. In a pot large enough to hold the pasta you selected to cook, season enough water with olive oil and salt.
2. Bring the water to a boil.
3. Place your pasta in the pot.
4. Boil the pasta until al dente.
5. Rinse the pasta and set it aside.
6. In a skillet, melt the butter.
7. Raise the temperature of the heat and allow the butter to brown but not burn.
8. Place the cooked pasta in the skillet with the brown butter and toss.
9. Salt and pepper to taste. Sprinkle with cheese.

NOTES:
1. Margarine will not brown as butter does.
2. Salted butter may be used, but limit any additional salting.
3. Other oils may be used.

PASTA WITH MEAT SAUCE

INGREDIENTS
1 pound pasta, any type
Salt
Olive oil

1. In a pot large enough to hold the pasta you selected to cook, season enough water with olive oil and salt.
2. Bring the water to a boil.
3. Place your pasta in the pot.
4. Boil the pasta until al dente.

5. Rinse the pasta and set it aside.

SAUCE TYPES
The sauce you select depends on the meat and taste you have. Below are some ideas:
1. Youvetsi – usually made with orzo, beef or lamb, onions and spices. The tradition is the pasta, par cooked or raw, is placed in a ceramic pot with the meat and sauce and baked. This gives you an unbelievable taste. This also may be placed in a slow cooker.
2. Tomato Sauce with ground pork
3. Tomato Sauce with ground meat
4. Kapama I with chicken
5. Kapama II with beef

NOTES:
1. I prefer whole wheat pasta for both taste and nutrition.
2. Garlic cloves may also be used to season the water.
3. Create the sauce from the selection above. Add the cooked pasta to the selected sauce and allow it to simmer.
4. For those of you who are busy and don't have the time to afford in making an elaborate meal, pre-make the sauce with the meat. Place uncooked pasta in a slow cooker with the premade sauce and extra water. Place the setting on low and cook for three hours. CAUTION: Consider the size of your slow cooker and the size of the meal it will hold.

PASTAS WITH MEATLESS SAUCES

INGREDIENTS
1 pound pasta any type
Salt
Olive oil

1. In a pot large enough to hold the pasta you selected to cook, season enough water with olive oil and salt.
2. Bring the water to a boil.
3. Place your pasta in the pot.
4. Boil the pasta until al dente.
5. Rinse the pasta and set it aside.

SAUCE TYPES
The sauce you select depends on the meat and taste you have. Below are some ideas:
1. Meatless Tomato Sauce with herbs
2. Meatless Tomato Sauce with spices

NOTES:
1. I prefer whole wheat pasta for both taste and nutrition.
2. Garlic cloves may also be used to season the water.

3. Create the sauce from the selection above. Add the cooked pasta to the selected sauce and allow it to simmer.
4. For those of you who are busy and don't have the time to afford in making an elaborate meal, pre-make the sauce. Place uncooked pasta in a slow cooker with the premade sauce and ½ cup water. Place the setting on low and cook for three hours. CAUTION consider the size of your slow cooker and the size of the meal it will hold.

PELOPONNESE STYLE PASTICHIO

MEAT FILLING
2 pounds ground meat or lamb
1 tablespoon mixed cinnamon, nutmeg
2 plum tomatoes chopped or 1 large beefstake
2 onions chopped
1/3 cup grated kefalotiri or parmesan cheese
Olive oil

PASTA
#2 Macaroni, ziti, or any short circular pasta
Olive oil
1/3 cup grated kefalotiri or parmesan cheese

BÉCHAMEL SAUCE
Refer to recipe

THE PASTA
1. Boil the pasta until it is cooked firm but just before al dente.
2. Strain the cooked pasta in a colander and allow to slightly cool.
3. Place olive oil on your hands.
4. Run your hands through the pasta while placing it in a bow ensuring that the oil covers all the pasta.
5. Take the cheese and sprinkle generously over the pasta. Use your hands to toss the pasta and make sure that the cheese is evenly distributed.
6. Set the bowl aside.

MEAT FILLING
1. Place oil in the skillet with the cinnamon, nutmeg, tomatoes and onions.
2. Sauté until the onions and tomatoes have cooked down.
3. Add the ground meat and continue to sauté until the meat is semi-cooked.
4. Remove the meat from the heat, add the cheese and mix.
5. Set the skillet aside.

THE BÉCHAMEL SAUCE
1. Refer to Recipe

1. Use a deep baking pan. Lay a layer of pasta as the base, making sure that the entire bottom is covered. Keep some pasta in reserve.
2. Take the skillet of meat and carefully layer the meat over the pasta, use all the meat from the skillet.
3. Take the remaining portion of pasta and cover the meat.
4. Now cover with the béchamel sauce. Make sure you have enough sauce to cover the entire pan. The rule of thumb is that no noodles show through. If noodles show, it means that your sauce was either too thin or you did not have enough sauce.
5. Bake at 350°F until golden brown.

NOTES:

1. You do not need to layer the pasta and meat as in Steps 13 and 14.
2. You could place all the pasta on one level, followed by the meat and topped by the Béchamel sauce.
3. Cardamom may be added to the spices.
4. If you wish to add a tomato sauce, I prefer those in a glass jar or carton.

ASIA MINOR PASTICHIO PIE

INGREDIENTS

Meat Filling
2 pounds ground meat or lamb
1 tablespoon oregano
2 plum tomatoes, chopped
2 onions, chopped
1/3 cup grated kefalotiri or parmesan cheese
Olive oil

Pasta
#2 macaroni, ziti, or any short circular pasta
Olive oil
1/3 cup grated kefalotiri or parmesan cheese

Béchamel Sauce
Refer to recipe you would like

Phylo
2 sticks unsalted butter, melted
1 pound phylo dough

FIRST, MAKE THE MEAT FILLING.

1. Place oil in the skillet with the oregano, tomatoes and onions. Sauté until the onions and tomatoes have cooked down.
2. Add the ground meat and continue to sauté until the meat is semi-cooked.

3. Remove the meat from the heat, add the cheese, and mix.
4. Set the skillet aside.

SECOND PASTA
1. Boil the pasta until it is al dente.
2. Strain the cooked pasta and allow to slightly cool.
3. Place olive oil on your hands.
4. Run your hands through the pasta ensuring that the oil covers all the pasta.
5. Sprinkle the cheese generously over the pasta. Use your hands to toss the pasta and make sure that the cheese is evenly distributed.
6. Set the bowl aside.

THIRD BÉCHAMEL SAUCE
1. Select the sauce you wish to make.

FOURTH CONSTRUCTION
1. Melt the remaining butter.
2. Use a 9" X 12" pan and grease with butter.
3. Open your box of phylo and unroll the phylo.
4. Arrange the phylo so that it covers all the sides of the pan and the ends are hanging over the pan. The center of the pan is also included in the phylo covering.
5. Baste the first layer of phylo with butter.
6. Add two more layers of phylo, again covering all sides of the pan.
7. Baste the third layer of phylo.
8. Add one more layer of phylo.
9. Take the pasta that has been set aside in the colander, and lay it evenly in the pan on the phylo sheets.
10. Make sure the pasta is even.
11. Lay phylo over the pasta. Again, the phylo will lay over the pan with the ends hanging over the ends of the pan.
12. Take the meat and spread it evenly over the inside of the pan.
13. Cover the meat portion of the pastichio with phylo.
14. Now the Béchamel Sauce is added to the pie. Again, spread the sauce evenly.
15. Lift the side overhanging panels and bring them toward the center of the pie, and butter this layer.
16. Add three straight sheets that cover the inside of the pieces brought in and the pie alone. Butter between each layer.
17. Bake at 350°F until golden brown.

NOTES:
1. This is more considered a Pastichio pie.
2. This may be an interesting recipe in that people, who are looking for a single portion, may purchase mini loaf tins or a Texas muffin tin, use short penne or ziti and construct single portions that can be frozen either before or after baking.

3. This should also be considered as a wonderful luncheon or dinner side dish that looks elegant and does not have the serving problem, but can be elegantly displayed on a dish.

QUINCE PILAF WITH ALMONDS AND DATES

INGREDIENTS
2-4 quince
½ chopped dates
½ Retsina wine
1 cup Arborio, short grain rice, or long grain rice
½ cup almond slivers
Zest of one lemon, and then slice the lemon to be used during preparation
¼ cup fresh dill, chopped
2 tablespoons fresh marjoram
1 onion, chopped
Dash of cinnamon
Olive oil
Cinnamon stick
1 teaspoon sugar
1 lemon
Salt and pepper

1. Soak your chopped dates for at least 2 hours to 24 hours in the Retsina.
2. Parboil the quince for 15 minutes. Do not remove the skin. Slice the top off the quince to act as a "hat" or "topper" for your stuffed quince. Place these pieces in a bowl of water with some lemon slices.
3. Now core the quince, extracting the seeds and core from the fruit.
4. Once the core is removed, using a grapefruit spoon or paring knife, remove some of the pulp from the fruit. Be careful not to puncture the bottom or shell of the quince and set that aside in the lemon water bath.
5. In a skillet, place enough olive oil to cover the bottom and heat.
6. Sauté the quince pulp, onions, herbs, cinnamon, zest, almonds, rice and dates (this includes the wine remaining from the soaking).
7. Keep stirring, noticing the change in the color of the rice and onions. This should be about 5 minutes. Add salt and pepper to taste.
8. Once the fluid has either been absorbed or evaporated, remove the skillet from the flame and stuff your quince.
9. Place your quince in a baking pan cover with the "hats" left in the bowl. Add 1 cup water with a few pieces of cinnamon stick and sugar.
10. Cover with aluminum and bake at 375°F for about 45 minutes or until rice is done.

NOTES:
1. Don't limit yourself to the dried fruits listed here. Try cherries, blueberries or cranberries.
2. If you are serving a number of people, you might want to place the rice in a baking dish with the other ingredients and chopped quince. Bake until rice is done.

3. Check that the people you are serving are not allergic to nuts. If so, remove the nuts from the recipe.
4. If the group that will be enjoying this dish is free from allergies, try adding different types of nuts.
5. Allergies also occur with the use of dried fruits. If you have anyone with this allergy, use fresh fruit such as apples, berries and pears.
6. If you have a problem finding quince use apples as a substitute

SPANAKORIZO

INGREDIENTS
1 pound fresh spinach
1-2 medium tomatoes
1-2 onions
¼ bunch fresh dill or fennel
½ cup long grain rice
½ bunch fresh parsley
2 cloves of garlic pressed
½ teaspoon cumin
Olive oil

1. Chop the herbs and onions (any type white, yellow, Vidalia or red) and place them in the skillet with the pressed garlic, cumin and about ½ cup of olive oil. Sauté until the onions are cooked down.
2. Chop the tomatoes and add them to the skillet and continue sautéing until it starts to cook down.
3. Add the spinach and sauté until limp.
4. If the spinach is sticking or the skillet seems dry, add more oil.
5. Add the rice and sauté until the rice becomes white.
6. Add 2 cups of water to the skillet. Reduce heat to low medium and simmer until rice is cooked.

NOTES:
1. If you have sensitivity to dill, you may want to substitute fennel for this dish.
2. I have tried this recipe with frozen spinach. It is OK, but fresh is the best. If you use the frozen spinach, do not sauté. Add the frozen spinach after sautéing the rice.
3. Garlic may be increased or decreased as needed.
4. If you wish to use a sauce, consider those in a jar or carton. You may also use a juicer or blender to expedite the breaking down of the tomatoes, just don't forget to use the pulp.

STUFFED ARTICHOKE WITH VEGETABLE PILAF

INGREDIENTS
Whole artichokes
Cherry tomatoes

Artichoke hearts (not marinated, frozen or jarred)
Onions, pearl and green
Dill and parsley, chopped
Kefalotiri or parmesan cheese
½ cup toasted bread crumbs
Olive oil
Salt and pepper to taste
1 cup white wine
Rice

1. Parboil the artichoke flowers for about 10 to 15 minutes.
2. Remove the flowers from the water and cool.
3. Place the flowers, one at a time, under cool running water at your sink. The running water will open the petals exposing the center closed leaves.
4. Using your thumb and three fingers, place them on the around the center leaves and gently twist the leaves from the choke removing the spiny leaves from the interior of the flower.
5. Take the hollowed flower and snip the pointed leaves with a kitchen scissors.
6. Chop off the point ends of the leaves and add them to the skillet.
7. Add olive oil to the skillet and heat.
8. Sauté the cut artichoke leaves with the rice, herbs, green and pearl onions, salt, and pepper in the skillet.
9. Once the rice begins to whiten, add additional artichokes and halved cherry tomatoes to the skillet and continue to sauté.
10. Once the onions become glossy and somewhat limp, fill the center of the flowers with the rice mixture, until it reaches the top leaves.
11. Mix the bread crumbs with the grated cheese and sprinkle it atop each flower.
12. Soak each flower with wine.
13. Add the cup of white wine with the amount of water needed to fill your baking pan. Cover with foil and allow the artichokes to steam in the oven at 300°F for 1 hour.
14. At the last 15 minutes of baking remove the foil and allow the bread crumbs to become crisp.

NOTES:
1. The type of vegetables used may be altered. You may add carrots, peppers, Vidalia onions, to the sautéed mixture.
2. Ground beef, lamb, chicken or turkey may also be added to the sautéing if you wish.
3. Omit the dill if you have someone sensitive to it and replace with tarragon or marjoram.

TRAHANA SOURDOUGH

INGREDIENTS
1 cup sourdough trahana
1 pound lamb, beef or chicken
1 tomato (optional)
1 stick butter
1 onion, sliced

2 cloves of garlic, chopped
1 cup red wine
Olive oil
Grated cheese – parmesan, kefalotirie, or mezethra

1. Chop the onions, tomato and garlic.
2. Sauté the onions and garlic in a skillet with olive oil.
3. Add the tomato and trahana and sauté.
4. Add the meat and continue to sauté.
5. Add 1 cup of wine.
6. Add water (1 cup for stew – 2 to 3 cups for soup).
7. Stew until meat is cooked.
8. Brown the butter and top the entire stew or soup.

NOTES:
1. Trahana comes in three forms: spicy, sourdough or sweet for cereals. For the purposes of this book we will only concentrate on the first two forms. The spicy trahana has a tomato and red pepper base, whereas the sourdough is plain with milk as a base.
2. Trahana can only be found in Greek or International stores. The pasta itself can be made from scratch. Those recipes will be submitted at a later date.
3. The smaller you cut the chunks, the quicker the meat will cook.
4. The great deal with trahana is that you can make this either a stew or soup. If you make it into a soup, you might want to consider using a slow cooker.

Chapter 8: Pitas – Pies

TIROPITA TRIANGLES

INGREDIENTS
½ pound feta cheese
3 whole eggs
½ pound manouri or ricotta cheese
1 pound phylo dough
1 stick butter
1 damp towel

1. Crumble the feta into a bowl.
2. Add the manouri and combine.
3. Lightly beat the egg with a fork and add to the feta combination in the bowl. Knead with your hands.
4. In a small pot, melt the butter.
5. Remove the phylo from the box and plastic. Keep the phylo in the plastic wrap until you have decided the size of your triangles.
6. Divide the phylo dough using a knife to score the appropriate width of your triangles. After the scoring has been defined and you have defined equal pieces, cut the phylo.
7. Place the phylo not being used under a damp, NOT WET, cloth.
8. The other section of the phylo should be unwrapped from the paper and laid out.
9. Depending on the thickness of the phylo, you may want to use 2 or 3 sheets.
10. Brush the butter between each layer of phylo, as you lay one layer upon the other.
11. In the lower corner of your strip, as it lies vertically before you, place a teaspoonful of the cheese mixture. If you are making small tiropita, use about a teaspoonful. The larger the triangle will use about 1 tablespoon of filling.

12. Starting from the lower end of the strip containing the cheese, fold the corner over to touch the direct opposite end of the strip forming a small triangle. From this point fold the strip as you would fold a flag. Your finished product will be a triangle.
13. Place the triangle on a greased cookie sheet folded side down. Once the cookie sheet is filled, brush the triangles with butter and bake at 330 °F until golden.
14. They may be enjoyed hot or cold. If you have made too many, they may be frozen prior to baking by layering them between parchment sheets.

NOTES:
1. The wider the width, the larger the triangle, the more the filling.
2. The cheese mixture must be somewhat loose in this recipe and continually stirred. The looseness of the cheese mixture provides for a fluffier pie or pita.
3. The shortening listed is butter, but margarine or olive oil will do as well.
4. Phylo comes in various forms of thickness from Horiatiko, which is the thickest and most resilient, to #3, which is the thinnest.
5. The thinness of the phylo determines the number of sheets to be used.
6. When determining the size of the pita consider when and how you will be serving the pie. Then when you remove the phylo dough from the box, you can gauge the size or width of your pie. 2" appetizer; 4" side dish; 5"-6" lunch, tea or light dinner.
7. This method also helps you determine how much phylo you will need for the filling you have made.
8. If you have the general type of phylo, remember to cover the portion you have not used with a damp, NOT WET, towel.

ARNOPITA

INGREDIENTS
1 pound roast lamb or ground lamb
1 tablespoon each oregano, thyme, mint and parsley
1 cup each carrots, peas, pearl onions and diced potatoes
1 pound phylo dough
1 stick of butter
Olive oil
½ pound feta cheese
2 stalks green onions
1 cup sliced olives

1. If you have roast lamb leftovers, slice the pieces of remaining lamb into thin strips and place them to the side.
2. Dice the carrots and potatoes and add them to a skillet with the peas and pearl onions.
3. In a skillet, heat the olive oil with the herbs and the vegetables.
4. You need to see the vegetables become bright and the onions glisten.
5. Sauté the slices of lamb in the skillet. Turn off the heat and allow the lamb to sit with the vegetables.
6. If you are using ground lamb, slightly brown the lamb in the skillet.

7. In the butter warmer, melt one stick of butter.
8. Cut the phylo in square pieces to compensate for the depth of the muffin pan and fold over or a design you wish to make (check notes).
9. Baste the muffin pan, between each layer of phylo - at least 4 layers.
10. Place one tablespoon of vegetables in each port of the pan.
11. Add some slices of lamb to each port.
12. Sprinkle some feta cheese.
13. Add more vegetables if there are any left.
14. Butter the phylo ends so they are moist.
15. Cut 6" pieces of floral wire for each pie you have made.
16. Bring the ends of phylo up, as if pointing upward. Take one of the silver wires and proceed to place it around the neck of the pita making a small parcel. Be careful not to puncture the pies. Do this for all the pies.
17. Bake at 325°F until golden.
18. Remove the pitas from the oven and let them cool.
19. Take the green onions, only the green portion, and cut them into strips with a scissors or sharp knife.
20. Remove the wire from one of the pitas and replace it with a green onion strip that you will tie on to the neck of the pita in a knot or bow.
21. Enjoy warm.

NOTES:
1. This is a fun recipe if you have leftover roast lamb or just want something light.
2. The best form for this pita is a Texas muffin pan.
3. Phylo comes in various forms of thickness from Horiatiko, which is the thickest and most resilient, to #3, which is the thinnest.
4. The thinness of the phylo determines the number of sheets to be used.
5. If you have the general type of phylo, remember to cover the portion you have not used with a damp, NOT WET, towel.
6. The silver wire will not harm the pita. It will keep the filo up and make it look like a gift.

HORTOPITA

INGREDIENTS
2 pounds of leafy greens mix (That means any combo you like. You pick!)
1 bunch leeks
1 large onion
1 sprig each fennel, dill, parsley,   marjoram, anything else you want, chopped finely
Watercress
1 tablespoon olive paste
Olive oil
3 eggs
¼ pound feta cheese
8 ounces ouzo
3 tablespoons rice
Salt and pepper to taste
Phylo

Combination of olive oil and unsalted butter

1. Chop the herbs and add them to a deep skillet with olive oil.
2. Chop the onion and leeks, and add them with olive paste and rice to the skillet.
3. Heat the skillet to a medium high temperature.
4. When the onion and leeks have cooked down start adding your greens. The onions should be glossy and the leeks become bright green and limp.
5. Continue stirring as the greens are cooking. All the greens must be cooked down.
6. Place the greens into a bowl, mix in eggs and cheese.
7. Salt and pepper to taste.
8. Heat ½ stick of butter with ½ cup of oil.
9. When butter is melted, remove the mixture from the heat and add the ouzo.
10. Prepare a cookie sheet by either brushing it with any butter or oil you have remaining, or simply cover it with a baking sheet. Preheat your oven to 350°F for standard oven or 325°F for convection oven (light fan).
11. Take a single sheet of the Horitiko folded in half lengthwise or 2 sheets of thin phylo buttered and folded in half.
12. Brush the phylo with the butter, then take a heaping tablespoon of the greens and place them on the buttered phylo.
13. Fold the phylo as a flag, when you finished butter the pie and place it on a cookie sheet.
14. Bake for approximately 20 minutes or until golden in color.

NOTES:
1. The greens selected for this dish are dependent on what the individual has growing around their homes, either wild or cultivated. The outdoor markets in Greece feature a wide selection of greens which could give this meal something to rave about. Due to the array of different types of greens, this recipe is difficult to replicate. It is hard to copy the same mixture of greens unless you have used premeasured bags.
2. The most important ingredient in this pita is the arrangement of flavors you get from the greens.
3. The three tablespoons of rice play an important role in your pie making. Greens tend to exude water during the cooking process, when introduced to the filling absorbs the water that would otherwise spoil your pie.
4. Phylo comes in various forms of thickness from Horiatiko, which is the thickest and most resilient, to #3, which is the thinnest.
5. The thinness of the phylo determines the number of sheets to be used.
6. When determining the size of the pita consider when and how you will be serving the pie. Then when you remove the phylo dough from the box you can gauge the size or width of your pie. 2" appetizer; 4" side dish; 5"-6" lunch, tea or light dinner.
7. This method also helps you determine how much phylo you will need for the filling you have made.
8. If you have the general type of phylo remember to cover the portion you have not used with a damp, NOT WET, towel.

KOLOKITHOPITA (PUMPKIN PIES)
Ingredients
 1 box filo pastry
 1 lb. unsalted butter, melted
 1 fresh sugar pumpkin or 1 large can prepared pumpkin
 4 eggs
 8 oz. feta
 ½ cup honey (optional)
 1 cup raisins (optional)
 1/2 pint half and half, milk or whipping cream
 pepper (optional)

1. If you are using fresh pumpkin. Cut the pumpkin into quarters and place it in a roasting pan with water. (If you are using can pumpkin go to step 4)
2. Cover the pan with aluminum foil and steam bake the pumpkin until soft at 300°F, about ½ hour.
3. You will know the pumpkin is ready by taking a fork and piercing the outer shell. If you find the pumpkin shell and meat soft, remove the pan from the oven and scoop the meat into a bowl.
4. Melt your butter. Half will be used in step 5 and half will be needed for wrapping your pies.
5. In a fairly large mixing bowl combine the eggs, feta, melted butter, honey, raisins, and pepper. Add each ingredient one at a time until thoroughly combined. If you are making a sweet pie you should include the honey and raisins. If you are making a side dish to the meal add the pepper and omit the honey and raisins.
6. Add the pumpkin meat and combine.
7. Remove your filo dough from the box. Filo comes in various thicknesses and is carried in many stores. Stores usually carry pastry thickness. If you can purchase the "country thickness" or the thickest texture they have that would be the best for this recipe.
8. Dampen your kitchen towel and lay it over the filo.
9. On your clean and dry table, extract one sheet of filo and lay it in front of you.
10. Take the melted butter with your pastry brush and brush the filo sheet. Do not dry brush and do not over saturate the brush.
11. Repeat step 9 and 10.
12. You now have two layers of filo before you. Pick up the short end and take it to the opposing side. You have now folded the sheets in half.
13. Spoon at least 2 tablespoons of the pumpkin mixture to the short end closest to you, in the center. Spread the mixture so that it is 1" away from the left and right.
14. Bring the two ends of the filo that are on either side of the mixture inward to cover the filling slightly.
15. Pick up the end of the filo closest to you (that is the area with the mixture) and roll it forward as if you were rolling an egg roll. Make sure to keep the sides tucked inwards.
16. Place the pita or pie onto a greased cookie sheet and butter.
    17. Repeat steps 9 through 16 until you have used up your filling.

18. Bake at 325°F until golden brown.

NOTES:
1. Make sure your mixture is not too runny; thicker is better.
2. If you wish to add spices like cinnamon, nutmeg, clove and allspice that would give the pita (pie) a great flavor.
3. The pita may also be made as a triangle or if you wish something untraditional Greek you may place the filo in muffin or cupcake tin. Baste the individual cupcake ports with butter. Cut you filo into squares, placing a sheet at a time in each port buttering between layers. It is preferred to have 8 layer thickness if you are using thin filo. If the filo is thick, use three layers.
4. Guests always like the extra touch! If you can make leaves, flowers, etc. with the extra filo; do it!

KOTOPITA

INGREDIENTS
1 pound chicken breast, leg quarters or 1 whole roasted Greek-style chicken
2 cups pitted Kalamata or black olives, chopped
½ bunch each mint and marjoram, chopped fine
1 medium size white or Vidalia onion, minced
1 bunch green onions, chopped
Olive oil
1 pound phylo
½ pound of unsalted butter
Salt and pepper

1. You may use chicken leg quarters or a whole-roasted chicken. I roasted the chicken in oregano, thyme, and parsley with olive oil and lemon. The chicken can even be leftovers. De-bone your chicken. The removal of the skin is up to you. I keep the skin in the mixture chopped to add extra flavor. Chop the meat into chunks and set it aside in a bowl.

2. Add olive oil to a skillet and sauté chopped olives, mint and marjoram, onions dry and green, until the white onion is translucent.

3. Remove the skillet from the heat and empty the contents into the bowl with the chicken and mix the meat with the scented oil until everything is combined.

4. Add the cheese if you wish at this point if you are not using a béchamel sauce.

5. Take the wine and pour it over the chicken mixture, continue stirring until the wine is completely distributed. Use about ½ cup if you are not using a béchamel sauce.

6. If you wish to add béchamel sauce, find the appropriate recipe in the sauce section, otherwise melt your butter and proceed to step 7.

7. Take a single sheet of the Horitiko folded in half or 2 sheets of thin phylo buttered and folded in half.

8. Lay the chicken on the buttered phylo, about 1" from the top in the center of the phylo strip.

9. Sprinkle with cheese if you have not used béchamel sauce.

10. Place one tablespoon of the sauce onto the chicken.

11. Fold the top sheet of phylo over the chicken, and bring in the sides and roll forward. Follow the diagram on the separate sheet. Butter the pita when finished rolling and place it on a cookie sheet.

12. Prepare a cookie sheet by either brushing it with any butter or oil you have remaining, or simply cover it with a baking sheet. Preheat your oven to 350°F for standard oven or 325°F for convection oven (light fan). Bake for approximately 20 minutes or until golden in color.

NOTES:
1. For the chicken pies, you might want to use disposable small loaf pans, Texas muffin tins or even scone tins to expedite the construction of the pies and to improve their appearance.
2. Béchamel Recipe of your selection.
3. Phylo comes in various forms of thickness from Horiatiko, which is the thickest and most resilient, to #3, which is the thinnest.
4. The thinness of the phylo determines the number of sheets to be used.
5. When determining the size of the pita consider when and how you will be serving the pie. Then when you remove the phylo dough from the box you can gauge the size or width of your pie. 2" appetizer; 4" side dish; 5"-6" lunch, tea or light dinner.
6. This method also helps you determine how much phylo you will need for the filling you have made.
7. If you have the general type of phylo, remember to cover the portion you have not used with a damp, NOT WET, towel.

KREATOPITA

INGREDIENTS
1 pound ground meat or lamb
3 cloves garlic, minced
3 stalks celery, minced
1 stalk leeks, minced
1 teaspoon each cumin, nutmeg and coriander
1 pound feta cheese, crumbled (optional)
1 ½ cups pine nuts (optional)
½ teaspoon white pepper

½ pound unsalted butter
1 pound thick phylo
Salt to taste

1. Sauté the garlic, spices, leek, pine nuts and celery until glossy.
2. Add the meat. Sauté slightly but do not overcook!
3. Remove from the stove and allow to cool. When cooled, add the feta and combine thoroughly.
4. Salt and pepper to taste.
5. Melt the unsalted butter.
6. Open the box of phylo dough. If the sheets are thick, you need only use one sheet at a time, folded in half, lengthwise. If the sheets are thin, use 2 at a time folded in half lengthwise.
7. Butter the sheet, and place about 1 tablespoon of the mixture in the top center of the strip. Fold the end inward first, and then continue to roll downward as if you are rolling an eggroll.
8. When completed, place on a cookie sheet and baste with more butter. Continue until the entire mixture is used.
9. Bake at 325°F for 40 minutes or until golden brown.

NOTES:

1. Phylo comes in various forms of thickness from Horiatiko, which is the thickest and most resilient, to #3, which is the thinnest.
2. The thinness of the phylo determines the number of sheets to be used.
3. When determining the size of the pita, consider when and how you will be serving the pie. Then when you remove the phylo dough from the box, you can gauge the size or width of your pie. 2" appetizer; 4" side dish; 5"-6" lunch, tea or light dinner.
4. This method also helps you determine how much phylo you will need for the filling you have made.
5. If you have the general type of phylo, remember to cover the portion you have not used with a damp, NOT WET, towel.

PRASSOPITA – LEEK PIE WITH POTATOES

INGREDIENTS
3-4 medium leeks, washed well and sliced
1 large egg
1 tablespoon cream
2 potatoes, peeled and grated
¼ cup olives
1/3 cup Parmesan cheese
2 tablespoons dill
Sea salt to taste
Dash of Turkish pepper
Olive oil
Phylo
Ouzo

1. Chop the leeks to form ringlets and place in a bowl.
2. Heat the oil in a skillet with pepper, salt, olives and dill.
3. Add the leeks and sauté until bright green. Be gentle during the sautéing not to damage the ringlets. When ready set the leeks aside to cool.
4. In a sauce pot, heat about ½ cup of olive oil. Add ouzo and remove from heat.
5. Try to use a circular baking pan if you can, if not a rectangular pan is fine.
6. Brush the pan with the oil mixture.
7. Proceed to lay the phylo, this time working from the center of the pan outward, overlapping the sheets, but continue around the pan.
8. Then lay a sheet of phylo in the center of the pan and brush with the olive oil mixture.
9. Continue Steps 7 and 8 for at least six layers.
10. When you have reached your six layers, brush the bottom and sides well. Fold the ends that are hanging over the pan inward and press them against the side of the pan.
11. Brush with the olive oil and ouzo.
12. Distribute the grated potatoes and cheese over the freshly brushed phylo.
13. Next lay the flat green leaves over the grated potato.
14. Take the circular pieces and lay them on top of the green leaves, displaying the flat portion.
15. Sprinkle with the olives from the skillet with the olive oil.
16. Gently beat the egg. Add 1 tablespoon of cream and drizzle the egg mixture over the exposed leeks.
17. Brush the exposed leeks with the remaining olive oil and ouzo.
18. Preheat the oven to 345°F and bake the pie until gold, about 45 minutes to 1 hour.

NOTES:
1. Phylo comes in various forms of thickness from Horiatiko, which is the thickest and most resilient, to #3, which is the thinnest.
2. The thinness of the phylo determines the number of sheets to be used.
3. When determining the size of the pita consider when and how you will be serving the pie. Then when you remove the phylo dough from the box you can gauge the size or width of your pie. 2" appetizer; 4" side dish; 5"-6" lunch, tea or light dinner.
4. This method also helps you determine how much phylo you will need for the filling you have made.
5. If you have the general type of phylo, remember to cover the portion you have not used with a damp, NOT WET, towel.
6. The use of ouzo was incorporated in Roumelli, just outside of Athens. The people there had a problem with the scent of leeks and used ouzo to cover the smell. If you don't want to use ouzo, tarragon does just as well.

MEAT BOUREKAKIA

INGREDIENTS
1 pound ground beef or lamb (small chunks of meat may also be used)
1 onion, chopped finely
¼ cup each walnuts and pine nuts
½ cup dry red wine
2 sprigs fresh mint, chopped finely
1/3 cup kasseri or parmesan cheese

2 + 1 eggs beaten
1 stick butter
Salt and pepper to taste
Olive oil
¼ cup sesame seeds, toasted
1 pound phylo (preferably Horitiko - thick)

1. Using a heavy skillet, place enough olive oil to cover the bottom about ¼" deep.
2. Add your mint, nuts and onions to the oil and sauté until the onions are translucent on medium heat.
3. Add the meat and wine, and brown lightly, about 2 minutes.
4. Place the contents of the skillet into a mixing bowl and add cheese and 2 beaten eggs.
5. Salt and pepper to taste.
6. Mix the contents thoroughly.
7. Melt the butter in a small saucepan.
8. Select how you would like your pies - as mezes or meal. If it is a starter to a meal then you would use 2 teaspoons of the mixture. If pita is for lunch then 2 tablespoons would be sufficient. Follow the attached diagram.
9. The size of the pita or pie is directly related to the way it is being served. For example, if you were serving this as an appetizer, I would cut the phylo into fourths, lunch side dish I would cut the phylo into thirds and if it was the main course at a light lunch, tea or dinner, the phylo would be cut in half.
10. Toast the sesame seeds by placing them in a dry skillet and heating them, stirring continually. When they are a light brown color remove them from the heat and allow them to cool.
11. Once you have completed forming all your pitas, take the remaining beaten egg and brush the tops and sprinkle with the toasted sesame seeds.
12. Prepare a cookie sheet by either brushing it with any butter or oil you have remaining, or simply cover it with a baking sheet. Preheat your oven to 350°F for standard oven or 325°F for convection oven (light fan). Bake for approximately 20 minutes or until golden in color.

NOTES:
1. Phylo comes in various forms of thickness from Horiatiko, which is the thickest and most resilient, to #3, or the type you find in the grocery store, which is the thinnest.
2. The thinness of the phylo determines the number of sheets to be used.
3. When determining the size of the pita, consider when and how you will be serving the pie. Then when you remove the phylo dough from the box you can gauge the size or width of your pie. 2" appetizer; 4" side dish; 5"-6" lunch, tea or light dinner.
4. This method also helps you determine how much phylo you will need for the filling you have made.
5. If you have the general type of phylo, remember to cover the portion you have not used with a damp, NOT WET, towel.

PRASSOPITA

INGREDIENTS

2-3 bunches of leeks
1 bunch of spinach
½ bunch of dill or tarragon
1 onion
3 eggs
½ pound feta cheese
Olive oil
8-10 ounces of ouzo
1 stick of butter
1 pound phylo

1. Chop the leeks first lengthwise down the center and then in small half circles. Place them in a colander washing them to ensure all the dirt is removed.
2. Rinse your spinach and set it aside.
3. Chop the onion and herbs and place them in a skillet with olive oil and start sautéing.
4. When you begin smelling the herbs, add the leeks and sauté.
5. When the leeks become bright green, add the spinach and sauté.
6. The spinach must turn a deep glossy green color, before the entire mixture is removed from the skillet and cooled in a bowl.
7. Crumble the feta and add to the bowl.
8. Crack the eggs in a cup and beat them with a fork until combined. Add them to the bowl.
9. Using your hands, combine the leek mixture, making sure all the ingredients are evenly distributed.
10. Set the bowl aside and let the flavors mingle.
11. Melt 1 stick of butter.
12. Add the ouzo to the butter.
13. Cut the phylo sheet to the size you like.
14. Baste your phylo sheet or sheets based on the number of sheets you will use.
15. The amount of filling you add is directly related to when you are serving you pie.
16. Prepare a cookie sheet by either brushing it with any butter or oil you have remaining, or simply cover it with a baking sheet. Preheat your oven to 350°F for standard oven or 325°F for convection oven (light fan).
17. The size of the pita or pie is directly related to the way it is being served. For example, if you were serving this as an appetizer I would cut the phylo into fourths, lunch side dish I would cut the phylo into thirds, and if it was the main course at a light lunch, tea or dinner, the phylo would be cut in half.
18. Brush the phylo with the butter, then take a heaping tablespoon of the greens and place them on the buttered phylo.
19. Fold the phylo as a flag. When finished, butter the pie and place it on a cookie sheet.
20. Bake for approximately 20 minutes or until golden in color.

NOTES:

1. Phylo comes in various forms of thickness from Horiatiko, which is the thickest and most resilient, to #3, which is the thinnest.
2. The thinness of the phylo determines the number of sheets to be used.
3. When determining the size of the pita consider when and how you will be serving the pie. Then when you remove the phylo dough from the box you can gauge the size or width of your pie. 2" appetizer; 4" side dish; 5"-6" lunch, tea or light dinner.
4. This method also helps you determine how much phylo you will need for the filling you have made.
5. If you have the general type of phylo, remember to cover the portion you have not used with a damp, NOT WET, towel.
6. The use of ouzo was incorporated in Roumelli, just outside of Athens. The people there had a problem with the scent of leeks and used ouzo to cover the smell. If you don't want to use ouzo, tarragon does just as well.

PSAROPITA

INGREDIENTS
1 pound Swai fish fillets
3 tomatoes
1/3 bunch parsley and tarragon
1 cinnamon stick
1 teaspoon nutmeg
½ teaspoon each cardamom and allspice
1 teaspoon rice
1 onion
1 green pepper
1 tablespoon sugar
Olive oil
1 bay leaf
1 cup sliced Kalamata olives
1 box phyllo

1. Prepare the sauce by chopping the herbs and placing them in a skillet with the spices, olives, rice and bay leaf in olive oil.
2. Chop the tomatoes, onions, green peppers. Add them to the skillet with the spice mixture and cook down. Add more oil if necessary.
3. When the sauce forms, add the sugar and stir.
4. Arrange the fish on a baking sheet. Add the sauce and bake for 30 minutes.
5. Remove the fish from the oven and cool.
6. Prepare a cookie sheet by either brushing it with any butter or oil you have remaining, or simply cover it with a baking sheet. Preheat your oven to 350°F for standard oven or 325°F for convection oven (light fan).
7. Take a single sheet of the Horitiko folded in half lengthwise or 2 sheets of thin phylo buttered and folded in half.
8. Brush the phylo with the butter. Take a heaping tablespoon of the vegetables and place them on the buttered phylo.

9. Add the filet of fish with some sauce. Be careful, too much sauce could ruin the pita.
10. Fold the phylo as a flag. When you finished, butter the pie and place it on a cookie sheet.
11. Bake for approximately 20 minutes or until golden in color.

NOTES:
1. Though any fillet fish would be great for this recipe, the discovery of Swai and this recipe could not be separated in my mind's eye. You make the decision.
2. Phylo comes in various forms of thickness from Horiatiko, which is the thickest and most resilient, to #3 which is the thinnest.
3. The thinness of the phylo determines the number of sheets to be used.
4. When determining the size of the pita consider when and how you will be serving the pie. Then when you remove the phylo dough from the box you can gauge the size or width of your pie. 2" appetizer; 4" side dish; 5"-6" lunch, tea or light dinner.
5. This method also helps you determine how much phylo you will need for the filling you have made.
6. If you have the general type of phylo, remember to cover the portion you have not used with a damp, NOT WET, towel.
7. The size of the pita or pie is directly related to the way it is being served. For example, if you were serving this as an appetizer I would cut the phylo into fourths, lunch side dish I would cut the phylo into thirds and, if it was the main course at a light lunch, tea or dinner, the phylo would be cut in half.
8. This is also a great recipe if you have leftover fish.
9.

SPANAKOPITA

INGREDIENTS
¼ pound feta cheese
3 whole eggs
1 pound spinach
½ bunch green onions
1 teaspoon dill or tarragon
1 lb. phylo dough
1 stick butter

1. Crumble the feta into a bowl.
2. Thinly slice the onions and place them into a skillet with olive oil and the dill, and sauté.
3. Add the spinach and continue to sauté until all the spinach is cooked.
4. Place the sautéed ingredients along with the olive oil into the bowel with the feta.
5. Lightly beat the eggs with a fork and add to the spinach combination in the bowl, and knead with your hand.
6. In a small pot, melt the butter.
7. Remove the phylo from the box and plastic. Keep the phylo in the plastic wrap until you have decided the size of your triangles.
8. Divide the phylo dough using a knife to score the appropriate width of your triangles. After the scoring has been defined and you have defined equal pieces, cut the phylo.
9. Place the phylo not being used under a damp, NOT WET, towel.

10. The other section of the phylo should be unwrapped from the paper and laid out.
11. Depending on the thickness of the phylo, you may want to use 2 sheets or 3.
12. Butter between each layer of phylo, as you lay one layer upon the other.
13. In the lower corner of your strip, as it lies vertically before you, place a teaspoon full of the spinach mixture. If you are making small Tiropita use about a teaspoon full. The larger the triangle will use about 1 tablespoon of filling.
14. Starting from the lower end of the strip containing the mixture, fold the corner over to touch the direct opposite end of the strip forming a small triangle. From this point fold the strip as you would fold a flag. Your finished product will be a triangle.
15. Place the triangle on a greased cookie sheet folded side down. Once the cookie sheet is filled, brush the triangles with butter and bake at 330 °F until golden.
16. They may be enjoyed hot or cold. If you have made too many, they may be frozen prior to baking by layering them between parchment sheets.

NOTES:
1. The shortening listed is butter, but margarine or olive oil will do as well.
2. Phylo comes in various forms of thickness from Horiatiko, which is the thickest and most resilient, to #3, which is the thinnest.
3. The thinness of the phylo determines the number of sheets to be used.
4. When determining the size of the pita consider when and how you will be serving the pie. Then when you remove the phylo dough from the box you can gauge the size or width of your pie. 2" appetizer; 4" side dish; 5"-6" lunch, tea or light dinner.
5. This method also helps you determine how much phylo you will need for the filling you have made.
6. If you have the general type of phylo, remember to cover the portion you have not used with a damp, NOT WET, towel.

Chapter 9: Poultry

TURKEY WITH OLIVE OIL AND HERBS

INGREDIENTS
1 turkey, 18 to 23 lbs.
1 cup lemon juice
½ cup olive oil
1 tablespoon each parsley, oregano, rosemary and thyme
5 cloves of garlic
Salt
½ teaspoon Turkish red pepper

PREPARE SAUCE
1. Press the garlic cloves into a bowl.
2. Add the dry herbs, olive oil, lemon juice and red pepper. Heat in a sauce pot.
3. Salt to taste.
4. Bring the contents to a boil, extinguish the heat and allow the mixture to settle.

TURKEY
1. Rinse the turkey with cold water and place it in a roasting pan.
2. Lift the skin by the breast, thigh and legs being especially careful not to rip or puncture the skin.
3. Stuff the turkey with the selected dressings.
4. Cover the area under the lifted turkey skin with the sauce before adding a small portion of your dressing. Be careful not to add too much dressing in that area – keep in mind expansion.
5. Baste the entire bird with the oil mixture.
6. Set the oven at 350°F and roast covered for the first few hours of baking.
7. Remove the covering for the final 45 minutes.

NOTES:
1. Refer to the poundage to verify how long your turkey should bake.
2. Only use a fresh bird with no other basting additives to alter the taste of the recipe.
3. More or less garlic may be used.
4. Black pepper may be substituted for the Turkish red pepper.
5. Basting is not necessary if you take some of the dressing and place it under the skin by the breast and thighs. This will keep the white meat moist and give you an interesting cut when carving the breast.
6. You may add wine or brandy in lieu of the lemon juice.
7. If you do not have a cover for the roaster or the bird is too big, make a tent with aluminum foil.

CHICKEN AND QUINCE IN RED SAUCE

INGREDIENTS
2-4 quince
1 frying chicken, quartered
1-2 sticks unsalted butter
2 cups flour
1 yellow or Vidalia onion
2 tomatoes, chopped
1 cinnamon stick
½ teaspoon sugar
1 tablespoon dried mint
Salt and pepper

1. Quarter, core and chop your quince. Place them in a bowl of cold water and lemon juice.
2. Season your flour with salt and pepper.
3. Dredge your chicken pieces in the flour and set them aside on a plate.
4. Melt 4 tablespoons of butter in a large skillet and brown your chicken pieces. Remove the pieces from the skillet and place them in the pot you intend on using.
5. Melt 2 more tablespoons of butter and sauté the quince until golden. Use a slotted spoon to remove the quince from the skillet and place them into the pot.
6. Melt the remaining butter in the skillet and sauté the onions, mint and tomatoes until you reach a sauce.
7. Add a cinnamon stick, ¾ cup of water and sugar. Cook for 1-2 minutes more to reach a boil.
8. Empty the skillet contents into the pot.
9. Cook on low to medium heat for 45 minutes in a Dutch oven or covered skillet. If you are using a slow cooker, place the setting on high and cook for 4 to 5 hours. (Slow cookers are the best since they replicate the conditions on the Islands where the cooks either cook slowly or use the stone ovens.)

NOTES:
1. Large pot, slow cooker, covered cast iron skillet or Dutch oven, are great for this recipe as it cooks the chicken uniformly and slowly.
2. For this recipe you might also try using fresh nutmeg, allspice and a touch of clove

CHICKEN WITH OKRA IN TOMATO SAUCE

INGREDIENTS

1 roasting chicken
Olive oil
1 layer onions, cut in thin slices
1 green pepper, sliced
1 pound of okra, fresh or frozen
½ bunch fresh parsley or 1 tablespoon dried
½ bunch fresh dill weed or 1 tablespoon dried
2 tomatoes, diced
White vinegar
Balsamic vinegar
1 cup red wine
Salt and pepper
Garlic, sliced to taste

1. Wash your chicken and remove excess fat from the openings.
2. Place the chicken in a roasting pan.
3. If you are using fresh okra, be careful not to cut into the pod itself. Trim the top crown off and place it in a liquid mixture of 2 parts white vinegar and one part water for at least one hour. The liquid must cover the okra. This procedure helps remove the slime.
4. Lightly cover bottom of skillet with olive oil and heat to medium high.
5. Sprinkle sliced onions and green peppers over bottom of pan and sauté.
6. Add the garlic and herbs and continue to sauté.
7. Add the tomato and sauté until it becomes sauce.
8. Place okra around the chicken in a roasting pan and add sautéed ingredients over the chicken and okra.
9. Sprinkle with balsamic vinegar, wine and bake at 350° F for 1½ hours.
10. Baked covered for 1 hour, uncover and bake for 15 minutes to thicken if necessary.

NOTES:
1. This recipe may be made in a crock pot. Deposit the skillet ingredients over the okra with the wine and vinegar and cook on low for 3 hours.
2. Water may replace wine for a simpler taste.
3. Walnut oil may replace olive oil.

CHICKEN WITH OLIVE OIL & LEMON JUICE

INGREDIENTS
1 roasting chicken
½ cup olive oil

Juice of 2 lemons
1 tablespoon each parsley, oregano and thyme
3 cloves of garlic
Salt and pepper
6 Yukon potatoes

1. Wash your chicken and remove the excess fat from around the openings.
2. Press the garlic and add it to a sauce pan.
3. Add the herbs, oil and juice.
4. Heat the mixture until it sizzles and you can smell the herbs.
5. Chop your potatoes. Peeling is optional.
6. Place the chicken in a roasting pan. Arrange the potatoes around the chicken.
7. Cover the chicken and potatoes with the oil mixture.
8. Spoon the solid ingredients evenly over the chicken and the potatoes.
9. Salt and pepper to taste.
10. Place the chicken in the oven and roast at 345 °F until the chicken is golden and the potatoes are brown.

NOTES:

1. Heating the oil, juices and herbs is a form of Corfu style of cooking. The cooks from this area have remarked that unless the herbs are heated with the oils, the flavors will not reach their peak. Therefore, by heating the ingredients together you are actually melding the flavors and you will get better results.
2. Yukon potatoes are used because of their excellent flavor.
3. Chopped olives may also be added to the oil mixture to dress up this recipe.
4. Garlic may be used to taste.
5. Lemon zest added to the oil also enhances the taste of the chicken.
6. Carrots and celery may be added to the potatoes to make a complete meal.
7. This may be made in a slow cooker on low for 4 to 6 hours depending on the chicken size and the amount of vegetables you have added.

CHICKEN YUVETSI

INGREDIENTS
1-2 pounds whole chicken
Olive oil
Salt and pepper
3 onions, chopped
1 cup orzo
2 tomatoes, chopped
Thyme
1 bay leaf
2-3 cups stock

1. In a pot add the chicken neck along with the bay leaf and bring the 3 cups of water to a boil.
2. Cut your chicken into quarters or debone. Cut the meat into small cubes and set it aside.
3. Dice the tomatoes and onions. Place in a deep skillet or wok with olive oil, salt and pepper, cinnamon stick, cloves and thyme.

4. Sauté these ingredients, until the sauce begins to form.
5. Add the chicken and cook, stirring until brown.
6. Add the orzo and stir until glossy.
7. Add 2 cups of stock and allow the orzo to cook.
8. When the stock has cooked down, taste the orzo. If you feel this is the right consistency, stop and serve.
9. If not, add additional stock and continue to cook until done.

NOTES:
1. Traditionally this is made with beef, lamb or goat, but the flavor is so appealing that many have adapted this recipe to chicken.
2. If you are making this in a terra cotta baking container, add ½ cup liquid in addition to that mentioned in Step 6 in the quick method above. Bake at 340°F for 1 hour.
3. If you are using a slow cooker, keep the liquid amount the same as Step 6. Leave the mixture to cook overnight or from the morning until you come home. If you are checking the fluid level during the day and you feel you need more liquid, go ahead and add the additional fluid. But the liquid level in the slow cooker will not reduce the same as in the oven or on the stove. The tomatoes and onions will increase the fluid in the cooker.

GROUND MEAT DRESSING FOR TURKEY

INGREDIENTS
2 pounds lean ground meat
2 sticks unsalted butter
½ teaspoon clove
1 teaspoon each cumin, nutmeg and cinnamon
4-5 carrots, minced
3-4 stalks of celery
1 cup pine nuts
1 cup each walnuts, almonds and chestnuts
1 cup long grain rice
1 bunch green onions, chopped
1-2 cups of wine
2-3 eggs
1 apple, peeled and chopped
Turkey giblets
1-2 cups turkey broth
Salt and pepper

1. Place the giblets in a pot of water, seasoned with salt. Bring the water to a boil to create your broth. The giblets and the neck may be minced and used in the dressing.
2. In a separate pot melt your butter.
3. Add your spices, vegetables, rice and nuts and sauté.
4. Add 1 cup of broth and slow boil the rice mixture.
5. Add the apple to the mixture and continue to heat.
6. While the rice mixture is heating. Add the meat and eggs to a bowl and knead.
7. Add the wine to the meat and continue to knead.
8. Add the meat to the rice and brown slightly.
9. Salt and pepper to taste.

10. Remove the skillet from the heat and add the additional cup of wine.
11. There are two methods in cooking the remainder of the dressing:
    a. Stuff your turkey with the par-cooked ground meat and roast with the bird. This is a common practice, but I would advise that you cook the meat a little more toward medium instead of medium rare.
    b. The alternative roasting method is placing the meat mixture into a roasting pan and allowing it to cook independent from the bird. This ensures that the meat is cooked thoroughly. You may add any additional broth. Allow 30 minutes at 350°F

NOTES:
1. Nuts may be omitted in the event someone has an allergy. You might want to substitute dried bread, chopped yellow onions, raisins and/or chopped potatoes.
2. This is a heavier dressing than most American palettes are accustomed to. You may use ground pork or lamb, but the only problem is cooking the meat thoroughly. I would prefer the second method.
3. Veal or buffalo meat would be great but are expensive.
4. Be careful with your giblets. Make sure they are a good color, such as a bright red and not yellowish or brownish. If your giblets are the latter color, use low sodium turkey broth. You do not want to additional salts changing the flavor of your meal.

ISLAND DUCK WITH BRANDY

INGREDIENTS
1 duck
10 ounces of brandy
Olive oil
Juice of one lemon
½ bunch each fresh thyme and oregano
½ cup honey
5 celery stalks
Salt and pepper to taste

1. Find a pot that will fit the entire duck, submersed.
2. Add water to the pot, but not too much so as not to be displacing when the duck is added.
3. Place the duck before you on a cutting board.
4. Bring the water to a boil.
5. With a sharp knife continually stab the duck until it is covered in jabbing sites.
6. Place the duck into the boiling water for 10 minutes. Make sure that all sides of the duck are in the boiling water.
7. Remove the duck and set it aside to cool.
8. Discard the water.
9. In a sauce pan, combine ½ cup of olive oil with the herbs, lemon juice and honey, and heat.
10. Allow the herbs to mingle with the oil and the juices. When it comes to a sizzle, add the brandy and extinguish the heat.

11. Place the duck in a roasting pan on a bed of celery stalks.
12. Coat the interior of the duck cavity and the outside of the entire duck with the brandy mixture.
13. Roast the duck at 350°F for about 1 ½ hours or until golden.

NOTES:
1. Pomegranate syrup may replace the brandy.
2. The stabbing of the duck is important, because it allows the fat to leave the duck during the boiling process.
3. This recipe may be used with hay, and will take the place of the celery, which will absorb any additional oils that exude from the duck during roasting.
4. Cherry rice pilaf is a must with this dish.
5. Lemon zest adds flavor if you wish to add this to the sauce.

ISLAND STYLE QUAIL IN VINE LEAVES

INGREDIENTS
4 quail or Cornish hens
4-8 grape leaves
6 mini wooden skewers
2 lemons zest
Thyme sprigs
1 cup honey
1 cup brandy + 8 oz.
¼ cup of olive oil
Sea salt and fresh ground pepper
1 cedar plank soaked

1. Soak the cedar plank and mini skewers in water and 8 oz. of brandy for 24 hours.
2. Zest the lemons and slice the fruit.
3. Place the fruit in a sauce pot

Add the honey, oil and the thyme sprigs to the sauce pot.

4. Rinse the grape leaves.
5. Snip off the stems and arrange them in groups of four for each of the quail. The grouping should be joined at the stem and overlapping, forming a cross shape.
6. Grind the salt and pepper and combine with the lemon zest.
7. Rub the ground mixture on the quail.
8. Bring the sauce pot to a boil and reduce heat to a simmer for 10 minutes.
9. Turn off the heat and add the brandy.

10. First remove the fruit and place in each quail cavity.
11. Spoon the remainder of the liquid over the quail.

Fold the leaves encasing the entire quail and secure with a mini skewer.

12. Place the cedar plank in a roasting pan with 2 cups of water.
13. Gently place the wrapped quail onto the planks, making sure to keep the birds intact.
14. Pour the remainder of fluid in the sauce pan over each wrapped quail.
15. Cover with aluminum and bake at 325°F for 45 minutes. Uncover and bake for an additional 15 minutes.
16. *Serve the birds on a plate with the leaves partially opened.*

NOTES:

17. This recipe is awesome with the Cherry Rice Pilaf.
18. Recipe works well with Cornish hens.
19. My students Linda Eirich and B.J. Tommey developed another recipe by turning the above into an appetizer using chicken wings. The only stipulation is that the wings cannot be boneless.
20. Other types of wood are acceptable such as, apple, maple, mesquite, pecan, etc. Wood has been used in Greek cooking from the beginning, especially during in-ground smoking.

QUAIL IN WINE SAUCE

INGREDIENTS
6-8 quail
2 medium onions, chopped
3 large tomatoes, diced
2 garlic cloves, minced
2 cups or more wine
1 ½ cups water
2 cloves, whole
1 cinnamon stick (optional)
1 bay leaf
½ cup extra virgin olive oil

1. Heat the oil, onions, garlic, bay leaf, cinnamon stick and clove in a skillet until the oil starts to sizzle.
2. Once the onions become clear and you start to see them glossy, add the quail and brown on both sides.
3. Add the tomatoes and sauté for a minute.
4. Add the wine and ½ cup water.
5. Cover and simmer at a medium heat 20-30 minutes.
6. If you notice sticking, add more wine.
7. Serve over rice.

1. If you wish to use Cornish hens, about 4, you might want to brown the hens prior to the start of making the sauce. Place the hens in a roaster cover with the sauce and bake for 45 minutes covered at 325°F.
2. The slow cooker is also an option for cooking. You will have to gauge it on low heating for no more than 3 hours.

KLEFTIKO CHICKEN

INGREDIENTS
1 whole chicken, lamb, beef or fish
1 or 2 of any carrots, celery, onions, mushrooms, green onions and potatoes
Fresh mint, oregano, thyme, rosemary and/or parsley
½ cup olive oil
Lemon juice
½ pound of feta cheese
Salt and pepper

1. Juice your lemon. Extract the seeds from the juice and discard, but save the lemon halves.
2. Clean your chicken. Remove the fat from around the neck area. Rub your chicken with the remaining lemon halves you have just juiced.
3. Lift the skin of the chicken at the breast area, taking care not to pierce the skin layer. Use your fingers to gently pull away the tendons holding the skin to the meat.
4. Strip the leaves from the herb's stalk. Place them in the skillet with olive oil and slowly heat. Once the herbs become fragrant, turn the heat off and set the skillet aside.
5. Chop the selected vegetables and mix them together in a bowl.
6. Crumble your feta and combine with the vegetables.
7. With a tablespoon add the oil into the cavity of the chicken and rub.
8. Lift the skin and deposit a few tablespoons of oil under the skin.
9. Prepare a roaster with aluminum foil, baking parchment, or baking bag; you may also use a clay roaster, smoker or slow cooker.
10. Add as much of the vegetables as possible into the cavity. Whatever remains is added around the chicken, salt and pepper and seal.
11. Bake the chicken in the oven at 325°F for about 45 minutes to 1 hour or until thoroughly cooked.
12. Remove the vegetables from the cavity and serve as a side dish to the chicken.

1. This recipe is derived from history. During periods of war when rebels hid in the mountains, they often had to steal their food to survive. The food was wrapped in oil cloth, with vegetables and other cheeses. A hole was made in the ground, where wood, probably pine or cedar, was set on fire. The oil cloth was added to this hole and covered with soil. This was probably one of the first times smoking was used for a meal. The covering of the hole ensured that the enemy would not see any smoke, and their food would be cooked quickly.
2. The skin pocket will expose the breast, legs and thighs to the seasoning making the meat moist and the skin crispy.
3. Heating the herbs slowly will lock all the flavors together.
4. If you are using a slow cooker, place carrots or celery to the bottom of the ceramic pot and place the chicken and additional vegetables around. Add enough fluid to cover the base vegetables and cook on low for at least 5 hours or until done.
5. If you are smoking, soak your wood chips for at least 10 to 24 hours prior to cooking. Consider soaking in wine, brandy, whiskey or fruit juices. Suggested wood chips are apple, maple, cedar, walnut or maple. Place the meat you are cooking in the smoker with the vegetables in the pan. Cover and cook for 2 hours at least or until done.

ROAST DUCK WITH ALMONDS

INGREDIENTS
1 duck
2 cups sliced almonds
2 sprigs each mint, basil and parsley, chopped
10 fresh or soft dried figs, chopped fine
1 large pomegranate or ½ cup pomegranate syrup
1 teaspoon juniper berries, crushed
6 strands of saffron
1 cup mavrodaphne
Olive oil
Sea salt and fresh ground pepper
2 handfuls of fresh hay

1. Pre-heat the oven to 400°F.
2. Wash the duck in cool water.
3. Stab the duck repeatedly around its entire body.
4. Rub the duck inside and out with ground pepper and salt. Set aside.
5. In a skillet, heat the olive oil with the herbs, figs, pomegranate, juniper berries, and saffron.
6. Add the almonds.
7. Add the wine and simmer for 5 minutes for flavors to blend.
8. Lay half of the hay evenly in a roaster, making sure that the hay is not extending out of the roaster.
9. Generously coat the entire duck, inside and out, with the wine mixture and almonds.

10. Take the remainder of the hay and blanket the duck.
11. Seal your roaster and make sure that no hay is extruding from the pan.
12. Bake for 1 ½ hours.
13. Remove from the oven. Carefully open the roaster and remove the hay covering.
14. Serve on the bed of hay to add some fun to the meal.

NOTES:
1. Northern Greeks liked using hay to keep the meats warm after cooking. The hay also enhanced the flavor of the food during the cooking process and absorbed the excess oils.
2. The hay method of roasting is not reserved only for duck, but used also for lamb, beef and goat.

ROASTED STUFFED DUCK

INGREDIENTS
1 duck, dressed
3 apples
3 sprigs of rosemary
1 bunch celery
2 sticks unsalted butter
1 cup walnuts or chestnuts
2 onions, sliced thin
2 cups brandy
Juice of 1 lemon
Salt and pepper to taste

1. Clean and wash your duck. Towel dry.
2. With a sharp knife, continually stab the duck throughout its body. Make sure you stab evenly and cover the entire body.
3. Take the bunch of celery and cut the heart from the stalks. This is the portion of the celery that extends from the root area up to where the stalks begin to spread.
4. Core and peel one apple.
5. Quarter the apple and the celery heart and place them in the cavity of the duck.
6. Using a small skewer or turkey lacer to seal the opening of the duck.
7. Melt the butter in a large pot with the rosemary.
8. Place the duck and giblets into the pot with the melted butter and brown.
9. Once you have browned the duck, add water to the pot and parboil.
10. Reduce the heat on the broth to a medium high heat.
11. Remove the duck from the pot. Pull off the pins or lace and remove the apple and celery heart from the cavity.
12. Peel and chop the remaining apples and celery. Hold half of the apple to the side. Place half in water and lemon juice.
13. Combine the nuts, chopped apple, and celery and place the ingredients in the broth with the giblets. Simmer for a few minutes.
14. Stuff the duck with the simmered ingredients, and cover the opening with a large apple half.

15. Place the duck in a roaster.
16. If there is any stuffing remaining, drizzle it over the duck with the broth.
17. Bake at 350°F for 45 minutes.
18. At 45 minutes pour the brandy over the duck and continue baking for 15 more minutes.

NOTES:

1. This is a very unusual process developed in the islands of Greece. It allows you to enjoy the natural flavor of the duck without the heavy sauces associated with this particular game meat.
2. The boiling of the duck allows the fats to be expelled into the water but more so absorbed in the cavity by the celery heart and apple.
3. The initial stuffing is discarded and the duck is refilled with nuts, apples and celery which may later be eaten. The final addition of the brandy allows a simple sweetness to be added.
4. On the Island of Chios, the above mixture of nuts, apples and celery is replaced with dried apricots, as a family friend John Balasis explained. As with the apple above, the initial apricots are discarded and replaced with more dried apricots for the final roasting.

TURKEY IN GARLIC AND YOGURT SAUCE

INGREDIENTS
1 turkey, 18 to 23 lbs.
1 quart plain yogurt
½ cup olive oil
¼ cup lemon juice
1 tablespoon each parsley, mint and thyme
5 cloves of garlic
Salt
½ teaspoon Turkish red pepper

PREPARE SAUCE 6 HOURS AHEAD OR THE NIGHT BEFORE
1. Press the garlic cloves into a bowl.
2. Add the dry herbs, olive oil, lemon juice, red pepper and yogurt and combine.
3. Salt to taste.
4. Place the bowl in the refrigerator to allow the flavors to mingle.

TURKEY
1. Rinse the turkey with cold water and place in a roasting pan.
2. Lift the skin by the breast, thigh and legs being especially careful not to rip or puncture the skin.
3. Stuff the turkey with the selected dressings.
4. Remove the sauce you prepared and rub the entire turkey with the yogurt mixture.
5. Set the oven at 350°F and roast covered for the first few hours of baking.
6. Remove the covering for the final 45 minutes.

NOTES:

1. Refer to the poundage to verify how long your turkey should bake.
2. Only use a fresh bird with no other basting additives to alter the taste of the recipe.
3. More or less garlic may be used.
4. Black pepper may be substituted for the Turkish red pepper.
5. Basting is not necessary if you take some of the dressing and place it under the skin by the breast and thighs. This will keep the white meat moist and give you an interesting cut when carving the breast.
6. Make sure you thickly coat the entire bird with the yogurt.
7. If you do not have a cover for the roaster or the bird is too big, make a tent with aluminum foil.

Chapter 10: Beef, Lamb & Pork

YOUVARELAKIA

<u>INGREDIENTS</u>
1 pound ground beef or lamb
1 cup cooked rice
1 medium onion, minced
¼ cup parsley, minced
1 tablespoon mint
1 large egg
Olive oil

Avgolemono Sauce Recipe

1 box of orzo or elbow macaroni

1. Sauté the onions, herbs and rice in a skillet, until the rice kernels become white.
2. Combine the herb mixture with the egg and meat in a bowl.
3. Form small meatballs and place them on a plate.
4. Heat the olive oil in your skillet.
5. When the olive oil is heated, brown the meatballs.
6. Remove the browned meatballs from the skillet and place them in a pot with water.
7. Bring the water to a boil.
8. Add pasta.
9. When pasta is done, reduce the heat to simmer.
10. Add the selected Avgolemono Sauce and enjoy.

NOTES:
1. The meatballs may be floured and fried if you like but is not necessary.
2. This is a very simple recipe that may be adapted to a slow cooker. If you use a slow cooker, place the setting on low and cook for 4 hours. Then add your noodles, cook for ½ hour or until noodles are done. Turn off the heat and add your Avgolemono sauce. Do not forget to continue stirring the sauce in the broth until it is tempered
3. Though not a tradition you can try this recipe with ground pork.
4. This recipe is just as good without the Avgolemono Sauce.

ATHENIAN MOUSAKA

INGREDIENTS
1 pound ground beef, lamb or pork
1 large onion
2-3 tomatoes, diced
1 teaspoon each allspice, clove, cinnamon and nutmeg
2 tablespoons brandy or sweet wine (optional)
2-3 large eggplants, thinly sliced lengthwise
2-3 russet or Yukon potatoes
Olive oil
Salt and pepper to taste

Béchamel Sauce selected

Sauce
1. Place olive oil in the skillet with the spices and heat.
2. Chop the onion into slices and add them to the skillet.
3. When the onions have caramelized, add the diced tomatoes.
4. Stir the tomatoes until they have cooked down and become sauce.
5. Now add the ground meat and brown.
6. Stir the meat in the skillet making sure that the onions and tomatoes mingle with the meat.
7. When the meat is cooked, add the brandy or sweet wine and stir for a few minutes.
Preparing the Eggplant and Potatoes
8. Peel and slice your potatoes into thin circles, place them in water until needed.
9. Prepare a cookie sheet with baking paper or aluminum. Coat the sheet with olive oil and sprinkle with nutmeg, salt, and pepper.
10. Cut the eggplant lengthwise in thin slices. Repeat the sprinkle on the top of the eggplant slices as well. Lay the slices on the cookie sheet and bake at 300°F until the eggplant is limp, about 5 or 10 minutes.
11. Remove the cookie sheet from the oven.
Construction
12. Grease your roasting or baking pan (depending on how thick you want your Moussaka) with olive oil.
13. Take your potatoes first and line the bottom of the pan.
14. Next, place a layer of your eggplant over the potatoes.
15. Now place a layer of meat sauce over the eggplant.

16. Repeat Steps 12 to 15 until you finished all of your vegetables and sauce.
17. Add béchamel sauce.
18. Bake at 330°F for about 1 hour or until the béchamel is golden brown and sauce thickened.
19. Remove it from the oven and allow it to sit for about 10 minutes before cutting.

NOTES:
1. This may be a vegetarian dish by removing the meat and adding other vegetables such as zucchini, carrots, turnips, nuts or greens.
2. The uses of different spices such as cinnamon, allspice, clove and nutmeg are common to center or mainland Greece.
3. The use of potatoes as a base is important, especially with the vegetarian recipe. Vegetables emit a good amount of liquid as they cook. The potato absorbs the liquid and makes the moussaka tastier and better.

BEEF YOUVETSI

INGREDIENTS
1-2 pounds lamb or beef
1 bone, either lamb or beef
Olive oil
Salt and pepper
3 onions, chopped
1 cup orzo
2 tomatoes, chopped
1 sprig of thyme or 1/2 teaspoon dried thyme
3 cloves
1 cinnamon stick
3 pearls of allspice
1 bay leaf
1 cup sweet red wine
2–3 cups stock
Parmesan or kefalotirie to sprinkle

1. In a sauce pot add 2 cups of water, the soup bone and one bay leaf and bring it to a boil. Boil the broth to reduce to 1 cup.
2. Cut your meat into small cubes and set it aside.
3. Dice the tomatoes and chop the onions into wedges.
4. In a skillet with olive oil, add the diced tomatoes, onions, spices, bay leaf and thyme.
5. Sauté these ingredients until the sauce begins to form.
6. Add the meat to a clay pot along with the wine, orzo, sauce and broth minus the extra bay leaf.
7. Bake at 340°F for 1 hour or until the orzo is al dente.
8. Salt and pepper to taste.

NOTES:
1. This was a traditional Sunday meal in many parts of Greece. The various clay pots were brought to the baker who would place them in his ovens and bake them until the family was ready to pick

up their pot up after church services. It was a luxury to have an oven at your residence in early years, so this meal was considered a special treat.

2. When using a terra cotta or clay cooker always remember to soak your cover for at least one hour in cool water. This will give the baking the moisture it needs for a successful dish.
3. Slow cooking and moisture is the secret for this simple meal.
4. If you are using a slow cooker, keep the liquid amount the same. Leave the mixture to cook on low for at least 6 hours or high for 4 hours. Do not exceed 9 hours unless you have temperature control on your slow cooker and may calibrate to a low temperature. The slow cooker replicates the recipe accurately.
5. This recipe may also be made as a quick meal in a wok. Sauté the ingredients as described above, add the meat and brown. Then add the orzo and broth, bring to a boil. Reduce the heat and cover. Simmer for 30 minutes and serve.
6. The only drawback is the roaming spices that might be a problem if a guest or family member bites into one of the magic nuggets. For ease of mind, use a half lemon bag or a piece of cheese cloth to make a bouquet and keep everyone safe from roaming spices.

EGG LEMON PORK STEW WITH ARTICHOKES, CELERY AND ONIONS

INGREDIENTS
2-3 pounds pork roast
1 jar or 1 bag of frozen artichokes (unseasoned)
1 bunch celery with leaves
2 white or yellow onions
1 tablespoon dill and/or coriander
1-3 cloves of garlic
4 eggs, separated
2 cups wine (1 cup for the stew and 1 cup for the Egg Lemon Recipe
Salt and pepper to taste
Olive oil or 1 stick unsalted butter

Avgolemono Sauce of choice

1. Cut the roast into thin slices, cubes or strips, whichever you prefer. Set aside.
2. Chop your garlic, dill, celery, artichokes and onions. Keep the celery leaves separate.
3. Heat your oil in a deep skillet with the garlic, dill, coriander, onions and celery leaves.
4. Once the onions have become limp, add your meat.
5. Brown your meat. Add the celery and artichokes.
6. Add 1 cup of wine.
7. Reduce the heat and simmer until cooked. The manner in which you cut your meat makes a difference in the length of time we allow the stew to simmer. Slices or strips of meat cook faster than cubes.
8. Avgolemono Sauce just before serving.

NOTES:
1. Cutting the pork into slices allows the meat to cook faster in this recipe.
2. Pork recipes, especially this stew, are considered a winter dish, especially during the new year.

3. A slow cooker may be used. Prepare everything in a skillet. Combine the ingredients in the slow cooker and heat on low for 5 hours. Make sure there is sufficient fluid for the cooking period.
4. The egg lemon sauce will be added and if allowed to sit for a short period will thicken to make a wonderful sauce that will be perfect for some crusty bread.

EGGPLANT MOUSSAKA 1

INGREDIENTS
Meat Sauce
3 medium tomatoes, cut into cubes
4 garlic cloves, minced
1½ pounds lamb or beef, ground
2 large onions, minced
3 medium green peppers, minced
2 tablespoons cumin
1 teaspoon oregano and coriander
1 cup red wine
½ bunch fresh parsley, chopped
Salt and pepper
Olive oil
2 tablespoons of tomato paste (optional)
3 tablespoons lemon juice

6 medium Yukon gold potatoes sliced or baking potatoes
4 large eggplants sliced lengthwise about ½" in thickness
Salt and pepper

Bechamel Sauce selection

MEAT SAUCE

1. Chop the tomatoes and parsley and add them to the skillet with the minced onions, green peppers and garlic, olive oil, herbs and spices. Heat the oil and sauté until a sauce is formed.
2. Add the meat when your onions begin to gloss. The scent of the spices and garlic should be mingling in the air and the green peppers should have cooked down. You might want to mix your tomato paste with a little olive oil to make it easier to combine. Do not overcook the meat, but make sure it is browned.
3. Place the meat sauce in a bowl and set it aside.
4. Peel your potatoes and cut them into 1/2" slices. Place the sliced potatoes into a bowl of cold water and lemon juice (about 3 tablespoons).
5. Cut the stems from your eggplant and slice them lengthwise. Place the eggplant into cool water along with the potatoes to avoid discoloring.
6. <u>Do not fry the eggplant</u>. This takes too long and it is not a good idea though it is a tradition. Most cooks would agree that if they could skip this process they would be happy. Instead grease a cookie sheets with olive oil. Lay the sliced eggplant on the sheet and season each

slice with salt, pepper and olive oil. Bake at 300°F for 10 minutes or until glossy. Do not over-bake. You want the slices limp enough to work with, but not too limp.

7. When all the eggplant slices have baked, you may now arrange your pan. For the old fashion style of mousaka, layer the bottom of your pan with potato slices, then eggplant, then meat sauce. The potato slices will absorb the excess liquid that has not been drained from the meat sauce. When adding the meat sauce, use a slotted spoon this will allow most of the liquid to drain making your mousaka firmer.
8. Select the béchamel sauce recipe you wish as a crown to your mousaka.
9. Add the bechamel sauce to your moussaka when completed.
10. Bake at 350°F for 45 minutes to 1 hour or until golden.

NOTES:
1. If you wish a stronger tomato flavor, add jar or carton of tomato sauce. These products have less acidity and work well with the recipe.
2. If you do not care for the cumin spice, you may use the alternative mainland spices of 1 teaspoon each of cinnamon, allspice, nutmeg and 1/4 teaspoon of clove.
3. Consider the type of cinnamon that you are using. For a spicier taste use brown cinnamon, otherwise for a sweeter taste use red cinnamon.

GREAT-GRANDMOTHER IRENE'S SOUVLAKI ASIA MINOR STYLE

INGREDIENTS
Lamb, beef, pork or chicken *
Olive oil
Red wine
Thyme and oregano
Cumin
5-6 onions, large
5 garlic cloves, chopped (to taste add more cloves for a stronger taste)
Bamboo skewers

1. Cut the meat into cubes about 1" to 1 ½". Trim **some** of the fat from the meat.
2. Set the cubes aside.
3. Chop the garlic.
4. Slice the onion. Lay a layer of the onions in a roasting pan that you will use to marinade the cubes of meat.
5. If you are using wood skewers, they must soak in water prior to use.
6. Place about 5 or 6 pieces of the garlic on the onions, making sure it is distributed evenly in the pan.
7. Sprinkle the onions with thyme and oregano.
8. Sprinkle the onions with a pinch of cumin.
9. Place a layer of meat over the onions.
10. Pour olive oil over the meat. Do the same with the wine. For chicken and seafood use white wine.
11. Repeat Steps 4 through 9 until all the meat is used.
12. Place the meat in the refrigerator until you are ready to put it on the grill or roast in the oven.

13. When you are ready to grill or roast, take the meat from the refrigerator and skewer the pieces onto the bamboo skewers. Amount of pieces per skewer is up to you.
14. If you are grilling, baste the souvlakia repeatedly. If you are oven roasting, set the temperature to 375°F. Add a layer of onion slices to the bottom of the roasting pan with a little wine and olive oil. Lay your skewers on the onions. Roast covered for 10 minutes. Remove the cover and continue to roast until brown.

NOTES:
1. Lamb, beef, pork, chicken and even seafood could be used with this recipe. Lamb, beef and pork can be marinated the longest - up to 5 days. Chicken and seafood can be safely marinated for 24 hours.
2. The wine you use is important. Do not use a wine that is expensive. Inexpensive wine should always be used for a marinade. Your decision is whether the wine should be sweet or rich. In either case, it is the alcohol that tenderizes the meat.
3. To keep true to my great-grandmother's recipe, I have not used any other type of alcohol for marinating. Try the recipe in its original form first. Then if you wish to experiment with other flavors, i.e., vodka, tequila, ouzo, etc., go ahead. The secret to great cooking is to experiment. Sometimes it is positive - other times negative. What is important is that when you make a discovery, it is yours.
4. **DO NOT USE THE MARINADE FOR BASTING.** A new bowl of basting should be prepared for that purpose.
5. Pressing the garlic allows for more flavor to be distributed during the marinating.
6. You have probably seen stalks of oregano that are sold, dried in its entirety. It is this dried bundle that my great-grandmother used to baste her souvlakia. The bundle would sit in the bowl with oil and wine and be used only when the souvlakia seemed dry. In the meantime, the neighbors would be overcome by the aroma wafting from the rising smoke.
7. For those of you using the oven technique, consider soaking a wood plank in wine and water for at least 24 hours. For safety's sake, place the plank in a roasting pan with some of the fluid. Lay the souvlakia on the plank and roast. This replicates the techniques used on the Island or when people grilled in Greece. Wood was used for outdoor and sometimes indoor cooking.

GREEK MEATLOAF

INGREDIENTS
1 lb. ground meat total or any combination of beef, lamb, pork or turkey
Olive oil
1 small onion, minced
1 large carrot
1 tomato, chopped
½ cup burgal
1 teaspoon cinnamon
2 teaspoons basil
2 eggs
½ teaspoon nutmeg
½ cup Mezethra

2 hard-boiled eggs
1 raw egg
Salt and pepper to taste

Tomato Sauce you select

1. Place the ground meat in a bowl.
2. Hard boil two eggs.
3. Heat the olive oil in a skillet with the cinnamon, basil and nutmeg.
4. Shred the carrot.
5. Chop the tomato and onion into small cubes.
6. Add the onion, carrot and tomato and sauté until the onions are clear.
7. Pour the sautéed skillet ingredients over the ground meat and add the burgal.
8. Knead the ingredients into the meat with the raw egg, making sure that the flavor is equally dispersed.
9. Sprinkle the meat with the cheese and continue to knead.
10. Remove the hard boiled eggs from the shell and set them aside.
11. Form the loaf into two halves. Place the hard boiled eggs into the center and join the two halves.
12. Bring the halves together and bake at 350°F until done.
13. Cut into thick slices, add a tomato sauce and enjoy.

NOTES:
1. If you have wheat sensitivity, omit the burgal and add another raw egg as a binder.
2. Green pepper may be minced and added along with the carrot to place more flavors in the meat loaf.
3. Hot pepper such as Turkish red pepper and other hot spices may also be added if your guests or family like the extra kick. Keep the heat to ½ teaspoon. The hot flavor should not overtake the tastes of the other ingredients, but mingle and enhance.
4. The use of hard boiled eggs by my mother was a decorative addition that she liked. They may be omitted.

GREEK SAUSAGE

INGREDIENTS
1 ½ pounds ground lamb, pork, beef, or breakfast sausage
1 garlic clove, pressed
Zest of one orange & lemon
½ teaspoon coriander
½ teaspoon Turkish red pepper
1/3 cup Retsina wine
1/8 to ¼ of a teaspoon of cumin
Sea salt to taste
Casings (optional)

1. Mix all the ingredients in a bowl.
2. If you are using the casings use a sausage stuffer. Make sure to tie ends.
3. Place a little oil in a skillet and brown well or grill.

NOTES:

1. The use of breakfast sausage is a quick and simple way for making Greek Sausage.
2. The longer the ground meat is allowed to sit in the refrigerator, the better the flavors will meld.
3. Turkish red pepper may be replaced with white pepper.

GREEK STYLE GROUND MEAT

INGREDIENTS
1 lb. ground beef
1 large onion
2 tomatoes, diced
1 green pepper
1 bay leaf
1 teaspoon allspice, cinnamon, and nutmeg
2 tablespoons brandy or sweet wine
½ teaspoon of Turkish or cayenne pepper (optional)
Olive oil
Salt and pepper to taste

1. Mince the onion and green pepper and place them in the skillet.
2. Add olive oil to the skillet with the spices and heat.
3. Sauté until the onions and green pepper start to cook down.
4. When the onions have caramelized, add the diced tomatoes.
5. Stir the tomatoes until they have cooked down and become sauce.
6. Add the ground meat and cook.
7. Stir the meat in the skillet making sure that the onions and tomatoes mingle with the meat.
8. When the meat is cooked, add the brandy or sweet wine and stir for a few minutes.
9. Remove from heat and serve on a toasted bun.

NOTES:

1. As a child when I would ask for "Sloppy Joes," my mother, who was opposed to prepared foods, would make this recipe.
2. The amount of spices and pepper can be changed for your personal taste.
3. This recipe works well with soy meats for something vegetarian.
4. The types of meats may be mixed: pork, beef, turkey and chicken.

DADDY'S KARVOUMA

INGREDIENTS
5 lbs. of lamb or beef
1 teaspoon dried rosemary, oregano, coriander and thyme, crushed
1/4 teaspoon cumin
3 cloves of garlic, chopped
4 large onions, sliced in wedges
2-3 cups deep red wine
Olive oil

Sea salt
White pepper
Turkish red pepper

1. Crush herbs either with a mortar and pestle, in a coffee grinder or buy ground herbs.
2. Finely slice the onions. Place the onions in a deep pot along with the herbs, garlic, peppers and 1/4 cup of oil, just enough to cover the bottom of the pot and sauté.
3. Continue to stir until the onions are clear and the herbs are fragrant.
4. Cut the meat into cubes about 1" in size and add that to the pot and continue to stir.
5. Add additional oil if necessary and wine and allow the contents to simmer slowly.
6. Salt to taste
7. Serve over steamed rice or pasta.

NOTES:
1. This recipe was handed down to my father from his grandfather. There were many times that his grandfather would create a great fire on the beach and my great-grandmother would bring this huge black kettle to the fire. The herbs, onions, garlic and meat would be added to the mixture and stirred continually with a paddle. Once the meat was cooked, it was placed in vats along with the oil, spices and salt and stored on one of his many sponge boats that would go out on voyages. The sailors would eat from these vats during their long voyages.
2. A greater value is given to freshly ground herbs. You will definitely note the difference in the scent and taste of the herbs.
3. Though the salt is limited in this recipe, the sailors added much more for the sake of preserving the meat.

DADDY'S KEFTETHES

INGREDIENTS
1 pound ground meat or lamb
2 cloves of garlic minced
½ bunch each oregano, thyme, parsley, and mint, (chopped fine)
1-1 ½ cups of dried bread
1 tomato
1-2 cups red wine
1-2 eggs
½ teaspoon white pepper
Salt to taste
Olive oil for frying

1. Chop the herbs and garlic finely and add to bowl.
2. Finely chop the tomato and place in bowl.
3. Add the meat. Start to knead the ingredients together.
4. Moisten the breadcrumbs with wine, but not overly saturated. Add the breadcrumbs to the meat.
5. Salt and pepper to taste.
6. Add the egg and continue to knead.
7. Let the meat mixture sit in the refrigerator for an hour.
8. You may fry the hamburgers in olive oil as is tradition or you may bake them. Bake them at 325°F for 30 minutes or until golden brown.

NOTES:

1. One of my father's secrets to a perfect hamburger included hand cutting the meat. This was a technique brought down from my great-grandmother and involved using two butcher knives - one knife in each hand. Both hands worked simultaneously chopping the meat, then turning and re-chopping. The final result was a "chili style" coarse chop. This made the hamburger juicer and irresistible.
2. If the meat seems like it is not holding together when you form the hamburgers, then you may add another egg.
3. DO NOT FLOUR. The flour will blacken the oil when frying.
4. You may wish to work with the herbs or pepper, using some and not others. Mint and oregano is a must and has always been added in Dad's hamburgers.

LAMB IN PITA

INGREDIENTS

Lamb steaks about ½" thick from the shank portion of the leg or shoulder, cut as many slices as needed
1 teaspoon each oregano, thyme and mint
1 cup sliced black olives
¼ pound feta cheese
1 package of frozen artichoke hearts or 1 can artichoke hearts
2 onions, sliced thin
2 cloves, garlic
Olive oil
Salt and pepper to taste
2 sticks unsalted butter
1 pound phylo (If store bought, you will need 2-4 sheets per steak depending on thickness)

Avgolemono Sauce

1. Place enough oil in your skillet to cover the bottom.
2. Sauté your herbs, minced garlic and onions in your skillet until cooked down.
3. Take your lamb steak and lightly brown both sides in the oil mixture. Be careful not to overcook. Set the steak on a plate and continue to brown the other steaks.
4. Prepare the selected Avgolemono Sauce
5. Slice the artichoke hearts and set them aside.
6. Melt the remaining stick of butter.
7. Lay your first sheet of filo before you brush with butter or oil. Lay another sheet over the first layer and fold in half. If you are using homemade phylo, a single layer is enough.
8. Lay the steak in the center. Place some of the onions on the steak.
9. Followed by slices of artichokes.
10. Sprinkle the steak with feta cheese and olives.
11. Place two heaping tablespoons of the egg lemon sauce on the steak.
12. Fold the phylo over, encasing the steak with the other ingredients.
13. Butter each fold to ensure closure. Baste the top.

14. Place the pita on a greased cookie sheet.
15. Repeat Steps 10 to 14 until all steaks are used.
16. Bake at 325°F until golden.
17. If you have any Avgolemono Sauce left, you might want to place a little over the warm pita.

NOTES:
1. The lamb steaks may be browned in either butter or oil
2. Fresh artichokes take a great deal of preparation and are very expensive. For this recipe unseasoned artichokes from the can, jar or frozen may be used.
3. I prefer using the Avgolemono Sauce with the wine and butter for this recipe.
4. The thicker the phylo, the fewer sheets needed for each steak. If the sheet is Horiatiko or village type which is thickest, use only one sheet.

PORK & CELERY IN EGG LEMON SAUCE

INGREDIENTS
1-2 pounds of pork, lamb or beef
1 bunch of celery
1 onion, sliced
1 tablespoon each parsley and dill
  Olive oil
  Water
  2 small lemons or 1 large lemon
  Fresh ground sea salt and pepper

Avgolemono Recipe of your selection

1. Sauté the onion, parsley and dill in a skillet until golden.
2. Cut meat into strips.
3. Chop celery into large chunks; include the leaves if you wish.

QUICK COOK METHOD
1. Place the sautéed onions, herbs and celery in a large pot.
2. Add meat to the sautéed ingredients.
3. Salt and pepper to taste.
4. Brown meat on medium heat.
5. Add 2 cups of water and bring to a boil until the celery is tender.
6. Reduce the heat.
7. Follow Avgolemono 1 recipe.
8. Turn off heat once foamy and serve hot.

SLOW COOKER METHOD
4. Place the sautéed onions, herbs and celery in the crock pot.
5. Add meat and 2 cups water.
6. Salt and pepper to taste.
7. Place heat on low and stew for 4 to 5 hours.

8. Follow Avgolemono 1 recipe.
9. Close heat and serve hot.

NOTES:
1. By cutting the pork into strips, cooking time will be shorter. Cubes are also acceptable.
2. Traditional recipe for Avgolemono is referred above, but you may also use the other varieties.
3. Tarragon or mint may also be used instead of dill.

PORK FILLING FOR PITA

INGREDIENTS
3 pounds ground pork
½ teaspoon each cumin, thyme and oregano
2 cloves of garlic, minced
Olive oil
1 onion, minced

1. Heat the olive oil, garlic, herbs and spices with the onions.
2. Cook the onions down.
3. Add meat and sauté.

NOTES:
1. This is a simple recipe for preparing pork for a quick sandwich.
2. This may be used on Greek pizza
3. Also used as a breakfast meat.

PORK ROAST

INGREDIENTS
5 pounds pork roast, picnic, shank (do not cut off the rind)
4 cloves of garlic
1 tablespoon each oregano, thyme and/or rosemary
Olive oil
1 lemon or 8 ounces of red wine
Salt and pepper

1. Chop the garlic into chucks and press with a knife. Lay the blade portion of the knife over the chunk of garlic and press until the chunk is pressed.
2. Take a paring knife and make horizontal cuts into the skin at the fatty areas. Place the blade through and twist to form a pocket. Place the garlic in the pocket. Distribute the cuts around the entire roast.
3. Use a small sauce pot and heat at least 1 cup of olive oil, lemon juice and selected herbs. The mixture must reach a sizzle.

4. Using a basting brush, apply the oil mixture over the entire roast. Once coated, you may either pour the remaining portion of the oil over the roast or use it to baste during the roasting process.
5. Roast at 375°F until the skin is crispy.

NOTES:
1. All pork must be roasted until well done.
2. Wine may be used in lieu of lemon juice.
3. The horizontal piercing of the skin to the fatty area helps distribute the garlic taste throughout the meat. The garlic flavor is not concentrated in the meat.

PORK SAUSAGE WITH LEEKS AND ORANGE

INGREDIENTS
Pork sausage, Greek sausage or roasted pork
1 large bunch of leeks
1 medium onion, minced
½ cup long grain rice
½ bunch parsley, chopped
½ bunch mint
Rind of one orange and/or lemon
Celery or carrots for the bottom of your pot

Avgolemono Sauce of your selection

1. Mince your meat and set it aside.
2. Place olive oil in your skillet.
3. Cut off the upper green portion of your leeks. Make sure to leave at least an inch of green on the leek bottom.
4. Take a sharp knife and score halfway into the leek bulb center. You should be able to easily peel off each layer of the leek. Gently wash each layer, if necessary.
5. When you reach the interior portion of the leek, where the stalks are no longer large but become exceedingly smaller, remove that portion and mince. Add to skillet.
6. Mince the green portion you cut off and add it to skillet.
7. Mince onion, parsley and mint and add it to skillet.
8. Grate lemon and/or orange and add to skillet.
9. Add your rice to the skillet and sauté the mixture until limp. Remove the skillet from the heat and set it aside to cool.
10. Layer the bottom of the pot with celery or carrots.
11. Stuff the trimmed leeks with the mixture and place them in a pot.
12. Once all the leeks are stuffed and placed into the pot, place a dish upside down over the stuffed leeks. Add about 2 cups of water – enough to keep the pot moist.
13. Cover and cook for about 30 minutes. If necessary add more water to the pot and continue to cook until the rice is done.
14. Remove and drizzle with olive oil and lemon juice.

1. Stuffing vegetables is a Greek tradition. The varieties and methods are fun and tasty.
2. The leeks may also be made vegetarian style.

KLEFTIKO LAMB IN PHYLO

INGREDIENTS
Lamb steaks about ½" thick from the shank portion of the leg or shoulder, cut as many slices as needed
2 sprigs of rosemary
1 cup sliced black olives
½ pound feta cheese
1 package of frozen artichoke hearts or 1 can artichoke hearts
2 onions, sliced thin
1 cup peas and carrots
Olive oil
Salt and pepper to taste
1 pound phylo (if store bought, you will need 2 to 4 sheets per steak depending on thickness)

Avgolemono Sauce

1. Place enough oil in skillet to cover the bottom.
2. Sauté rosemary, minced garlic and onions in your skillet until you start to smell their fragrance.
3. Lightly brown both sides of lamb steak in the scented oil mixture. Be careful not to overcook. Set the steak on a plate and continue to brown the other slices.
4. Prepare the selected Avgolemono Sauce
5. Slice the artichoke hearts and set them aside.
6. Lay your first sheet of phylo before you, brush with the remaining oil from the skillet. Lay another sheet over the first layer, and fold in half. If you are using homemade phylo, a single layer is enough.
7. Lay the steak in the center, placing some of the onions on the steak.
8. Followed by a tablespoon each artichoke, peas and carrots.
9. Sprinkle the steak with feta cheese and olives.
10. Place two heaping tablespoons of the egg lemon sauce on to the steak.
11. Fold the filo over encasing the steak with the other ingredients.
12. Oil each fold to ensure closure. Baste the top.
13. Place the pita on a greased cookie sheet.
14. Repeat Steps 6 to 13 until all steaks are used.
15. Bake at 325°F until golden.
16. If you have any Avgolemono Sauce left you might want to place a little around the warm pita.

1. The lamb steaks may be browned in oil.
2. Fresh artichokes take a great deal of preparation and are very expensive. For this recipe unseasoned artichokes from the can, jar or frozen may be used.
3. I prefer using the Avgolemono Sauce with the wine and butter for this recipe.
4. The thicker the phylo, the fewer sheets needed for each steak. If the sheet is Horiatiko or village type, which is thickest, use only one sheet.

ROAST BEEF

INGREDIENTS
2 pounds roast beef
2 onions, large
4 Yukon gold potatoes
2 tablespoons each dried oregano and thyme
7 artichoke hearts
Juice of 2 lemons
3 garlic cloves
½ cup chopped olives or 1 tablespoon olive paste
Olive oil

1. Lay the roast on a cutting board. With a knife cut 3 to 4 slits in the roast, forming pockets. Do not cut across the roast. The pockets should be short of the width of the roast.
2. Press the garlic cloves and place them in a skillet, with the herbs and olive oil and heat.
3. Slowly add the artichokes and olives, and continue heating.
4. Chop the onions and continue heating.
5. Add the lemon juice and continue heating.
6. When the flavors have melded together, remove the oil from the heat.
7. Place the sautéed onion mixture into the pockets.
8. Chop the potatoes and surround the roast.
9. Drench the roast and potatoes with the remaining oil and onions.
10. Place the roast in the oven at 350°F, and bake for 45 minutes.
11. Remove the roast and thinly slice. The roast should be very rare.
12. Place the slices back in the roasting pan with the juices, potatoes and artichokes.
13. Heat for another 30 minutes at 300°F
14. Serve with crusty bread.

NOTES:
1. The pockets allow the juices to seep into the meat as it par cooks.
2. You may also place the juices, vegetables and sliced beef in a slow cooker on low to cook for 1 to 2 hours.

ROAST LAMB

INGREDIENTS
1 leg of spring lamb, shank or shoulder
4 cloves of garlic
Olive oil
1 tablespoon fresh ground sea salt
1 tablespoon each of the dried herbs thyme, oregano, parsley and mint
Juice of two lemons
Pepper to taste

1. Juice the lemons into a bowl and set them to the side along with the halved emptied rinds.
2. Using a paring knife, poke the fatty areas of the lamb horizontally, making a pocket. Do this throughout the entire piece of meat.
3. Press each clove of garlic.
4. Take the pressed portions of garlic and insert them into each horizontal pocket.
5. Place aluminum foil in the roasting pan with the dull side showing; lay the lamb on the foil.
6. Rub the lamb with the lemon halves and pour the lemon over the meat.
7. Rub the meat with salt and the other herbs.
8. Drizzle the meat with olive oil.
9. Seal the foil and bake at 375°F for 1 hour. Open the aluminum for the final 15 minutes to allow the lamb to become crusty.

NOTES:
1. Greeks prefer young lambs. Though some will put larger lambs on the spit, the young or spring lamb is preferred.
2. Anyone who has taken my classes knows that salt is used within limits. I never use salt excessively. I use it to enhance the food. In this recipe the salt is used for a different reason. It is used to help drain the fat from the lamb meat, making it more appealing when it has finished roasting.
3. The poking of the fatty areas is an interesting trick. It allows the salt to penetrate to help melt the fat, the garlic to baste the meat and herbs to season the meat completely.
4. The rubbing of the meat with the used lemon halves is traditionally performed to cleanse the meat and tenderize it with the lemon skin. The lemon juice will assist in flavoring as well as cutting the fatty taste of the lamb.
5. The aluminum helps the meat to perspire during the roasting.
6. Decrease the herbs and salt to a teaspoon, and only 2 cloves of garlic, if you are making a shank.

SAUSAGE AND PEPPER STEW

INGREDIENTS
Sausage Recipe
2 large onions
1 large green pepper
3 medium tomatoes

3 garlic cloves
1 bay leaf
1 ½ teaspoon oregano
½ cup red wine
Salt and pepper
½ teaspoon Turkish pepper
Olive oil

1. Heat a skillet with olive oil, garlic, bay leaf and Turkish pepper.
2. Form the sausages from the recipe given. Brown the sausages in the heated oil.
3. Remove the links and set the sausages aside to drain.
4. Slice the onion into ringlets and place them in the skillet.
5. Slice green pepper and add that also to the skillet.
6. Chop your tomatoes. Add them to your skillet and sauté.
7. Add the sausages and wine to the pot and simmer for 45 minutes to 1 hour.
8. Add water or more wine if needed during the simmering.

NOTES:
1. This is an easy and quick recipe.
2. You may use other sausage, but the traditional is the orange rind.
3. Pepper content may be either increased or decreased to taste.

STIFATHO

INGREDIENTS
1 ½-2 pounds beef, veal, venison, pork, rabbit or fish
4 cloves of garlic
1 cup dark red wine for beef, veal, venison or rabbit
or 1 cup white sweet wine for pork or fish
1 large bay leaf
1 cinnamon stick
10 cloves
¼ cup olive oil
1 pound pearl onions
1 medium onion (any type, Vidalia is great)
¼ teaspoon cumin
½ bunch parsley
½ cup raisins or currents
Salt
½ teaspoon white pepper
Zest of one orange or lemon
3 tomatoes
1 tablespoon raw sugar

1. Press the four cloves of garlic into a sauce pan.
2. Add the oil, bay leaf, cumin, parsley, raisins, zest, pepper and cinnamon. Heat slowly.

3. While the spices are heating, use a toothpick to puncture the medium onion with 10 holes. Make a design using the entire onion. Insert the cloves into the onion. Place the decorated onion into the crockpot.
4. When the spices have become fragrant, add the pearl onions and, using a wooden spoon, sauté the pearl onions gently.
5. Cut the meat into 1" cubes and brown in the spiced oil.
6. Place the meat in the slow cooker once it is browned.
7. Add the spiced oil.
8. Puree the tomatoes and add them to the slow cooker, along with the wine.
9. Salt to taste.
10. Add sugar if necessary.
11. Place the crockpot on low and stew for 4 hours.

NOTES:

1. This dish is especially famous for its flavor. It is an onion stew. Stifatho is primarily made with veal, but other meats, even seafood, may be substituted.
2. Wine varies dependent upon the meat being used.
3. Juicing or pureeing the tomatoes prior to use will help provide the rich sauce needed for the dish.
4. Jar tomato sauce may be used, if you wish a shortcut.
5. The use of the medium onion was developed by my mother. The single medium onion is used for the cloves. Using a toothpick, puncture the onion and insert each clove individually, making a mosaic design. The larger onion will swell as it cooks with the stew, keeping the cloves intact and allowing its flavor along with the clove to permeate through the stew.
6. The raisins and zest provide a fruity flavor to this stew.
7. My mother cooked this slowly on the stove, sometimes simmering the content for 2 to 3 hours. The use of a slow cooker is, in fact, more accurate in cooking technique. Traditionally, the stew was prepared in a clay pot and slow cooked in stone ovens. The result was a succulent stew that enhanced any meat used.
8. The use of white pepper enhances the other flavors, instead of overpowering the other flavors.

STUFFED LAMB CHOPS

INGREDIENTS
1 pound lamb chops, butterflied
2 Vidalia onions
½ pound manouri or feta cheese
1 bunch green onions
8 ounces of olives, chopped
1 tablespoon each mint, parsley, oregano rosemary
3 cloves of garlic
Olive oil
Lemon zest
Salt and white pepper

1. Chop the onions into thin strips and place in the skillet with olive oil.
2. Finely chop the garlic, green onions and herbs and include them in the skillet.
3. Chop the olives and zest of one lemon and add to the oil in the skillet along with the juice of the lemon.
4. Sauté until the ingredients become fragrant.
5. Remove the skillet from the heat and place the mixture in a bowl.
6. Once the mixture is cool, add the manouri and combine thoroughly
7. Arrange chops on a greased sheet.
8. Take one teaspoon of the spread and place it in the center of the butterflied opening.
9. Baste the chops with the remaining oils in the skillet
10. Bake at 325°F for 40 minutes or until done.

NOTES:
1. The use of dried herbs is acceptable.
2. Manouri is Greek ricotta. You may substitute feta cheese, but you are increasing the amount of salt in the meal. The manouri has more of a feta taste. It is closer to a combination of feta with whipped cream cheese or ricotta. I would consider ¼ of a pound each.

STUFFED LAMB STEAKS

INGREDIENTS
1 pound lamb, ½ inch slices (2 slices per person); or long strips of lamb steaks for each person. Using the leg, remove the bone and cut the steaks from the meat available
1 pound frozen artichokes
½ pound manouri or feta cheese
1 bunch green onions
8 ounces of olives, chopped
1 tablespoon each mint, parsley, oregano, thyme
Olive oil
Lemon zest
Salt and pepper
½ green pepper (optional)

1. Chop the artichoke hearts into thin strips and place in the skillet with olive oil.
2. Finely chop the green onions and herbs and add them to the skillet.
3. Shred the green pepper, olives and zest of one lemon adding to the skillet.
4. Sauté until the ingredients become fragrant.
5. Remove the skillet from the heat and place the artichoke mixture into a bowl.
6. Once the artichoke mixture is cool, add the manouri and combine thoroughly
7. Arrange the first layer of the lamb steaks on a greased baking sheet and baste with olive oil, salt and pepper to taste.
8. Place one tablespoon of the artichoke spread in the center of the steak. If the lamb steak is one long strip, place the tablespoon of artichoke spread down the center of the strip stopping about 1 inch to the end.
9. Lay the second steak over the spread, or if using the strip, roll the strip forward (shorter length), trapping the artichoke spread in the roll.
10. Bake at 325°F for 30 minutes or until done.

NOTES:
1. The lamb steaks should resemble strips about ½ inch thick, about 3 inches wide. If you wish to use the two steak method, the steak should be 4 to 6 inches long.
2. Some people have sensitivity to green pepper, you might want to remove it totally or substitute it with zucchini.
3. Manouri is Greek ricotta. You may substitute feta cheese, but you are increasing the amount of salt in the meal. The manouri has more of a feta taste. It is closer to a combination of feta with whipped cream cheese or ricotta. I would consider ¼ of a pound each.

LAMB SWEETBREADS

INGREDIENTS
Lamb or beef sweetbreads
Olive oil
5-8 ounces brandy, wine or lemon juice
1 teaspoon each oregano, thyme and parsley
4 cloves garlic

1. Rinse your sweetbreads in cool water and place them in a bowl.
2. Combine the herbs and pressed garlic in a small bowl.
3. Sprinkle and rub the sweetbreads with half of the garlic mixture.
4. Measure the liquid you wish to use (lemon juice, wine or brandy). Pour over the sweetbreads.
5. Pour enough olive oil to coat the sweetbreads.
6. Let them marinate for at least 24 hours in the refrigerator.
7. When you are ready to prepare, remove the sweetbreads from the marinade.
8. Place olive oil in a skillet with the remainder of the herbs and garlic and heat.
9. When the garlic caramelizes, add the sweetbreads and sauté until tender.

NOTES:
1. Garlic powder may be used in place of pressed garlic.
2. Dried herbs are great for this recipe, but fresh works well.

Chapter 11: Game

STUFFED RABBIT WITH OLIVES

INGREDIENTS
1 Rabbit, dressed
4 cloves garlic, crushed
2 tablespoon each thyme and rosemary
4 bay leaves
2 stalks of celery
1 tablespoon celery greens
½ cup green onions
Red wine
Olives
1 white onion or ½ lb. pearl onions
Olive oil
Salt and pepper

1. Marinate the rabbit in wine, 2 pieces of garlic, 2 bay leaves, celery leaves, 1 tablespoon of the thyme and rosemary for 5 hours or overnight. Discard marinate.
2. Heat oil in a skillet with remaining herbs, garlic, onions and bay leaves.
3. Once the oil is fragrant, brown the rabbit. Remove from the skillet and place in a bowl.
4. Add the chopped white onion, celery, additional herb and spices, greens and garlic and sauté.
5. Add the olives and continue to sauté.
6. Return the rabbit. Stuff the cavity of the rabbit with the sautéed ingredients.
7. Salt and pepper to taste.
8. Add 1 cup red wine, drizzle with olive oil and roast at 300°F until tender.

NOTES:
NOTES:
1. Have the additional herbs ready. This will help in stewing the rabbit.
2. Feta cheese may be included in the stuffing and sprinkled over the rabbit.
3. This dish must be cooked slow for the spices and wine to penetrate.

Roast Goat

INGREDIENTS
1 leg of goat
2 cups mavrodaphne
½ cup spiced honey (honey made from herbs)
2 Vidalia onions
5 cloves of garlic
12 mission figs
1 pomegranate
½ pound feta cheese
5 Yukon potatoes
Salt and pepper
Olive oil

1. With a sharp filleting knife, make an incision along the goat leg bone on both sides, making a deep pocket.
2. Mince the garlic, soft figs and onions and place them in the skillet with olive oil and honey.
3. Remove the seeds from the pomegranate, and add them to the skillet and sauté.
4. Place the goat leg in a roasting pan with the chopped potatoes.
5. When the onions and garlic are caramelized add ¼ of the feta crumbled. Using a spoon, gather the sautéed content and fill the pockets at the sides of the leg.
6. Whatever remains of the sautéed ingredient, sprinkle on the potatoes and goat.
7. Combine some olive oil and mavrodaphne and coat the exterior of the goat. Sprinkle with feta.
8. Salt and pepper to taste.
9. Bake at 350°F for 1 ½ hours or until tender.

NOTES:
1. Mastica liqueur may be substituted for the sweet wine.
2. Lamb may be used instead of goat.

Rabbit with Wild Greens

INGREDIENTS
3 pounds rabbit
3 bay leaves
½ teaspoon mastica, ¾ cup mastica liqueur or anise
1 bunch wild greens, mixture or dandelions
1 bunch green onions, chopped
1 onion
2 tomatoes, chopped
3 cloves garlic, pressed

1 cup or more dark red wine or one cup ouzo
Olive oil
Salt and pepper

1. Wash the rabbit.
2. Chop into parts, keeping the saddle whole and making the legs and arms parts. Place the parts into a bowl.
3. Add the red wine and mastica liqueur or use one cup ouzo for the marinade.
4. Add the oil and pressed garlic.
5. Let the marinade stand in the refrigerator overnight or at least 10 hours.
6. Strain the liquid from the marinade. Add the garlic and rabbit with the scallions to a skillet of heated oil.
7. Brown the rabbit in the oil with the scallions, bay leaves and garlic.
8. Add the tomatoes and some liqueur or wine and stew for 15 minutes.
9. Remove the rabbit after the stewing is complete and set it in a roaster.
10. To the remaining broth, add the chopped tomatoes, wild greens with the ½ teaspoon anise seed and bay leaves. Blanch for two to four minutes.
11. Remove the greens from the skillet and add to the roaster.
12. Preheat oven to 400°F.
13. Pour the heated content of the skillet over the greens and the rabbit.
14. Salt and pepper to taste.
15. Bake for 20 minutes.

NOTES:
1. The use of the liqueur or wine is a tenderizer as well as a flavor enhancer.
2. The use of greens is very important. Greeks love their greens and though there are other recipes that contain these leafy vegetables, this is a very unusual recipe. Other wild greens may be used in place of just dandelions.
3. If you do not care for liqueurs, the use of anise seed, anise greens, fennel and tarragon are great options that will offer similar tastes.

VENISON STIFADO

INGREDIENTS
2 ½ pounds of venison
1 medium onion, chopped
2 medium tomatoes, chopped
2 cloves of garlic, chopped
Seasoning A: If you are using fresh herbs, ¼ bunch any or all:
      Parsley, mint, dill, basil, thyme and savory (and any other herb you might like)
        If you are using dry herbs, 1 teaspoon of any or all:
      Parsley, mint, dill, basil, thyme and savory
Seasoning B: 1 tablespoon brown sugar, (1) cinnamon stick, (3) whole cloves,
2 bay leaves
4 stalks of celery, chopped
4 carrots, chopped
Olive oil
½ cup orzo or rice

Salt and fresh ground pepper

1. Cut your venison into cubes and set the cubes on a plate.
2. Dredge the venison cubes in flour seasoned with salt and pepper.
3. Place enough olive oil to cover the bottom of a skillet and heat.
4. First add the herbs and bay leaf to the skillet. Using a wooden spoon, stir the herbs on a low medium heat until they become bright green and fragrant.
5. Now add the onion and garlic to the skillet. Raise the heat to medium, and sauté the onion until it is golden.
6. Add the floured venison to the skillet and stir.
7. Add the celery and carrots to the skillet.
8. Add the pasta or rice to the skillet and sauté.
9. Raise the temperature to medium high heat, add a cup of water, and allow the skillet content to cook and the pasta to absorb the juices.

NOTES:
1. If you are using a buck or fairly tough meat, you might want to marinate it in red wine or balsamic vinegar until tender. I have marinated venison in wine and olive oil for five days. The olive oil and wine must cover the meat. I usually have a 2:1 ratio for olive to wine. Herbs, spices and garlic may be added to enhance the marinating, but stick with the spices and herbs from the recipe you are using so as not to clash with the flavors of the meal you are preparing.
2. Celery leaves are not traditionally used in Greek cooking, yet I have found them to add additional flavor to the recipes.
3. This particular recipe has a Selection A and B for seasoning. Select one; do not mix. They are two different flavor recipe.

Chapter 12: Seafood

Ingredients
2 pounds shrimp
1 each large green, red, yellow and orange peppers
2 zucchinis
2 onions
3 medium tomatoes, chopped
1 tablespoon each parsley and tarragon
½ pound feta cheese
3 potatoes, chopped
4 garlic cloves
Sweet wine
Olive oil
Salt and pepper

1. Rinse and dry your shrimp.
2. Heat the oil in the skillet with the peppers, zucchinis, onions, potatoes, tomatoes, parsley, tarragon and garlic.
3. When the potatoes are tender, add the shrimp and wine.
4. Sprinkle with feta and simmer until cooked.
5. Add the salt and pepper.
6. Cook until the shrimp are done.

NOTES:
1. This is a great and quick shrimp that is tasty.
2. You may complete the cooking in the skillet or place the shrimp and vegetables in a brown lunch bag coated with waxed paper or olive oil for baking.
3. Other vegetables may be added such as eggplant, mushrooms, etc.

SHRIMP IN WINE SAUCE

INGREDIENTS
1 pound shrimp
½ bunch parsley
½ bunch dill
2 onions
1 ½ cups dry red wine
Olive oil
Lemon rind
1 cup long grain rice
½ pound feta cheese
4 tomatoes
1 cup olives
White pepper

1. Chop the onions, olives, dill and parsley.
2. Heat some olive oil in a skillet with the herbs, olives, tomatoes, onions, lemon rind and pepper.
3. When the herbs become fragrant, add the shrimp.
4. Add the wine, rice and 1 cup water.
5. Cover the skillet and allow the rice to absorb the fluid.
6. Sprinkle with feta and serve.

NOTES:
1. You may juice your tomatoes if you would like a thicker sauce, but you must use the meat of the tomato with the juice.
2. Olive oil may be replaced with other oil flavors.
3. Retsina may substitute the dry red wine.

PLAKI WITH ZUCCHINI AND SAGE

INGREDIENTS
2 ½ pounds plaki
1 medium leek
2 zucchinis
2 onions
3 medium tomatoes, chopped
1 tablespoon olive paste
1 teaspoon sage
1 tablespoon parsley

3 potatoes, chopped
1 teaspoon juniper berries, ground
Sweet wine
Olive oil
  Salt and pepper

1. Rinse and dry your fish.
2. Heat the oil in the skillet with the olive paste, leek, zucchinis, onions, potatoes, tomatoes, parsley, juniper and sage.
3. When the potatoes are tender, add the fish and wine.
4. Add the salt and pepper.
5. Cook until the fish are done.

NOTES:
1. This is a great and quick fish that is tasty.
2. You may complete the cooking in the skillet or place the fish and vegetables in a pan and bake.
3. For individuals' sensitive to the tomato acidity, this is a great alternative.
4. Other vegetables may be added such as eggplant, mushrooms, etc.

OCTOPUS IN WINE SAUCE

INGREDIENTS
1 large octopus or 1 pound small octopi
½ bunch parsley
½ bunch dill
2 onions
1 ½ cups dry red wine
Olive oil
Lemon rind
1 cup long grain rice
½ pound feta cheese
4 tomatoes
1 large green pepper
1 cup olives
1 cup vinegar
White pepper

1. Boil the octopus in water and vinegar until tender.
2. Chop the octopus and set it aside.
3. Chop the onions, olives, dill and parsley.
4. Heat some olive oil in a skillet with the herbs, olives, tomatoes, onions, lemon rind and pepper.
5. When the herbs become fragrant, add the octopus.
6. Add the wine, rice and 1 cup water.
7. Cover the skillet and allow the rice to absorb the fluid.
8. Sprinkle with feta and serve.

NOTES:

1. You may juice your tomatoes if you would like a thicker sauce, but you must use the meat of the tomato with the juice.
2. Olive oil may be replaced with other oil flavors.

MASTIC-FLAVORED GRILLED FISH

INGREDIENTS
6 medium fish
2 stalks of celery, chopped with greens
1 onion, chopped
1 tomato, chopped
1 ½ teaspoons parsley
1 ¼ teaspoon mastic ground or 8 ounces mastica liqueur
Olive oil

1 cedar plank soaked in water for 24 hours

1. Chop the celery, onions and tomatoes large slices or wedges.
2. Pulverize the mastic to powder.
3. Heat about ½ cup oil in a large skillet with the mastic and parsley.
4. Lay the vegetables onto the plank. With a basting brush, coat the vegetables with the oil mixture.
5. Lay the fish onto the vegetables, and coat the fish with the remaining oil.
6. Bake at 325°F until done.
7. Serve with the vegetables.

NOTES:

1. Gum mastica may be replaced with its liqueur form. The gum form must be pulverized prior to use in the recipe.
2. Caution on the use of the gum. Using an excessive amount will make your food bitter.
3. Soak your plank in water with some liqueur to enhance the flavor of the fish.
4. Ouzo may replace the mastica.
5. Non-alcoholic replacements are anise, fennel and tarragon.

MARINATED FRIED FISH

INGREDIENTS
2 pounds fish, use small fish or fish steaks
¾ of cup flour
½ teaspoon salt
1/3 teaspoon white pepper
¼ teaspoon baking powder
¼ teaspoon each **ground** thyme, oregano and rosemary
¾ cup water
1 tablespoon olive oil
Fresh stalks of rosemary, thyme and oregano

Recipe for Skordostube

Olive oil for frying

1. Rinse the fish with water.
2. Dry the fish with paper towels and set it aside.
3. In a bowl combine the flour with the salt, pepper, baking powder and herbs.
4. Fill the skillet with enough oil to cover the bottom and heat.
5. Drop a little flour into the skillet to test the heat of the oil. If sizzling occurs immediately then the oil is ready.
6. Coat the fish in the flour then place them in the skillet and fry until golden brown.
7. Fry the fish for 5 minutes on each side until cooked or crunchy.
8. Place the fried fish in a clean glass container with lid, with the fresh stalks of herbs.
9. Make a large amount of the Skordostube (garlic-flavored vinegar) and pour that over the fried fish and seal the container with its lid.
10. Allow the fish to sit in the scented vinegar for at least 24 hours. The longer the fish marinates, the tastier it becomes.

NOTES:
1. This is my grandmother's recipe. Often it was very difficult to hold the fish that long. The flavor was unbelievable.
2. Your batter should be thin enough not to cake on the fish, but thick enough to leave a good coating. The best is to have extra flour and water on hand if you need to thicken or loosen the batter.
3. The use of ground herbs and spices is important. Excessive amounts of ground herbs can make the food bitter. Use small portions to make the batter tasty. Increase should be directly proportional to the amount of fish that you are frying.
4. White pepper has a mild peppery taste. If you want something stronger replace it with Turkish red pepper.
5. Alternate oils for frying are corn oil, sunflower oil or grapeseed oil.
6. Different types of vinegar may be used to alter the flavor of the Skordostube.

GRILLED SQUID

<u>INGREDIENTS</u>
1 pound squid
Olive oil
1 teaspoon each oregano, thyme, rosemary and parsley
4 cloves garlic
¼ teaspoon white pepper
½ cup lemon juice

1. Mince garlic and place it in a bowl along with olive oil, lemon juice, herbs and spice.
2. Place squid in a bowl and marinate overnight.
3. Remove squid from the oil and lay them on a mesh grill screen for seafood.
4. Secure the screen. Grill squid for 5 minutes on one side. Flip the screen and grill other side.

NOTES:
1. Serve the squid with rice and crusty bread.
2. More or less garlic may be added.
3. Salt to taste.
4. Alternate oil may be used
5. Smoking or using a plank is insanely great!

GRILLED OCTOPUS

INGREDIENTS
1 pound octopus
Olive oil
1 teaspoon each oregano, thyme and parsley
4 cloves garlic
¼ teaspoon white pepper
½ cup red wine juice
1 cup vinegar

1. Boil the octopus in a pot of water and vinegar.
2. When tender, remove the octopus and place in a bowl.
3. Mince the garlic and place in a bowl along with olive oil, red wine, herbs and spice.
4. Marinate the octopus overnight.
5. Remove the octopus from the oil and lay them on a mesh grill screen for seafood.
6. Secure the screen and grill the octopus for 5-10 minutes on one side and then flip the screen and grill, depending on its size.

NOTES:
1. Serve the octopus with garlic pasta.
2. More or less garlic may be added.
3. Salt to taste.
4. Alternate oil may be used.
5. Smoking or using a plank is insanely great!

GRILLED CUTTLEFISH

INGREDIENTS
1 pound cuttlefish
Olive oil
1 teaspoon each oregano, thyme, mint and parsley
4 cloves garlic
¼ pound feta cheese
¼ teaspoon white pepper
½ cup white wine

1. Mince the garlic and place it in a bowl along with olive oil, white wine, herbs and spice.
2. Place the cuttlefish in the bowl and marinate overnight.

3. Remove the cuttlefish from the oil and lay them on a mesh grill screen for seafood.
4. Secure the screen and grill the cuttlefish for 8 minutes on one side. Flip the screen and grill until tender.

NOTES:
1. Serve the cuttlefish with rice and crusty bread.
2. More or less garlic may be added.
3. Salt to taste.
4. Alternate oil may be used
5. Smoking or using a plank is insanely great!
6. Roasting is also a choice at 325°F; roast until tender 30 – 45 minutes.

GREEK SPICED FISH

INGREDIENTS
Cinnamon sticks and star anise (enough to cover the bottom of the roaster)
Whole fish or fillets: tuna, whiting or red fish - anything
Combination or one of each vegetable: Tomato, green peppers, green onions, zucchinis, green beans, celery, carrots and white onions
3 cloves garlic
Olive oil
½ teaspoon Turkish red pepper
½ cup Raki or Ouzo
Salt

1. Arrange the cinnamon sticks and star anise on the roaster. This will act as a grate for the fish or fillets.
2. Lay the fish on the grate.
3. In a skillet, sauté the sliced vegetables, sliced garlic, salt and pepper in olive oil.
4. Pour the raki or ouzo over the fish and vegetables.
5. When the vegetables are soft, place them over the fish.
6. Bake at 330°F for 35 minutes or until done.

NOTES:
1. If you don't care for the liqueur, you may use fennel or anise, about ½ teaspoon.
2. This recipe was developed along the lines of plank cooking. Instead of cooking on wood, you are baking on the cinnamon sticks.
3. This recipe may be altered to include more tomato sauce. You may add more tomatoes or use the jar or carton sauce.
4. The heat may be controlled by increasing or decreasing the amount of pepper in the recipe.

GREAT-GRANDPA GEORGE'S FISH IN GRAPE LEAVES

Grape leaves
Sardines, smelt, red fish or mullet
1 bunch dill fresh, chopped
Zest of 2 lemons
Juice of one lemon

½ teaspoons ground cumin
1 teaspoon Turkish red pepper
Capers
Olive oil
1 fish grill screen

1. If you are using fresh grape leaves, blanch them in boiling water to become limp for 3-5 seconds. Remove the small stem. If you are using the jar leaves, rinse them thoroughly but do not blanch.
2. Set the leaves on wax paper with the vein side facing up and set aside.
3. Clean and scale your fish. If you are using smelt, washing under light water is sufficient. Set the fish aside.
4. Chop the dill, zest the lemon, juice the lemon and combine them in a bowl with the cumin, red pepper, capers, and ¼ cup olive oil.
5. If your fish is large, you will probably need more than one leaf, probably up to 4 leaves or more. If you are working with smelt, you will probably use one leaf at a time.
6. Place a tablespoon of the mixture in the center of the leaf, making sure that the mixture covers all the leaf area. Place the fish in the center. Open its cavity and place some the mixture inside the fish and some of the mixture outside.
7. Roll the grape leaves around the fish. If the fish is large, the head and tail may be exposed, but the body should be covered.
8. Method of cooking:
   a. **Oven:** Use a roasting pan. Either line the fish in the greased pan or place them on a plank that you have soaked. The oven should be set at 325 °F. Bake the fish until flaky, the grape leaves will keep the fish tender and moist.
   b. **Grill**: If the fish is medium or large, you might consider using a soaked plank. The plank will keep the fish intact and will protect the fish from overcooking. Depending on the size, you should grill the fish for at least 15 to 20 minutes based on size.
   c. **Grill**: If the fish is very large, maybe a salmon fillet, you may use a fish rack. The fish rack is a special rack that allows you to keep the fish directly on the grill while being protected in a screen. Try grilling 5 to 10 minutes on each side. This is direct flame so you must be very careful not to burn your meal.

NOTES:
1. If you use smelt, the small fish make for exotic appetizers.
2. If grilling, the fish might need to be basted to avoid drying out.

FRIED FISH

INGREDIENTS
1 pound fish
¾ cup flour
½ teaspoon salt
1/3 teaspoon white pepper
¼ teaspoon baking powder
¼ teaspoon **ground** each thyme, oregano and rosemary
¾ cup water
1 tablespoon olive oil

Olive oil for frying

1. Rinse the fish with water.
2. Dry the fish with paper towels and set it aside.
3. In a bowl combine the flour with the salt, pepper, baking powder, herbs, water and olive oil.
4. Fill the skillet with enough oil to cover the bottom and heat.
5. Drop a little flour into the skillet to test the heat of the oil. If sizzling occurs immediately, then the oil is ready.
6. Dip the fish in the batter. Place them in the skillet and fry until golden brown.
7. Fry the fish for 5 minutes on each side until cooked or crunching.

NOTES:
1. Your batter should be thin enough not to cake on the fish, but thick enough to leave a good coating. The best is to have extra flour and water on hand to gauge if you need to thicken or loosen the batter.
2. The use of ground herbs and spices is important. Excessive amounts of ground herbs can make the food bitter. Use small portions to make the batter tasty. Increase should be directly proportional to the amount of fish that you are frying.
3. White pepper has a mild peppery taste, if you want something stronger replace it with Turkish red pepper.
4. Alternate oils for frying are corn oil, sunflower oil or grapeseed oil.

FISH WITH GARLIC GLAZE

INGREDIENTS
4 fish fillets (white fish, grouper, swai, or fillets of your preference)
¼ teaspoon parsley
Olive oil
Juice of 1 lemon
Salt and white pepper

1. Juice the lemon and mix it with an equal amount of olive oil.
2. Arrange the fish fillets on a greased baking sheet.
3. Coat the fillets with the olive oil and lemon mixture.
4. Heavily coat the fillets with the remaining oil.
5. Salt and pepper to taste.
6. Prepare Dad's Garlic Glaze
7. Bake at 325 °F until the fish is flaky and done.

NOTES:
1. This is a simple fish recipe for people who love garlic.
2. This recipe may be used with shellfish.
3. This recipe is great for the grill and may be used even with a plank.
4. This recipe may be used in a skillet.

FISH STUFFED WITH ONIONS & LEEKS

INGREDIENTS
1 large fish or 4 medium fish fillets

1 small leek
1 white onion
3 cloves of garlic
6 ounces ouzo
1 tablespoon dill or tarragon
Salt and pepper to taste
Olive oil

1. Place the fish on a cookie sheet greased with olive oil.
2. Slice the garlic, leeks and onions and place in a skillet with olive oil.
3. Add the herb, salt and pepper to the skillet and sauté.
4. Cook the leeks and onions down.
5. Add ouzo to the skillet and turn off the heat.
6. If you have a whole fish, first stuff the fish and the remaining sautéed ingredients should be placed over the fish.
    a. If you are making the fillets, place a single layer on the cookie sheet.
    b. Lay the leek mixture on each fillet on the baking sheet, making sure you cover the entire fillet.
    c. Lay the second fillet over each of leek mixture.
    d. Cover the stacks with the remaining leek mixture.
7. Bake at 325 °F for 40 minutes

NOTES:
1. Potatoes may be added to this recipe.
2. The fillets may be single levels.

FISH IN PAPER

INGREDIENTS
Brown paper bags (Lunch bags are OK. No bags with writing or glue)
Whole fish or fillets or shrimp any type, any amount
Salt and pepper
Fresh rosemary and tarragon
1 teaspoon capers
Olive oil
Juice of 2 lemons

1. Cut the brown paper bag larger than the fish or fillets you are preparing to bake.
2. Baste the cut bag with olive oil. Make sure you baste it entirely.
3. Place the capers inside the cavity of the fish, if whole, or over the fillet.
4. Place the tarragon and rosemary in the bag first. If you are using fresh herbs, one sprig of each will do. If dry is used, 1 teaspoon of each will be enough.
5. Lay the fish on the herbs and repeat Step 3 on top of the fish.
6. Sprinkle the fish with lemon juice.
7. Seal the bag by first folding the long way two folds, followed by twisting the ends.
8. You may place the fish directly on the rack or on a cookie sheet.
9. Bake for 15 to 20 minutes at 400°F.
10. Place on the dish and allow guest to open.

NOTES:

1. Baking in a brown paper bag is a traditional method in Greece. In fact, this method was used in some restaurants. The fish is moist. They may be individually added in a bag or multiple servings.
2. Wax paper may also be used if you seal the food through the folding.
3. I found it interesting that each of us was served a paper bag in one small restaurant with our fish and shrimp having been baked with our vegetables in the bag. It is a conversation piece and offers an outstanding meal for your guests.
4. Basting the bag thoroughly with olive oil is important.
5. If you are making individual bags, you might want to place your vegetables and par cooked rice in along with your fish.

BAKED FISH WITH HERBS

INGREDIENTS

4 fish fillets (white fish, grouper, swai or fillets of your preference)
¼ teaspoon each of dried oregano, thyme and parsley
2 cloves of garlic
Olive oil
Juice of 1 lemon
Salt and white pepper

1. Juice the lemon and mix it with an equal amount of olive oil.
2. Mix the herbs with the oil and lemon.
3. Slice the garlic thin and set aside.
4. Arrange the fish fillets on a greased baking sheet.
5. Coat the fillets with the olive oil mixture.
6. Sprinkle the baking pan with garlic and turn the fish over laying them directly onto the garlic.
7. Heavily coat the fillets with the remaining oil and sprinkle them with the remaining garlic slices.
8. Salt and pepper to taste.
9. Bake at 325 °F until the fish is flaky and done.

NOTES:

1. If you dislike seafood, you might want to try this recipe with swai. This recipe is simple and light and enhances the taste of the fish.
2. This is a general fish recipe and may also be used with shellfish, especially shrimp.
3. This recipe is great for the grill and may be used even with a plank.
4. This recipe may be used in a skillet.

STUFFED SQUID

INGREDIENTS
1 pound squid
4 tomatoes
3 cloves garlic
1 white onion
½ cup mushrooms
¼ cup chopped parsley
¼ cup chopped mint, dill or tarragon
½ cup short grain rice
½ cup chopped olives
½ cup pine nuts
¼ slivered almonds
½ cup zucchini
1 cup sweet white wine
Salt and white pepper
Lemon zest
Olive oil

1. Chop the garlic, mushrooms, herbs, zucchini, tomatoes, zest and olives.
2. Heat the oil in a skillet with the garlic, herbs, mushrooms, onions and olives.
3. Add the tomatoes and zucchini and sauté until it becomes sauce.
4. Add the rice and oil if necessary.
5. Add the wine and sauté until rice is white.
6. Add the pine nuts and almonds.
7. Wash and clean your squid.
8. Grease a baking pan.
9. Using a teaspoon, fill each squid with the rice mixture.
10. Place the filled squid in the baking pan. Continue filling until all the squid has been used.
11. Place the remaining filling around the stuffed squid.
12. Add the remaining ½ cup wine and ½ cup water and bake at 325°F for 45 minutes.

NOTES:
1. Raisins may be added for sweetness.
2. Chopped shrimp may be added for texture and taste.
3. You may also use grapeseed oil, sunflower oil, etc. Oil flavors enhance the taste of this food.
4. Retsina may also be used in lieu of sweet wine.

Chapter 13: Pastry

ASIA MINOR SARAGLIE (ROLLED BAKLAVA)

INGREDIENTS

Syrup

> 3 cups sugar
> 2 cups water
> 1 orange, sliced
> 1 lemon, sliced
> 2 sticks cinnamon

Pastry

> 1 box of phylo
> Rose or orange water (optional)
> Chocolate or carob (optional)
> ¼ cup each chopped pecans, walnuts, almonds and pistachios
> 2 tablespoons ground cinnamon
> 1 cup sugar
> Rind of each orange and lemon
> 1 tablespoon each of allspice and nutmeg
> 2 sticks unsalted butter
> 1 container of maraschino or candied cherries

Syrup

1. First start the syrup by combining the sugar and water in a saucepan with the orange slices, lemon slices and spices. Place on the stove at medium heat and stir the mixture to combine the ingredients.
2. Bring the syrup to a boil being careful not to allow the content to over-boil.
3. Reduce heat, and cook until clear, about 10 minutes or until thickened.
4. Set the syrup to the side

Pastry
5. Open the box of phylo. If you have dry sheets, set them to the side until you need them. These sheets will be crumbled and used as a filler to make the pastry fluffier.
6. In a deep bowl combine the nuts, orange rind, lemon rind, chocolate, sugar, and spices. Mix them all thoroughly, to ensure even distribution.
7. Prepare your baking pan by buttering all the sides.
8. Make sure that you have a damp clean cloth with you to lay over the phylo if needed.
9. Take two sheets of phylo at a time (3 if you want extra crunchy pastry). Place the sheets in front of you. If you choose the longer side, you will make a narrower roll. The short side will give you a shorter yet wider roll.
10. Butter the top sheet.
11. Take a handful of the nut mixture and evenly spread it over the sheet.
12. Sprinkle the nuts with scented water.
13. As you are standing in front of the sheet of pastry, fold the two vertical sides of the phylo ¾ ", overlapping the nut mixture slightly and butter.
14. Fold the horizontal end up ½ "and being to roll the pastry roll carefully. The roll must be firm, not loose, so maintain slight tension on the roll. Too much tension will rip the delicate phylo.
15. Have a greased baking sheet ready for use.
16. Place the roll in the baking pan and butter.
17. With a very sharp knife, cut the roll into 1" rounds. The sharper the knife the better the cuts and the less mixture you will lose.
18. Follow Steps 9 to 17 until you have used all your ingredients.
19. Bake the rolls at 325°F until golden.
20. Warm the syrup during the time the rolls are baking.
21. Remove them from the oven and immediately pour the syrup on the hot rolls. The syrup should reach halfway up the roll. If correctly performed you will hear a sizzling from the pastry. That ensures that the pastry is absorbing the syrup.
22. Allow the pastry to stand overnight uncovered.
23. Adorn with halved candied cherries or maraschino cherries and serve in cupcake foils.

NOTES:
1. Chocolate or carob is an optional ingredient. On the Island of Symi, my great-grandmother was known to use carob to sweeten some of her pastry. Carob may be purchased in most health food stores. Dark chocolate is often times a great substitute and equally as nutritious. In all of the chocolate recipes that I have, I use Sweetriots® because of the taste, variety and value.
2. The knife is a crucial part of this recipe. It must be sharp and the cut must be straight and even.

3. The choice of syrup depends on the timeframe you will be serving your pastry. If you intend on serving the pastry in the evening or the following day of preparation, honey syrup is permissible. Yet if you are looking to serve the pastry in a few days then opt for the sugar syrup. The sugar syrup will ensure that you have no "hard syrup" base on your pastry. A "hard syrup" base exists when the honey collects at the base of the pastry and leaves the upper portion dry and sticky.
4. The syrup must be added when the pastry is removed from the oven. The syrup must be warm and must be added using a ladle. If correctly applied a sharp sizzling sound will be heard.

VASILOPITA CAKE RECIPE

INGREDIENTS
5 eggs
2 sticks unsalted butter
1½ cups sugar
Zest from 1 orange and 1 lemon
¼ cup orange juice
¼ cup orange water or 1 tablespoon orange emulsion or extract (optional)
4-5 cups cake flour
2 teaspoons baking powder
½ teaspoon salt
¼ cup honey
1 stick of butter
2 cups powdered or confectioners' sugar
1 teaspoon milk
1 coin wrapped in aluminum
Cloves (whole) for decoration

1. Chill mixer beaters and a large glass or metal bowl for a few minutes.
2. Separate the egg whites from the yolks.
3. Place the whites in the chilled bowl first and beat the egg whites until stiff, then add the egg yolks and beat until creamy.
4. Add the butter and sugar to the egg mixture and beat for 5 minutes forming a batter.
5. Add the orange rind and continue to beat.
6. Add the orange juice and water.
7. In a smaller bowl, stir the baking powder and the salt into the flour.
8. Sift the flour mixture into the egg mixture.
9. Have some extra flour handy. If the batter is too loose, add 1 tablespoon of flour at a time. The batter needs to be soft and glossy but not sticky.
10. Place the batter into a greased 10-inch round spring form pan.
11. Tuck the coin into the center of the batter and push down to making sure the coin is embedded in the batter.
12. Preheat oven to 325°F degrees.
13. Use a small bowl to mix the orange water and honey together.
14. Brush the entire Vasilopita with orange water and honey.
15. Bake for 45–60 minutes, or until the dough separates from the sides of the pan.
16. While the cake bakes, make a fondant decoration:
    a. Soften (do not melt) 1 stick of butter until it can be easily molded in your hand.

b. Use a fork to combine the butter with 1 cup of sugar until it forms dough. If the butter is not workable, add a few drops of milk. If it is too loose, add sugar.
c. Place the butter and sugar mixture over the form you selected.
d. Press it in so that it fills all of the crevices.
e. Gently remove the fondant from the form and place it on waxed paper.
f. Store the form in the refrigerator until the cake has cooled completely.
g. Set the form in the center of the cake.
h. Outline with cloves.

NOTES:
1. Depending on altitude, gauge the use of flour. Add your flour slowly until you reach the correct batter texture. By adding the flour slowly you will avoid inconsistency with the cake texture.
2. The cake or bread is baked in a large circular baking pan or cake pan. The larger the better.
3. Emulsions and concentrations of flavors are fun to use, but understand they must be used sparingly to avoid their scent becoming overbearing and ruining your pita or cake.
4. Traditionally, the Vasilopita is considered a pita. In this case unlike the pies you have already worked with, the Vasilopita, depending on the area of Greece, maybe either bread or a cake with the coin or even coins embedded within.
5. The coins should be washed and then wrapped in aluminum foil. Traditionally, the coins were gold or silver. Whatever you place in the pita is acceptable. The person who receives the coin in their piece is especially blessed during the New Year.
6. The pita is cut according to tradition. The family prays together for a happy and healthy New Year. The head of the household will take a knife and make the sign of the Cross three times on the bread. The first piece of bread goes to Jesus Christ, the second to the Virgin Mary, St. Basil and the Saints of the Church, the next pieces fall in line with the head of the house and continue to the youngest and friends in attendance.
7. If the coin is not found in the group of cuttings, the blessings then revert back to the entire house, blessing everyone within.

KADDAFI

INGREDIENTS
Kaddafi phylo
2 sticks unsalted butter
1 ½ cups blanched chopped almonds
1 teaspoon cinnamon
2 cups sugar

Sugar and Honey Syrup Recipe

1. In a sauce pot, melt the butter.
2. Grease a pan with the butter and set it aside.
3. In a bowl combine the sugar, nuts and cinnamon and set to the side.
4. Open the box of shredded dough and comb it with your fingers gently separating into sections measuring approximately 3" to 4" in width and about 6" long. Try not to separate

the dough too far apart with gaping holes, instead keep the shredded dough fairly close together.
5. Cover the dough you are not using with a damp cloth.
6. Taking one strip at a time, sprinkle the nut mixture down the center of the length of section.
7. Drizzle with some melted butter down the center of the strip.
8. Using both hands, begin rolling the dough from the area closest to you forward making a tight roll. The key is to keep the strip together and roll the nuts into a bundle that resembles shredded wheat cereal.
9. Placed the tight bundle onto the greased pan with the end side facing downward.
10. Repeat Steps 6 to 9 until all the dough is used.
11. Drizzle, the bundles with the remaining butter.
12. Bake at 325°F until golden.
13. Remove the pan from the oven and while hot, pour a ladle of syrup over each bundle. The syrup should reach just about halfway up the side of the pan. Allow the rolls to absorb the syrup.
14. Remove the bundles, place them in cupcake tins and sprinkle with cinnamon. Serve when cooled

NOTES:
1. There exists a long-standing feud about the best time to baste this pastry. One group insists before rolling, while the other group maintains after rolling. I solved the dilemma. I do both. This adds an extra hint of butter that makes all the difference.
2. The pastry should be made 24 hours prior to being served. The period of time allows the pastry to absorb the syrup used in the recipe.
3. Only almonds are used in this recipe. The Kaddafi is considered the "blond" baklava. Recipes have been known to include walnuts, but the original recipe uses only almonds.
4. Kaddafi dough is intimidating until you have played with it a few times, keep a damp towel handy until you are used to making your bundles.
5. There is no problem laying each bundle side by side, in fact that would ensure that the bundles remain tight.
6. Orange or lemon rind may be added to the nut mixture for a variation to the flavor.
7. For a real difference sprinkle with some Sweetriots® dark chocolate coconut chips prior to rolling the bundle.

ASIA MINOR CHOCOLATE BAKLAVA

INGREDIENTS
1 box of phylo
Orange water (optional)
½ cup chocolate or carob chips (optional)
1 cup each chopped pecans, walnuts, almonds and pistachios
½ cup ground cinnamon
1 cup sugar
Rind of one orange and one lemon

1 tablespoon each of allspice and nutmeg
2 sticks unsalted butter
Sugar Syrup Recipe

Nut Mixture
1. Open the box of phylo. If you have dry sheets that crumble easily, set them to the side to be used later. These sheets will be crumbled and used as a filler to make the pastry fluffier.
2. In a deep bowl combine the nuts, orange rind, lemon rind, chocolate, sugar and spices. Mix them all thoroughly, to ensure even distribution.
3. Prepare your baking pan by buttering all the sides.

Assembly of Baklava
1. Make sure that you have a damp clean cloth with you to lay over the phylo, if needed.
2. Cover your pan as shown in the figure on the next page. This will ensure that your phylo is laid correctly and no edge cutting is needed.
3. After 2 layers of phylo have been placed on the baking pan, you may butter all sides and center. Make sure that you alternate the sides you are laying the phylo (i.e., long side, the next layer should be short).
4. Carefully take the orange water and use an atomizer or sprinkle a little in the center of your pan
5. Follow Steps 6 and 7 until you have reached a phylo thickness of 8 layers. On the ninth layer go to Step 9.
6. Take your nut mixture and sprinkle about a handful onto the phylo. **You do not want a thick layer, just enough to cover the bottom**.
7. Lay the next layers of fresh phylo onto the pan.
8. Sprinkle with dried phylo.
9. Repeat from Step 9 until you are left with 3 sheets of phylo or have reach the top of your baking pan, stop and go to Step 13.
10. Your pan should be filled with layers of phylo and nuts, and the phylo wings hanging on all sides. Taking one of the long sides with both your hands, lift the side and bring it to the center of the pan.
11. Repeat this action with the other side of the pan, as well as with your short sides.
12. Now your baklava is totally wrapped with phylo. Your edges are as perfect as that of a Greek pastry chef. Butter the wrapping area and spray it with orange water.
13. Take your last 3 sheets, fold them in half, if necessary, and place each layer singly on top of your baklava covering the top folded area, buttering and spraying each layer. If this step is correctly rendered, you do not need to cut anything until the final sheet.
14. After the final layer is placed on the baklava, buttered and sprayed with orange water, take a sharp knife and diagonally score the pastry, first one way then the other to form diamond shapes in the top of the baklava. Your knife should not touch the bottom of the pan; it should only go down to the nut area.
15. Drip the remaining butter into the cracks and on the sides.

Baking & Syrup
1. Bake at 325°F in a convection oven (about 25 minutes), 350°F (about 45 minutes) in a regular oven until golden brown.
2. Immediately after removing the pan from the oven, pour the hot syrup on the baklava. If this is correctly done, you will hear the sizzling sound made by the nuts as they begin to absorb the hot liquid. In order for this process to work, both must be very hot. Don't worry if the

baklava appears to be floating in syrup. The syrup will be absorbed totally by the nuts and phylo and will be perfect in texture.

3. It is preferred that you make the baklava ahead of time so that it is allowed to sit overnight and absorb the syrup.

NOTES:

1. Carob was used by my great-grandmother Irene for this recipe. That would be a perfect ingredient for this recipe, if and when it could be found. A great substitute is found in dark chocolate chips.
2. The complicated form of "wrapping" the baklava was taken from Kalamata pastry chefs that explained whether it was baklava or galactobouriko. You are recognized by other chefs by the method of folding your phylo. The scary thing is they were right.
3. The other wonderful outcome of phylo wrapping is the layers of pastry leaf one can enjoy
4. This pastry is wonderful if you make it with walnuts alone or with the variety of nuts as in Asia Minor. The combination of nuts is up to you and the people you will serve, but consider the variety gives you the added flavor.
5. We know people who have nut allergies will abstain from this recipe. There are people who have sensitivities to certain types of nuts. It is always a must to ask people you are not sure of if they have sensitivities or allergies to any food you make.
6. Be careful not to over-grind your nuts, turning them to an almost "coffee ground" state. This will, without a doubt, destroy you pastry. Texture is good.

BASIC PHYLO 1

INGREDIENTS
3 + 1 cups of flour
1 teaspoon salt
1 cup warm water
Olive oil or vegetable oil

1. Place 3 cups of flour into a bowl.
2. Sprinkle the salt on the flour and mix.
3. Using your fingers, form a well in the middle of the flour mound.
4. Add the warm water into the well and mix into the flour.
5. You may use a fork or a mixer if necessary. Otherwise, your hands work just as well.
6. Knead the dough for about 10 to 15 minutes to make sure that it is totally combined and shiny.
7. Place the oil on your hands and use it to rub the outside of the dough forming it into a ball.
8. Place the ball on a large pre-cut piece of plastic wrap and seal the dough from the air.
9. Place the dough ball on a dish and let it sit for several hours at room temperature.
10. When you are ready to roll out the dough, cut the dough in half and then ¼ pieces. It is easier to cut the dough
11. into smaller, manageable pieces for your first time.
12. Sprinkle your dowel rod or rolling pin and the table top with flour.
13. Place the small dough ball on the floured surface and roll the dough in a circular form.
14. Don't be afraid to move the dough around as you roll.
15. Roll the dough to get it at the proper thinness or as thin as possible.

16. When you have worked the dough as thin as you would like, test the thinness by placing your face close to the surface of the table as possible and lightly blowing. If the phylo flounces up, you have the right thickness.
17. Use the phylo right away or sprinkle with flour and set it to the side with a damp towel.
18. If you would like to use it the next day, place cornstarch or flour and wax paper between the layers, and wrap it in plastic wrap.
19. Place it in the refrigerator for up to 2 weeks or up to 6 months in the freezer.

NOTES:
1. Add the flour slowly as you mix the dough to avoid extreme textures one way or other.
2. If you find the dough too dry. An example of dry dough is evident during the kneading process when layers remain separate and do not easily come together when pressure is applied. In this case, you may wet your hands with either water or oil, allowing the dough to absorb the moisture it needs. Repeat this process until the proper texture is reached, gradually adding fluid.
3. If the dough is extremely sticky and remains glued to your hands, you have not reached the correct flour balance. You must, therefore, add flour slowly to the mixture and continue kneading. When the dough has totally absorbed the flour and no longer is clinging to your hands, refrain from adding any more flour.
4. There are a variety of rolling pins available for use. For the purpose of phylo making a dowel rod is preferred, otherwise a French rolling pin is acceptable.
5. Work your rolling pin from the center out with your hands, applying equal pressure throughout the rod.
6. Though the type of rolling pin is your preference, the rolling pins mentioned allow for equal pressure to be applied throughout the pin, leaving you with even phylo leaf.

FLUFFY PHYLO - 2

INGREDIENTS
4 + 1 cups flour
2 tablespoons baking powder
3 tablespoons olive oil
1 teaspoon salt
1 can of beer

1. Place 4 cups of flour into a bowl.
2. Sprinkle the salt and baking powder on the flour and mix.
3. Make a well in the heap of flour using your fingers.
4. Add half the can of beer into the well and mix into the flour. Add the remaining portion of the beer, if necessary. Use all the flour.
5. Add two tablespoons of olive oil to the mixture.
6. You may use a fork or a mixer, if necessary. Otherwise, your hands work just as well.
7. Knead the dough for about 10 to 15 minutes to make sure that it is totally combined and shiny. Add additional flour to your dough to stiffen, if necessary.

8. Place the oil on your hands and use it to rub the outside of the dough forming it into a ball.
9. Place the ball on a pre-cut piece of plastic wrap and seal the dough from the air.
10. Place the dough ball on a dish and let it sit for several hours.
11. When you are ready to roll out the dough, cut the dough in half and then ¼ pieces. It is easier to cut the dough into smaller, manageable pieces for your first time.
12. Sprinkle your dowel rod or rolling pin and the table top with flour.
13. Place the small dough ball on the floured surface and work the dough in a circular form.
14. Don't be afraid to move the dough around. Work the dough to get it as thin as possible.
15. When you have worked the dough as thin as you would like; test the thinness by placing your face close to the surface of the table and lightly blowing. If the phylo flounces up, you have the right thickness.
16. Use the phylo right away or sprinkle with flour and set it to the side covered with a damp towel.
17. If you would like to use it the next day, place a sheet of wax paper and cornstarch or flour between the layers and wrap it in plastic wrap. Place it in the refrigerator for up to 2 weeks or up to 6 months in the freezer.

NOTES:
1. Add the flour slowly as you mix the dough to avoid extreme textures one way or other.
2. If you find the dough too dry. An example of dry dough is evident during the kneading process when layers remain separate and do not easily come together when pressure is applied. In this case, you may wet your hands with either water or oil, allowing the dough to absorb the moisture it needs. Repeat this process until the proper texture is reached, gradually adding fluid.
3. If the dough is extremely sticky and remains glued to your hands, you have not reached the correct flour balance. You must therefore, add flour slowly to the mixture and continue kneading. When the dough has totally absorbed the flour and no longer is clinging to your hands, refrain from adding any more flour.
4. There are a variety of rolling pins available for use. For the purpose of phylo making a dowel rod is preferred, otherwise a French rolling pin is acceptable.
5. Work your rolling pin from the center out with your hands, applying equal pressure throughout the rod.
6. Though the type of rolling pin is your preference, the rolling pins mentioned allow for equal pressure to be applied throughout the pin, leaving you with even phylo leaf.

SPARKLE PHYLO - 3

INGREDIENTS
4 + 1 cups flour
2 + 1 tablespoons olive oil
1 tablespoon white wine, white vinegar or lemon juice
1 teaspoon salt
¾ cups water

1. Place 4 cups of flour in a bowl.
2. Sprinkle the salt on the flour and mix.
3. Make a well in the heap of flour using your fingers.
4. To the water, add the wine and 2 tablespoons of olive oil.
5. Add the warm water into the well and mix into the flour.
6. You may use a fork or a mixer, if necessary. Otherwise, your hands work just as well.
7. Knead the dough for about 10 to 15 minutes to make sure that it is totally combined and shiny.
8. Place the oil on your hands and use it to rub the outside of the dough forming it into a ball.
9. Place the ball on a pre-cut piece of plastic wrap and seal the dough from the air.
10. Place the dough ball on a dish and let it sit for several hours.
11. When you are ready to roll out the dough, cut the dough in half and then ¼ pieces. It is easier to cut the dough into smaller, manageable pieces for your first time.
12. Sprinkle your dowel rod or rolling pin and the table top with flour.
13. Place the small dough ball on the floured surface and work the dough in a circular form.
14. Don't be afraid to move the dough around. Work the dough to get it as thin as possible.
15. When you have worked the dough as thin as you would like, test the thinness by placing your face close to the surface of the table and lightly blowing. If the phylo flounces up, you have the right thickness.
16. Use the phylo right away or sprinkle with flour and set it to the side covered with a damp towel.
17. If you would like to use it the next day, place a sheet of waxed paper and cornstarch or flour between the layers and wrap it in plastic wrap. Place it in the refrigerator for up to 2 weeks or up to 6 months in the freezer.

NOTES:
1. Add the flour slowly as you mix the dough to avoid extreme textures one way or other.
2. If you find the dough too dry. An example of dry dough is evident during the kneading process when layers remain separate and do not easily come together when pressure is applied. In this case, you may wet your hands with either water or oil, allowing the dough to absorb the moisture it needs. Repeat this process until the proper texture is reached, gradually adding fluid.
3. If the dough is extremely sticky and remains glued to your hands, you have not reached the correct flour balance. You must, therefore, add flour slowly to the mixture and continue kneading. When the dough has totally absorbed the flour and no longer is clinging to your hands, refrain from adding any more flour.
4. There are a variety of rolling pins available for use. For the purpose of phylo making, a dowel rod is preferred, otherwise a French rolling pin is acceptable.
5. Work your rolling pin from the center out with your hands, applying equal pressure throughout the rod.
6. Though the type of rolling pin is your preference, the rolling pins mentioned allow for equal pressure to be applied throughout the pin, leaving you with even phylo leaf.

INGREDIENTS
5 + 1 cups flour
1 cup thick yogurt (optional)
2 eggs
3 tablespoons olive oil
1 teaspoon salt
½ cup milk
Cornstarch

1. Place 3 cups of flour in a bowl.
2. Sprinkle the salt on the flour and mix.
3. Make a well in the center of the flour in your bowl using your fingers.
4. Add the milk, yogurt, 2 tablespoons of oil and eggs into the well and mix into the flour.
5. You may use a fork or a mixer if necessary. Otherwise, your hands work just as well.
6. Knead the dough for about 10 to 15 minutes to make sure that it is totally combined and shiny.
7. Place the oil on your hands and use it to rub the outside of the dough forming it into a ball.
8. Place the ball on a pre-cut piece of plastic wrap and seal the dough from the air.
9. Place the dough ball on a dish and let it sit for several hours.
10. When you are ready to roll out the dough, cut the dough in half and then ¼ pieces. It is easier to cut the dough into smaller manageable pieces for your first time.
11. Sprinkle your dowel rod or rolling pin and the table top with flour.
12. Place the small dough ball on the floured surface and work the dough in a circular form.
13. Don't be afraid to move the dough around as you are rolling it out. Work the dough to get it as thin as possible.
14. When you have worked the dough as thin as you would like, test the thinness by placing your face close to the surface of the table and lightly blowing. If the phylo flounces up, you have the right thickness.
15. Use the phylo right away or sprinkle with flour and set it to the side with a damp towel.
16. If you would like to use it the next day, place a sheet of waxed paper and cornstarch or flour between the layers and wrap it in plastic wrap. Place it in the refrigerator for up to 2 weeks or up to 6 months in the freezer.

NOTES:
1. Add the flour slowly as you mix the dough to avoid extreme textures one way or other.
2. If you find the dough too dry. An example of dry dough is evident during the kneading process when layers remain separate and do not easily come together when pressure is applied. In this case, you may wet your hands with either water or oil, allowing the dough to absorb the moisture it needs. Repeat this process until the proper texture is reached, gradually adding fluid.
3. If the dough is extremely sticky and remains glued to your hands, you have not reached the correct flour balance. You must therefore, add flour slowly to the mixture and

continue kneading. When the dough has totally absorbed the flour and no longer is clinging to your hands, refrain from adding any more flour.
4. There are a variety of rolling pins available for use. For the purpose of phylo making, a dowel rod is preferred otherwise a French rolling pin is acceptable.
5. Work your rolling pin from the center out with your hands, applying equal pressure throughout the rod.
6. Though the type of rolling pin is your preference, the rolling pins mentioned allow for equal pressure to be applied throughout the pin, leaving you with even phylo leaf.

SYRUPS

BASIC SUGAR

INGREDIENTS
2 cups sugar
1 cup water
Any or all cinnamon stick, cloves, allspice
Slices of orange, lemon or lime

1. Add the ingredients into a pot.
2. Bring to a boil.
3. Reduce heat and allow to cook until thick.

NOTES:
1. Use if the pastry will be eaten more than 24 hour after being made. Basic Sugar syrups are not heavy, they are easily absorbed and will not weigh heavily at the base of your pastry. Your pastry will reflect a professional appearance with a fresh, light taste.
2. The flavor may be altered by replacing those suggested in the recipe and adding other flavors you prefer through spices, concentrations, extracts or even liqueurs.
3. Be cautious with the amount of flavoring you use. Vary the amount based on the strength of the characteristic taste.

BASIC HONEY

INGREDIENTS
2 cups honey
1 cup water
Any or all cinnamon stick, cloves, allspice
Slices of orange, lemon or lime

1. Add the ingredients to a pot.
2. Bring to a boil.
3. Reduce heat and allow to cook until thickened.

NOTES:
1. Use if the pastry will be eaten within 24 hour after being made. As much as we love the traditional honey syrup, it tends to gather unappetizingly at the base of most pastries if it is not consumed within 24 hours. Unless you "water down" your syrup considerably, the honey crust that lays at the base of pastry will reveal its age. This was proven at a pastry

contest held at St. Haralambos Greek Orthodox Church in Niles, Illinois in the mid 1980s, when two food critics examined more than 100 pastries. Our conclusions were simple, the pastries that used a sugar-base syrup withstood the test of time, both by taste and appearance. My compliments to the Chicago Suntimes and Chicago Tribune!

2. The flavor may be altered by replacing flavors suggested in the recipe and adding other flavors you prefer through spices, concentrations, extracts or even liqueurs.
3. Be cautious with the amount of flavoring you use. Vary the amount based on the strength of the characteristic taste.

BASIC SUGAR/HONEY

1 cup honey
1 cup sugar
1 cup water
Any or all cinnamon stick, cloves, allspice
Slices of orange, lemon or lime

1. Add the ingredients to a pot.
2. Bring to a boil.
3. Reduce heat and allow to cook until thickened.

NOTES:
1. Use if the pastry will be eaten more than 24 hours after being made. This is the safest way of having the honey taste in syrup without giving up appearance. The honey is not too watery and keeps the pastry looking every bit as good as it should.
2. The flavor may be altered by replacing those flavors suggested in the recipe and adding other flavors you prefer through spices, concentrations, extracts or even liqueurs.
3. Be cautious with the amount of flavoring you use. Vary the amount based on the strength of the characteristic taste.

BOUGATSA

INGREDIENTS
½ pound phylo
1 cup fine semolina
4 eggs, beaten
¾ cup sugar
2 sticks butter, melted
4 cups whole milk
Ground cinnamon for dusting
Confectioners' sugar for dusting

1. In a large pot combine the milk and butter and heat slowly, melting the butter.
2. Separate the eggs. Beat the whites first, then the yolks.
3. Stirring continuously, add semolina, egg and then sugar, slowly alternating each ingredient until everything is used.
4. Cook the custard until it thickens and produces thick blistering bubbles.
5. Preheat the oven to 325 °F.
6. Brush a baking pan with the melted butter.

7. Lay a sheet of phylo in front of you.
8. Butter the sheet and fold it in half lengthwise. The shorter end will be in front of you and the longer end of the phylo will extend outward.
9. Place 2-3 tablespoons of custard at the end closest to you, an inch from the ends of the phylo.
10. Fold the overhang over the custard. Bring the two sides together and roll forward until the sheet is totally used and the Bougatsa resembles an eggroll.
11. Place the roll in the baking pan and butter.
12. Repeat Steps 8 to 12 until all the custard is used.
13. Bake until golden, about 30 to 40 minutes.

NOTES:
1. This is one of my favorite recipes for custard. It is simple, and once you have the technique set you may make them in various sizes.
2. Unlike other custards, this recipe may be served hot or cold. It is even better hot.
3. If you are serving this at a dinner party, consider having the rolls made just before guests arrive. Then pop them in the oven as you are sitting down for dinner. You may also turn the oven off and allow them to sit in a warm oven until you are ready to serve.

DIPLES

INGREDIENTS
5 eggs + 1 egg white
2 sticks unsalted butter
1 jigger brandy, cognac, mastica or amaretto
1 teaspoon almond extract
1 teaspoon baking powder
¼ teaspoon baking soda
2-3 ½ cups flour
Orange blossom honey
Corn oil for frying
½ cup ground walnuts
1 tablespoon cinnamon

1. Melt your butter and allow it to cool.
2. In a bowl beat your egg whites until fluffy.
3. Add the yolks and continue beating.
4. Add the flavoring, extract and butter and continue to beat. You should have a nice batter.
5. Start sifting the flour, baking powder and baking soda into the bowl.
6. As the mixture thickens, you might find it easier to switch from using beaters to kneading with your hands.
7. Flour your table and transfer the dough to the floured area. As with phylo, recipes gauge the need for additional flour by the sticky texture of the dough.

8. Add the flour carefully. You do not want to add too much flour. The diples dough is, in fact, a phylo recipe.
9. When the dough has absorbed the correct amount of flour, take out your dowel rod or French rolling pin.
10. Cut the dough into manageable pieces. I prefer quartering the dough. Use one piece at a time, and place the remaining pieces of dough in plastic wrap.
11. Flour both sides of the dough lightly, and start rolling out the dough. Don't be afraid to rotate the dough. The thinner the dough the better the diples. Sprinkle with flour as needed.
12. When you have reached the correct thinness, blow at the base of the table to see if the phylo flounces. If the phylo flounces, then you have reached your proper thickness.
13. Fill a skillet halfway with corn oil.
14. While the oil is heating, use a pizza cutter to cut strips to make them manageable:
    a. About 2" by 4" for bows; take each strip and twist it in alternate directions at the same time to form a bow.
    b. About 2" by 3" for knots; slit the center of the strip 1" lengthwise. Fold one side through the opening, making a knot.
15. Sprinkle some flour on the oil to test if it is ready. If the oil sizzles immediately, then you have reached the right temperature.
16. Using a slotted metal spoon, drop your bows or knots into the hot oil. Quickly flip the dough so that it fries equally on the opposite end.
17. Remove the dough from the oil when it starts to change color. Do not wait too long, the oil is hot and they will continue to brown for a few seconds after you have removed them.
18. If you find that the dough is darkening too fast, reduce the heat.
19. Place the fried dough on paper towels to drain.
20. Heat the honey in a sauce pan.
21. When the honey is hot, dip the diples into the honey and transfer them to wax paper.
22. After all the diples have been fried and dipped in honey, sprinkle them with cinnamon and ground walnuts and enjoy.

NOTES:
1. Traditionally, Greek women use a pot of oil to fry their diples. This is because they like making the curl forms, which I have not described above for two reasons. First this is an introductory level of Greek cooking and this procedure, though interesting, is dangerous for a novice. My students had practiced for quite some time before attempting the task on their own. Second, the technique of frying the dough using two forks is a technique in itself and must be carefully used.
2. The use of a skillet instead of a pot is for safety's sake. Yes, the pot of oil allows the diples to drop, but the use of a skillet provides more control and uses less oil.
3. Flavoring alternatives may include orange, lemon or lime rind.
4. A ravioli cutter may be used if you wish to make a fancy edging on your strips.
5. Have extra flour to the side.
6. Traditionally, Greek women would use a plasti or broomstick (of course detached from the broom) to get the correct thinness of the pastry leaf. The thinness of the leaf makes

all the difference. The longer, thinner and more even in shape your rolling pin is, the better the dipla.

7. When eating a dipla, you should feel the crispness and the fried dough should melt in your mouth, leaving you with a sweet memory and making you crave more. Thick pastry traps the oils, does not allow for honey penetration and has really no taste. Thinness is everything in this recipe!

GALACTOBOURIKO

INGREDIENTS
1 gallon vitamin D milk
1 teaspoon vanilla extract or 1" piece of vanilla bean
1 ½ cups sugar
2 cups extra fine semolina or farina
6 eggs
1 pound unsalted butter (1 stick for the phylo, 1 stick for the filling)
Rosewater or oil (optional)
1 pound phylo

Syrup Recipe of choice.

CUSTARD
1. In a chilled bowl, beat the egg whites.
2. Add the egg yolks and continue to beat until creamy.
3. Place the milk, sugar, vanilla and one stick of butter in a large pot and heat slowly.
4. Traditionally, you may add a few drops of rose oil to the milk, if you wish scented custard. Use only rose oil, not the water.
5. Stir continually making sure that you do not burn or scald the milk.
6. When the butter has melted and sugar has dissolved, slowly add the eggs and semolina.
7. Using a wooden spoon and continually stirring the milk, alternate the eggs and semolina.
8. Make sure that you dissolve each before adding the other ingredient.
9. Continue this step until both ingredients are used and your custard begins to thicken.
10. The custard will thicken within a few minutes. Keep stirring to make sure that nothing sticks to the base of the pot. The custard is ready when you see a blister-type of bubble.
11. Set the custard to the side to cool.
ASSEMBLY
12. Make sure that you have a damp clean cloth to lay over the phylo if needed.
13. Cover your pan as shown in the figure on the next page. This will ensure that your phylo is laid correctly and no edge cutting is needed.
14. First lay two sheets lengthwise.
15. Next lay two sheets widthwise.
16. The next sheet should first be folded in half. The folded sheet should be placed in the center of the pan, covering the overlays of the previous steps.
17. After 2 layers of phylo have been placed on the baking pan you may butter all sides and center. Make sure that you alternate the sides you are laying the phylo (i.e., long side, the next layer should be short).
18. Carefully take the rosewater and using an atomizer, spray a small portion in the center of the pan.
19. Follow Steps 14 through16 until you have reached a phylo thickness of 8 layers.

20. Take the cooled custard and spread it on the laid phylo.
21. Don't forget to remove the vanilla bean (if it was used).
22. Bring the lengthwise sheets of phylo toward the center.
23. Repeat this action with the widthwise phylo sheets that are hanging, bringing them to the center.
24. Butter the folded sheets generously and, if you like, spray them with rosewater.
25. The final two sheets of phylo should be folded in half widthwise.
26. Take the folded sheets and lay them into the folded area of the Galactobouriko, neatly covering the folds.
27. Butter generously.
28. Bake at 325°F until golden.
29. During the baking time, make the syrup you have selected.
30. When you remove the pastry from the oven, while still hot, drench with syrup.
31. You need to see the syrup go up the side of the pan at least halfway to 2/3 of the way.
32. Allow the pastry to absorb the syrup, if possible, overnight.
33. Cut in diagonal pieces.

NOTES:
1. My great-grandmother and grandmother both used rose oil in their pastry. My mother loved the exceptional scent and insisted on carrying on the tradition. This is very exotic. If you use the rose oil, it is added to the custard. If you use rosewater, scent the phylo only.
2. The complicated form of "wrapping" the Galactobouriko was taken from Kalamata pastry chefs that explained whether it was baklava or galactobouriko, you are recognized by other chefs by the method of folding your phylo. The scary thing is, they were right.
3. The other wonderful outcome of phylo wrapping is the layers of pastry leaf one can enjoy
4. Scents other than rosewater may be used, such as orange water.
5. Orange or lemon rind may also be added to the custard as a scent.

GALATOPITA

INGREDIENTS

6 cups whole milk
2 sticks
3 1/2 cups sugar
2 cups semolina

7 large eggs
1 inch vanilla bean
1 cup water
1 stick cinnamon
1 lemon
Ground cinnamon

PREPARE SYRUP – PREPARE THE SYRUP WHILE THE PHYLO IS BAKING
1. In a sauce pot combine the water, 2 cups sugar, fruit slices and cinnamon stick and bring it to a boil.
2. Boil the syrup until it is reduced and thickens slightly.
3. The syrup is ready when there is a distinct color change and water scent.

4. Separate the eggs. Beat the whites first, then the yolks.
5. In a large pot combine the milk, vanilla bean and butter and heat, slowly melting the butter.
6. Stirring continuously, add the semolina, the egg, and then sugar, slowly alternating each ingredient until everything is used.
7. Cook the custard until it thickens and produces thick blister-type bubbles.
8. Remove the vanilla bean.
9. Use a double pan baking method. Place the custard into the greased baking pan. Place that pan into a pan with water and bake at 350°F until golden.
10. Remove from the oven and while still hot apply the syrup to the sides and center covering the entire galopita. Use all the syrup.
11. Set the pan to the side to cool and absorb the syrup.
12. Cut the pieces into diamond size and garnish with sprinkled cinnamon and, if you would like, a maraschino cherry.

NOTES:
1. This is a different form of custard making. The flavours may be changed by substituting the vanilla bean with a cinnamon stick. You may also want to use vanilla extract.
2. The syrup is a must and cannot be omitted.
3. You may top this with a warm fruit preserve or powdered sugar.

KADDAFI EKMEK

PHYLO
1 lb. Kaddafi dough
2 st. unsalted butter
¼ lb. pecans, walnuts or almonds

SYRUP
2 cups sugar
1 thin sliced orange or lemon
1 cup water
1 cinnamon stick

CUSTARD
1 cup whole milk
1 st. unsalted butter
1" piece of vanilla bean or 1 tablespoon of vanilla extract
1 cup sugar
5-6 eggs

WHIPPED CREAM
1 pt. whipping cream
2-3 teaspoons powder sugar

Place 1 bowl in the freezer with the beaters to chill.

PREPARE PHYLO
1. Melt the butter in a skillet.
2. Add the nuts selected and sauté.
3. Spread the phylo in the appropriate greased cake pan or cupcake pan you wish to use.
4. Spread the sautéed nuts over the phylo.
5. With a spoon, sprinkle the melted butter over the phylo.
6. Bake the phylo until golden at 300 °F.
7. While the phylo is baking prepare the syrup.

PREPARE SYRUP – PREPARE THE SYRUP WHILE THE PHYLO IS BAKING
1. In a sauce pot combine the water, sugar, fruit slices, and cinnamon stick and bring it to a boil.
2. Boil the syrup until it is reduced and thickens slightly.
3. The syrup is ready when there is a distinct color change and water scent.
4. Using a small ladle, pour the syrup over the phylo removed from the oven, while it is still warm. Pour enough syrup to cover the entire phylo. **DO NOT ADD TOO MUCH SYRUP – REFER TO NOTES.**
5. Allow the phylo to cool and absorb the syrup.

PREPARE CUSTARD
1. Beat the eggs until thoroughly combined; and set it aside.
2. In a medium size pot, heat the butter until totally melted; do not brown.
3. Add the sugar and stir combining the two ingredients.
4. Add the vanilla and continue stirring.
5. Add the milk and stir over medium heat.
6. When the milk has totally combined with the ingredients start adding the eggs.
7. The key to this recipe is the beating and the heat. If you stop stirring, the custard will curdle. If you raise the heat too high, the custard will curdle. If the heat is too low, the custard will not thicken. If you have a handheld beater that can be used by a stove that is preferred.
8. Beat the heated mixture until thickened.
9. Remove the custard from the heat and allow it to cool.

PREPARE WHIP CREAM
1. Remove the bowl and beaters from the freezer.
2. Place the beaters in the beater and place the whipping cream in the container with 2-3 tablespoons of sugar.
3. Beat the contents until the whipped cream is formed.

CONSTRUCTION
1. By now the syrup is absorbed by the phylo.
2. If you are using a baking pan:
   a. Take a large dish and place it over the top of the baking pan.
   b. Holding firmly, flip the pan and dish over. Now the dish is on the bottom and pan on top.
   c. Remove the pan and place your serving dish over the golden kataifi.

     d.   Again holding firmly, but not crushing the phylo, flip the kataifi a second time exposing the nut topping.

     e.   Whatever nuts remain on the first dish should be reapplied to the phylo using a spatula.

3. If you are using a cupcake pan:
     a.   You may use a fork to remove the baked phylo
     b.   Place the phylo in cupcake foils
4. Take a spoon and place the custard over the phylo, be generous.
5. Take the whipped cream and spread generously over the custard.
6. Serve chilled.

NOTES:

1. Make your custard always from scratch. Greek pastry chefs are known for their custard. To use box pudding or any other substitute is an insult to your guests and to the tradition of the recipe. Custard takes practice, but once learned, your recipe will be popular.

2. **Too Much Syrup,** be careful to spoon only the amount of syrup you need when the kataifi is removed from the oven. I usually gauge halfway up the pan. If you add too much syrup your phylo will be a soggy mush and not reflect the crispy light phylo with the complement of the custard and whipping cream.

3. If someone in your party is allergic to nuts, substitute fruit for the nuts; consider strawberries, cherries, blueberries, etc. Sauté the fruit the same method as you have the nuts and add one tablespoon of sugar.

Chapter 14: Cookies

INGREDIENTS
DOUGH
4 cups olive oil
1 cup confectioners' sugar
½ cup brandy or amaretto
Juice from 1 orange
3-4 cups cake flour or fine semolina
3-4 teaspoons baking powder
½ teaspoon baking soda
½ teaspoon ground cloves and nutmeg
1 tablespoon cinnamon
Grated rind from 1 orange

FILLING
1 cup walnuts, chopped
½ teaspoon cinnamon
Rind from ½ orange

TOPPING
Ground walnuts
Cinnamon

Honey Syrup Recipe

1. Whip the olive oil with the sugar until creamy. This is a lengthy processes, about 10 to 15 minutes at a high pace.
2. Juice your orange.

. Add the orange juice and continue beating.
. Add the brandy, baking soda, rind and spices and continue beating.
. In a separate bowl, add the flour and baking powder.
. Slowly add the flour to the orange mixture and continue beating.
. Stop when the beating becomes difficult.
. Turn the dough out onto a floured surface and knead until it becomes soft, elastic, and the dough no longer sticks to your hands.
. Wrap the dough in a plastic wrap and allow it to settle.
10. While the dough is settling combine the orange rind with cinnamon and the chopped walnuts. Set this mixture aside.
11. Prepare the syrup and have it ready for the cooled cookies.
12. Grind about 5 walnuts and combine them with cinnamon and have this ready for after the cookies have been dipped in the syrup and placed in foil tins.
13. Place parchment on the cookie sheet and grease.
14. Remove the dough from the plastic wrap. Knead slightly.
15. Take an amount of dough that is about walnut size.
16. Form the dough into an oval and flatten.
17. Place ¼ of a teaspoon of the mixture from Step 10 lengthwise, down the center of the flattened oval.
18. Gently bring the sides of the oval cookie shape together encasing the cinnamon nut mixture.
19. Place the formed cookie on the cookie sheet with the seam side down.
20. Once you have finished forming all the cookies, bake them for about 15 minutes at 325°F.
21. When you remove the cookies from the oven, let them sit until they are cool - about 2 hours.
22. Heat the syrup. You don't want it boiling – just warm.
23. Using a slotted spoon, dip one or two cookies at a time and place them on a clean cookie sheet.
24. Take the ground walnuts and cinnamon that you prepared in Step 12 and sprinkle over all the cookies once they are bathed in syrup.

NOTES:

. The great debate among many Greek bakers is whether their cookie is a Phiniki or Melomakarono. What is the difference? Initially the cookie was introduced by the Phoenicians to the Greek culture. The Phenikia are originally made with semolina and olive oil. As time progressed and alternative products were made available, the Phiniki evolved to a Melomakarono. The Melomakarono was made with flour and sweet cream butter. The question is, which is better? I witnessed the making of the Phiniki in my early education and truly was amazed. First, that olive oil could be whipped to a creamy consistency. Secondly, that a cookie with olive oil as its base could be so good. Each baker develops their own secret recipe, in some instances combining both techniques, which is not surprising. Upon comparison, the cookie made with olive oil and semolina is not as crispy as that made of butter and flour. My recipe above prefers the cake flour instead of the semolina. This is a texture preference.
2. Fresh orange juice is a must, no imitations are accepted. If you do not have a juicer. Cut the orange in half and use a fork. Just remember to extract the seeds before using the juice. The pulp is used as well.

3. Do not over-knead; this could toughen the cookie.

AMIGTHALOTA

(Non-baked almond cookies)

INGREDIENTS
1 pound blanched almonds
2 ½ cups sugar
Rosewater or rose oil
10 ounces water
1 pound powdered sugar
1 whole clove for each piece

1. If your almonds are not already blanched, do so by dipping them in boiling water for a few seconds and then placing them in cold water. Work each almond until the brown skin is removed.
2. Place the almonds in a food processor and grind them finely.
3. Place the almonds in the pot with water, 2 tablespoons of rosewater and the sugar. Heat slowly on low, while stirring the mixture with a wooden spoon.
4. Continue to stir until the mixture comes away from the sides of the pan.
5. Let cool.
6. Put some rosewater or rose oil on your hands.
7. Place parchment paper on a cookie sheet.
8. Take a small portion of the cooled mixture and mold it into a pear shape.
9. Set the pear-shaped cookie on the parchment.
10. Sprinkle lightly with powdered sugar and a clove on top to resemble a pear.

NOTES:
1. This was one of my mother's favorite cookies. They took a little work but they were worth the time and effort.
2. My mother would incorporate rose oil in her pastries whenever she could get some from Greece. Rose oil is a concentrated form and you need just a few drops, 2 or 3 at most, for a recipe whether it was cookies or Galactobouriko. This is an acquired taste, but I was told as a young girl that it was used by my father's mother and grandmother in their baking traditions and that its incorporation into a recipe was a sign of a highly sophisticated baker.
3. Rose oil may be purchased at specialty, baking or health food stores.
4. Rose water is simpler to find, though the scent is much lighter and the flavor is not as intense.

KOULOURAKIA

INGREDIENTS
1 pound unsalted butter
2 cups granulated sugar

186

3 eggs + 4 egg yolks
½ cup cognac, mastica or whiskey
1 teaspoon vanilla
1 1/2 tablespoons baking powder
6-7 cups of flour
½ cup cream
¼ cup of oil
Sesame seeds are optional

1. Leave your butter out to soften the night before.
2. Separate your 4 eggs placing the yolks in a bowl. Place the whites in the bowl with the 3 whole eggs. Set the 4 yolks aside to use later.
3. Using an electric mixer, cream butter until fluffy.
4. Beat the yolk and whites with a fork combining them thoroughly.
5. Gradually start adding the sugar, beaten eggs, liqueur, vanilla and finally the cream.
6. Place 5 cups of flour into the sifter along with the 5 teaspoons of baking powder.
7. Combine the ingredients in the bowl with the sifted flour using your hand.
8. Make sure the powder is evenly distributed and before sifting more.
9. Continue adding more flour until the dough no longer sticks to your hands or the bowl.
10. Let the dough rest.
11. Place parchment on a cookie sheet.
12. Lightly beat the 4 egg yolks.
13. Add 1 tablespoon of the liqueur or flavoring combination and set aside.
14. Divide the dough into walnut-sized balls.
15. Place the ¼ cup of oil close to where you are rolling out the cookies. Place some oil on your hands to grease them.
16. Roll the balls of dough into long ropes. Take care not to put too much pressure on the dough or make the rope too long. This will result in the dough cracking. Try keeping the dough about 5" long.
17. Fold the rope in half and twist to form the braid.
18. Or bring the two ends together to form a circle.
19. Or lay the rope before you and gently work the rope into a spiral forming an "S".
20. Place the formed cookies onto the cookie sheet.
21. Once all the cookies are formed, take a pastry brush and lightly coat the cookies with the egg yolk mixture.
22. Bake at 325°F until golden brown.
23. Remove the cookies from the oven, cool and enjoy.

NOTES:
1. Try not to continually open the oven to gaze on the cookie status. It may cause cracking.
2. My mother was a stickler for organic ingredients and liqueurs. She was absolutely right.

3. The Koulourakia used to be made only for the Easter and Great Lent depending on the ingredients, of course. The Lenten cookies were sans the rich ingredients, but they were still great. The various shapes these cookies were made into represented eternal life in our Lord. Today, these cookies are made throughout the year, except during fasting periods, because so many individuals and children love them.
4. The recipe above is one way of making this cookie - my mother's way. There exist about 40 more flavors and alternate recipes for this cookie! Talk about being popular.
5. The use of oil on the hands helps to gloss the cookies as they are being formed. Whatever oil you select is fine.

MELOMAKARONA

INGREDIENTS
DOUGH
1 pound unsalted butter
1/3 cup confectioners' sugar
½ cup brandy or amaretto
Juice from 1 orange
3 - 4 cups cake flour
3 - 4 teaspoons baking powder
¼ teaspoon baking soda
½ teaspoon ground cloves, cinnamon and nutmeg
Grated rind from 1 orange

FILLING
1 cup walnuts, chopped
½ teaspoon cinnamon
Rind from ½ orange

TOPPING
Ground walnuts
Cinnamon

Honey Syrup Recipe

1. Allow the butter to soften to room temperature.
2. Beat the butter and sugar together until creamy.
3. Juice your orange.
4. Add the orange juice to butter and sugar and continue beating.
5. Add the brandy, baking soda and spices and continue beating.
6. In a separate bowl, combine the flour and baking powder.
7. Slowly add the flour to the orange mixture and continue beating.
8. Continue until beating becomes difficult.
9. Turn the dough out onto a floured surface and knead until it becomes soft, elastic and the dough no longer sticks to your hands.
10. Wrap the dough in a plastic wrap and allow it to settle.

11. While the dough is settling, combine the orange rind with cinnamon and the chopped walnuts. Set this mixture aside.
12. Prepare the syrup and have it ready for the cooled cookies.
13. Grind about 5 walnuts and combine them with cinnamon. Have this ready for after the cookies have been dipped in the syrup and placed in foil tins.
14. Place parchment on the cookie sheet and grease.
15. Remove the dough from the plastic wrap and knead.
16. Take an amount of dough that is about walnut size.
17. Form the dough into an oval and flatten.
18. Place ¼ teaspoon of the mixture in Step 11 lengthwise, down the center of the flattened oval.
19. Gently bring the sides of the oval cookie shape together encasing the cinnamon nut mixture.
20. Place the formed cookie on the cookie sheet.
21. Once you have finished forming all the cookies, bake the cookies for about 15 minutes at 325°F.
22. When you remove the cookies from the oven let them sit until they are cool - about 2 hours.
23. Heat the syrup. You don't want it boiling - just warm.
24. Using a slotted spoon, dip one or two cookies at a time and place them on a clean cookie sheet.
25. Take the ground walnuts and cinnamon that you prepared in Step 13 and sprinkle over all the cookies once they are bathed in syrup.

NOTES:
1. The great debate among many Greek bakers is whether their cookie is a Phiniki or Melomakarono. What is the difference? Initially the cookie was introduced by the Phoenicians to the Greek culture. The Phenikia are originally made with semolina and olive oil. As time progressed and alternative products were made available, the Phiniki evolved to a Melomakarono. The Melomakarono was made with flour and sweet cream butter. The question is, which is better? I witnessed the making of the Phiniki in my early education and truly was amazed. First, that olive oil could be whipped to a creamy consistency. Secondly, that a cookie with olive oil as its base could be so good. Each baker develops their own secret recipe, in some instances combining both techniques, which is not surprising. Upon comparison the cookie made with olive oil and semolina is not as crispy as that made of butter and flour. My recipe above prefers the cake flour instead of the semolina. This is a texture preference.
2. It is funny how our memories take us back in time just by the scent of a cookie. This particular recipe was always made in November, a week before Thanksgiving, and repeated for Christmas. You knew the time of the year not by the shows on the TV or music being played but by the fragrance that permeated the home - the smell of holiday cookies. This was the cookie that made us all try to snatch a piece and not get caught by my mother's eagle eyes. I truly believe that my mother knew how successful the recipe was by how many cookies were stolen.
3. Fresh orange juice is a must. No imitations are accepted. If you do not have a juicer, cut the orange in half and use a fork. Just remember to extract the seeds before using the juice. The pulp is used as well.

4. The butter must be softened. Take the butter out the night before or just before you leave for work. The soft consistency of the butter allows for equal disbursement of sugar and flavors in the cookie itself.

MOTHER'S KOURAMBIETHES

INGREDIENTS
2 egg yolks
8 ounces mastica, whiskey, brandy or amaretto
1 pound unsalted butter
3 - 4 cups cake flour
1 tablespoon vanilla
½ cup ground walnuts (optional)
3 - 4 teaspoons baking powder
2 ½ - 3 cups powdered sugar
Rosewater

1. Allow your butter to soften at room temperature. Take it out of the refrigerator at least 6 to 8 hours before use.
2. Place the butter in the bowl and beat it at high rate until creamy.
3. Slowly add the 1 cup of the powdered sugar, the liqueur selected, the vanilla and the egg yolks.
4. Blend the ingredients until smooth.
5. Add the ground walnuts to the batter.
6. Combine the flour with the baking soda, and, using a sifter, slowly add the flour mixture to the batter while continually beating on a medium setting.
7. When the batter starts taking on a dough consistency, remove the beaters. Remove the excess dough from the beaters.
8. Continue adding the flour and knead it into the dough.
9. When the dough ceases sticking on your hands, you have added a sufficient amount of flour.
10. Place parchment on a cookie sheet and grease.
11. Take about 1 tablespoon of dough and form it into a pear or ball shape. Place on a greased sheet.
12. Bake the cookies at 325°F until golden. The bottoms of the cookie should be a golden color.
13. Remove the cookies from the oven.
14. Place the cookies on a clean cookie sheet to cool.
15. Using an atomizer filled with rosewater, lightly spray the cookies.
16. Place the cookies in small cookie cups.
17. Place the powdered sugar in the sifter and bury the cookies in sugar.

NOTES:
1. Shaved walnuts are an optional ingredient.
2. Rosewater is an optional ingredient.
3. A family member, affectionately called Grandma Katerina Secaras, used to place a small piece of dark chocolate in the center of the cookie and encase it in dough as she made

her balls. The balls were baked and the chocolate melted inside and made a rich center. The cookies were wonderful.

4.   My mother sometimes cracked walnuts and placed them in the center of her balls for more texture and taste.

PAXIMADIA 1

INGREDIENTS
6 sticks of unsalted butter, softened
1/2 cup walnut, corn, peanut, coconut or any other oil
3 cups of sugar
6 eggs
1/2 teaspoon baking soda
1/2 cup whole milk or whipping cream
2 teaspoons cinnamon (to your taste)
Dash of allspice
8-10 cups of flour
1 teaspoon baking powder for each cup of flour
Rind from one orange (optional)

1.   Cream butter, oil and sugar together.
2.   Dissolve baking soda in milk and add to the butter mixture.
3.   Continue beating while adding one egg at a time.
4.   Add the cinnamon and allspice and continue to beat.
5.   Add rind and continue to beat.
6.   Add the flour one cup at a time with the teaspoon of baking powder
7.   When the dough thickens and become difficult to beat, remove it from the beater and begin to knead by hand.
8.   The dough is ready when it stops sticking to your hand. Be careful not to add too much flour. This is a slow process and you want to get just the right amount of flour to make the cookie correctly.
9.   When the dough is ready, form logs 3" or 4" wide and however long the log is - probably the size of your cookie sheet.
10. Bake at 350° F until lightly brown (325° F in a convection oven - light fan). Remove the cookie sheet from the oven.
11. Slice the logs while still hot. Use a sharp knife and have a bowl of water to the side to dip your knife and assist in the cutting process.
12. Rearrange the cut pieces on the baking sheet and bake until crispy but not burned.

NOTES:
1.   Paximadia maybe either a cookie or toasted bread.
2.   Traditionally this cookie was a memorial cookie, served primarily at wakes and memorials. Almost overnight the cookie gained a dramatic change in popularity. Now it is available in a variety of flavors.

3. Have fun adding chocolate chips, nuts, dried fruit or raisins. Be creative.
4. Liqueurs and brandy are great additions, just balance with flour and baking powder

PAXIMADIA 2

INGREDIENTS
6 sticks of unsalted butter, softened
1/2 cup walnut, corn, peanut, coconut or any other oil
3 cups of sugar
6 eggs
1 cup mastica, brandy or your favorite liqueur
1/2 teaspoon baking soda
1/2 cup whole milk or whipping cream
4 teaspoons cinnamon (to your taste)
1 teaspoon allspice, nutmeg
Pinch of clove
8 -10 cups of flour
1 teaspoon baking powder for each cup of flour
Rind from one orange or lemon (optional)

1. Cream butter, oil and sugar together.
2. Dissolve baking soda in milk and add to the butter mixture.
3. Continue beating while adding one egg at a time.
4. Add the cinnamon, nutmeg, allspice and clove and continue to beat.
5. Add rind and continue to beat.
6. Add the brandy or flavoring selection and continue to beat.
7. Add the flour one cup at a time with the teaspoon of baking powder
8. When the dough thickens and become difficult to beat, remove it from the beater and begin to knead by hand.
9. The dough is ready when it stops sticking to your hand. Be careful not to add too much flour. This is a slow process and you want to get just the right amount of flour to make the cookie correctly and not too dry.
10. Place the baking parchment on the cookie sheet.
11. Form the dough into logs 3" or 4" wide and however long the log is - probably the size of your cookie sheet.
12. Bake at 350° F until lightly brown. Remove the cookie sheet from the oven. It is important to take this cookie out just before it is ready.
13. Slice the logs while still hot. Use a sharp knife and have a bowl of water to the side to dip your knife between cuts. The water helps the cutting of the loaf.
14. Rearrange the cut pieces on the baking sheet and bake until crispy and slightly hard but not burned. The cookies will harden as they cool.

NOTES:
1. Paximadia may be either a cookie or toasted bread.
2. Baking parchment is a great tool, cutting down on cleanup.
3. Though it is not necessary, I like spraying some oil on the parchment.

4. Traditionally this cookie was a memorial cookie, served primarily at wakes and memorials. Almost overnight the cookie gained a dramatic change in popularity. Now it is available in a variety of flavors.
5. Have fun adding chocolate chips, nuts, dried fruit or raisins. Be creative.
6. Liqueurs and brandy are great additions - just balance with flour and baking powder

Chapter 15: Desserts

VASILOPITA CAKE RECIPE

<u>INGREDIENTS</u>
5 eggs
2 sticks unsalted butter
1½ cups sugar
Zest from 1 orange and 1 lemon
¼ cup orange juice
¼ cup orange water or 1 tablespoon orange emulsion or extract
4-5 cups cake flour
3 teaspoons baking powder
½ teaspoon salt
¼ cup honey
1 stick of butter
2 cups powdered or confectioners' sugar
1 teaspoon milk
1 coin wrapped in aluminum
Cloves (whole) for decoration

1. Soften the butter by leaving it out at room temperature for a few hours before you bake.
2. Chill mixer beaters and a large glass or metal bowl for a few minutes.
3. Separate the egg whites from the yolks.
4. Place the whites in the chilled bowl first and beat the egg whites until stiff. Add the egg yolks and beat until creamy.
5. Add the butter and sugar to the egg mixture and beat for 5 minutes.
6. Add the orange rind and continue to beat.
7. Add the orange juice and water.
8. In a smaller bowl, stir the baking powder and the salt into the flour.

9. Sift the flour mixture into the egg mixture.
10. Have some extra flour handy. If the batter is too loose, add 1 tablespoon of flour at a time. The batter needs to be soft and glossy but not sticky.
11. Place the batter in a 10-inch round spring form pan.
12. Tuck the coin into the center of the batter and push down to make sure the coin is embedded in the batter.
13. Preheat oven to 325°F degrees.
14. Use the whole cloves to make a design.
15. Brush the entire Vasilopita with orange water and honey.
16. Bake for 45–60 minutes, or until the dough separates from the sides of the pan.
17. While the cake bakes, make a fondant decoration:
    a. Soften (do not melt) 1 stick of butter until it can be easily molded in your hand.
    b. Use a fork to combine the butter with 1 cup of confectioners' sugar until it forms dough. If the butter is not workable, add a few drops of milk. If it is too loose, add sugar.
    c. Place the butter and sugar mixture over the form you selected or create a form for the New Year - for example a star or the four numbers representing the year.
    d. Press it in so that it fills all of the crevices if using a form or create the forms you want and lay them on wax paper.
    e. Paint the form with gel food coloring or leave as is.
    f. Store the form in the refrigerator until the cake has cooled completely.
    g. Set the form in the center of the cake.
    h. Outline with cloves.

NOTES:
1. Remember not to over-knead or beat your batter. You do not want your cake to be too tight.
2. Do not keep opening the oven to check on the baking. That forms cracks on your cake. Open the oven about 5 minutes before the allotted time. Use a toothpick or cake tester to judge the baking of the cake.
3. The fondant is not necessary, but it is a fun activity for children or adults in decorating the cake.
4. Make sure you grease and flour your pan before laying the batter. Always use a circular pan.
5. Do not forget to cover the coin with aluminum foil. Even though you clean the coin, you want to keep any germs or reaction the metal might make with the batter as it is baking.

Greek Apple Pie
INGREDIENTS
2-3 large apples
½ cup chopped walnuts
2 tablespoons ground cinnamon
1 sheet of puff pastry
8 tablespoons unsalted butter

½ cup raisins
4 ounces brandy
½ cup powdered sugar (optional)
9" pie pan, buttered

1. Remove one of the sheets of puff pastry from the box. Using a rolling pin, work the pastry sheet with the roller in all directions enlarging the sheet. Do not try to make it even.
2. Lightly fold the sheet into a quarter of the size to make it manageable. Lay the corner of the pastry sheet in the center of the pan and unfold the sheet leaving the pastry sheet hanging over the sides of the pan. Set the pan aside.
3. Melt the butter in a skillet. Add the raisins, cinnamon and walnuts and sauté until the nuts glisten.
4. Add the powdered sugar, continue to stir.
5. Add the brandy and stir for a minute. Remove the skillet from the flame and set it aside.
6. Cut the apples into wedges and hull. I prefer, for this recipe, to keep the peel on, but if you like you may peel the apples.
7. Arrange your apples artistically on the pastry sheet. The appearance of the apples is important, so lay the wedges carefully.
8. Take the glazed nuts and raisins and drizzle the mixture over the apples. Make sure the butter and nuts cover all the apples sections. Keep some butter in the pan for basting the pastry.
9. Now, in a carefree manner fold over the sides. It is acceptable to have the shell just fall on the apple sections. Baste with the remaining butter.
10. Bake at 325°F until golden.

NOTES:
1. A great many people believe that a recipe must be difficult if it is artistic. That is incorrect. This is a simple recipe and gives you the same flavors as the original. The only difference is that it's easy and beautiful.
2. The phylo recipe number 4 is perfect if you wish to make your own pastry leaf.

CHOCOLATE CHERRY HALVAH

Halva
1 cup farina or semolina
¼ cup butter or vegetable oil
Dark chocolate (If a bar, freeze prior to use; if powder, use as is)
¼ teaspoon cinnamon

Syrup
Cherry preserves
2 cups sugar
1 cups water

Syrup
1. Remove cherries from the preserve and set them aside.
2. Combine sugar, water and the preserve syrup in a pot and bring to a boil.

Halva

3. Grate the dark chocolate.
4. Create 2 cups of your selected syrup.
5. In a separate skillet, melt butter and add farina.
6. While stirring with a wooden spoon, brown farina over medium heat.
7. As it is browning, sprinkle some cinnamon and grated chocolate on the farina.
8. When farina has begun to brown, add all the syrup and stir until thick over low-medium heat.
9. Serve warm or cold with a sprinkle of cinnamon.

NOTES:

1. This has to be the easiest of all the deserts and the quickest to make when you have unexpected guests.
2. The chocolate and cherry is a modification of the original recipe. You may create your own modification once you have mastered the technique of making this recipe.
3. Sweetriots© makes a wonderful array of dark chocolate nibs (small pieces) that are perfect for this recipe. The flavors of the nibs are wonderful and give you a great selection of flavor.

CONTINENTAL BAKED PEARS

INGREDIENTS

1 package of puff pastry
2 pears, halved, cored and sliced thinly
Powdered sugar
1 egg yolk, beaten
1 cup chopped nuts
¼ pound unsalted butter
8 ounces brandy or liqueur
Mint (optional for decoration)

1. Thaw the puff pastry.
2. Roll the dough out to a circular shape and about 1/4" thickness.
3. Lay the pastry in a baking dish or pie dish. Do not be concerned with the sides hanging out of the pan.
4. Melt ¼ pound unsalted butter with the powdered sugar, allspice and nuts.
5. Sauté the nuts for about 5 minutes on a low flame.
6. Remove the pot from the heat and add brandy
7. Using a spoon, remove only the nuts from the butter mixture and place them on the pastry sheet.
8. Quarter, core and thinly slice your pears with their skins. Keep the skins on for color.
9. Arrange the pears in a circular formation; first clockwise then counterclockwise.
10. Sprinkle the nuts over the arranged pear slices.
11. Pour the brandy mixture over the pears, holding 1 teaspoon for the egg yolk.
12. Lift the edges of the puff pastry and drape over the pears, carelessly. Don't worry about covering all of the pears, just drape.
13. Beat the yolk with 1 teaspoon of brandy and brush onto the outside of the pie.

14. Bake at 400°F for 10 minutes; reduce to 300°F for the remaining 10 minutes.

NOTES:
1. A great many people believe that a recipe must be difficult if it is artistic. That is incorrect. This is a simple recipe and gives you the same flavors as the original. The only difference is that it's easy and beautiful.
2. The phylo recipe number 4 is perfect if you wish to make your own pastry leaf.
3. Sweetriots© makes a wonderful array of dark chocolate nibs (small pieces) that are perfect for this recipe. The flavors of the nibs are wonderful and give you a great selection of flavor.

ORANGE CRÈME CARAMELE

INGREDIENTS
1 cup sugar
1 cup orange water
6 eggs
3 oranges rind and fruit (slice fruit thinly)
1 cup powdered sugar
2 cups whole milk
½ cup whipping cream
Pinch of salt

1. Preheat your oven to 350°F.
2. Preheat a greased ramekin dish in the oven.
3. Rinse and chill a glass or metal bowl in the freezer.
4. Take a sauce pan and add about ½ cup of orange water, 1⁄3 of the orange rind and 1 cup of granulated sugar. Place it over a medium flame and stir until the sugar is dissolved.
5. Once the sugar is dissolved, raise you heat slightly and allow the sugar syrup to caramelize and turn a rich brown color.
6. When the rich brown color is reached, remove the dish from the oven and pour the sugar syrup in the ramekin dish. Make sure the syrup covers the entire bottom of the ramekin dish by tilting the dish in different directions until the dish is covered. Set the dish aside on a trivet.
7. Separate your egg whites and yolks.
8. Remove the chilled bowl from the freezer and proceed to beat the egg whites with a pinch of salt until stiff.
9. Once the egg whites are stiff, add the egg yolks and continue beating.
10. Add the powdered sugar, orange water and remaining rind and beat until thoroughly combined.
11. In a clean pot, heat the milk with the whipping cream until just before boiling. You will see the milk start to bubble and slightly run instead of coat the side of your pot.
12. Reduce the temperature slightly and add the egg mixture. Continue to beat the mixture over the flame. If you have a beater that can work well in a pot that is fine, otherwise a wooden spoon is acceptable.
13. Beat at a slow rate or stir until thickened.
14. Once thickened, set the pot aside to cool.
15. Take the thinly sliced orange and arrange slices in the ramekin dish so that your design lays on the caramelized sugar.
16. Pour the crème into the ramekin dish containing the orange design and caramelized sugar.
17. Place the ramekin dish in a deep roasting pan. Fill the pan halfway up the dish with water.

18. Bake for 20 minutes at 350°F.
19. Carefully remove the ramekin dish from the water-filled roaster.
20. Immediately place a serving plate over the dish.
21. Flip the dish over. Now the serving platter is holding the ramekin dish.
22. Quickly set the platter on the table and remove the ramekin before the caramelized sugar can set.
23. Garnish with mint and serve chilled or room temperature.

NOTES:
1. For the purposes of this recipe you may use small ramekin or soufflé dishes or one large soufflé dish.
2. Crème Caramele should not be confused with the French or Spanish Milk Flan. Though similar in appearance, the milk flan contains flour. Crème Caremele does not.
3. The addition of whipping crème adds richness to this recipe. It is optional and the recipe will work well with it omitted.
4. Sweetriots© makes a wonderful array of dark chocolate nibs (small pieces) that are perfect for this recipe. The flavors of the nibs are wonderful and give you a great selection of flavor.

GREEK ICE

INGREDIENTS
1 bottle of sweet wine Muscat, Pinot Grigio or Mavrodaphne
1 cup water
1 cup sugar
Gold flakes

1. In the pan combine all the above ingredients, making sure the sugar is dissolved.
2. Place the pan in the freezer and ice.
3. When the content is iced, use a metal spoon to scrape and place in the glasses for serving.

NOTES:
1. This is simple ice that many people find delightful and is very easy.
2. Try with brandy, ouzo or any other liqueur.
3. The sugar and water are important because without the water the ice will not form.
4. You may add gold flakes, fruit or any other items.

DADDY'S GREEK YOGURT

INGREDIENTS
½ gallon Vitamin D whole milk
5 tablespoons yogurt – Dannon plain Greek Yogurt (Cultured Grade A Milk)
1 candy thermometer
1 package of flour sack cloth
2 towels
2 bowls: 1 medium, 1 large
Floral wire

*IMPORTANT NOTE: In order for this recipe to work properly, you must use yogurt that has only Cultured Grade A Milk as its ingredient. If you use anything with an additive or containing other ingredients, your yogurt starter will curdle your milk!

1. In a heavy pot, bring the milk to just below a boil over a medium heat.
2. Remove the pot from the heat just when it reaches the boiling point – the milk shows the signs against the side of the pot. You see bubble activity to the side of the pot. You should avoid the formation of skin.
3. Remove 2 cups of milk and put in a bowl. Place the candy thermometer in the bowl to monitor the temperature of the milk.
4. Allow the milk to cool to about 120°F to 130°F.
5. Mix the 5 tablespoons of yogurt into the bowl of milk thoroughly until there are no lumps.
6. Add the starter to the pot and mix thoroughly.
7. Cover the pot with clean, lint-free towels, to keep the pot warm, and let it sit for 8-10 hours.
8. At the end of the 8-10 hours, lay the flour sack cloth as a single layer thick. Let the ends drape over sides of the bowl.
9. Place the activated thickened milk in the center of the flour sack. Bring the ends of the cloth together. Tie the ends together with the floral wire making sure the line is secure.
10. Tie the silver wire and suspend the yogurt over the small bowl for approximately 5 or more hours. The longer the yogurt is suspended the thicker it becomes. Gauge the fluid dispensed by the rate of drops descending from the bag, a minute or two between drops is perfect. The small bowl will collect the whey dispensed by the sack.
11. Remove the suspended bag from the hanging place and place the contents of the bag in a clean dry bowl and refrigerate.
12. Serve the yogurt chilled with raw honey and nuts (pecans and walnuts are preferred).

NOTES:
1. The whey may be used as a beverage and is considered very healthy by those in Asia Minor.
2. I have experimented with many varieties of plain Greek yogurt. All but Dannon had other additives and nutrients added to the basic recipe. Dannon All Natural® was the only brand that would work with this recipe.
3. If your scald the milk, the recipe will not work. The milk must be heated to approximately 150°F to 155°F.
4. From 1985 to the present this is the only recipe that was repeated continually. I would like to think that people want to take down each and every trick my father conveyed. I later discover, humorously, that it was not only the secrets they were trying to obtain, but the samples of yogurt! None of the students wanted jams or preserves for the yogurt, instead they asked for the traditional honey, ground nuts and cinnamon. The thick, creamy yogurt left everyone craving more and loving each spoonful.

HALVAH

INGREDIENTS
1 cup Farina or Semolina Extra Fine
1 stick butter
1 teaspoon Cinnamon

Select your Syrup

1. Create 2 cups of your selected syrup.
2. In a separate skillet, melt butter and add farina.
3. While stirring with a wooden spoon brown farina over medium heat.
4. As it is browning, sprinkle some cinnamon on the farina.
5. When farina has begun to brown, add all the syrup and stir over low-medium heat until thick.
6. Serve warm or cold with a sprinkle of cinnamon.

NOTES:
1. This has to be the easiest of all the deserts and the quickest to make when you have unexpected guests.
2. This is also the easiest recipe to modify.
3. Sweetriots© makes a wonderful array of dark chocolate nibs (small pieces) that are perfect for this recipe. The flavors of the nibs are wonderful and give you a great selection of flavor.

POACHED ORANGES IN SWEET WINE

INGREDIENTS
1 bottle sweet wine, preferably Mavrodaphne
2-3 cups sugar
5-6 oranges, tangelos, grapefruits or mandarin oranges, peeled
1 teaspoon lavender or rose blossoms (untreated used for cooking or tea only)
1 cup orange blossom honey

1. Pour the entire bottle of wine into a pot.
2. If you are using Mavrodaphne or another sweet wine such as a Muscat, use only 2 cups of sugar. Otherwise use the entire 3 cups. If the wine is too tart, the dessert might not have the sweetness needed.
3. Add the blossoms and heat the mixture slowly, stir until the sugar dissolves. Do not bring to a boil. Keep the heat on the range to a low medium.
4. Add the citrus fruit that is either whole or in slices.
5. Poach for 15 minutes at the slow heat. Try not to boil the mixture.
6. After 15 minutes remove the fruit from the pot and arrange on plates or a platter.
7. Add honey to the remaining liquid to form a syrup.
8. Drizzle generously over the arranged fruit.
9. You may serve warm or chilled.

NOTES:
1. This is a simple dessert that is presented elegantly.
2. Fruit is a popular dessert in Greece, especially during the summer months.
3. If you have a question about the wine you are using, sample it first before working with it in the recipe.
4. The syrup is optional, but does add a lot to the recipe.

Rizzogalo (Rice Pudding)

INGREDIENTS

1 cup Arborio rice
1" piece of vanilla bean
1 gallon vitamin D whole milk
1 pint whipping cream (optional)
3 eggs
1 stick unsalted butter
1 cinnamon stick
1 cup sugar

1. Beat the eggs together
2. In a large pot, add the gallon of milk, pint of whipping cream, rice, vanilla bean, butter and cinnamon stick.
3. Slowly heat the pot on low medium heat.
4. Using a wooden spoon, stir the content of the pot until the butter is melted.
5. Slowly add the egg and the sugar to the pot alternating and stirring continually until both are totally added.
6. Heat until thickened.
7. When the pudding is thickened enough, remove the pot from the heat and place it either in a large bowl or small serving bowls.
8. Allow the pudding to cool.
9. Place the pudding in the refrigerator until chilled.
10. Serve with sprinkled cinnamon.

NOTES:

1. This was my grandmother's recipe, and no doubt, had been passed down from generations before. My mother had to prepare the pudding while I was at school with my sister. Otherwise it barely made it to the refrigerator.
2. Warm or cold, this was a great recipe.
3. The use of the whipping cream is optional, but it does give it that rich taste it had back then when foods were natural.
4. This is also a special recipe in that it teaches us that not only sauces and syrups may be flavored, but milk as well. The vanilla bean and cinnamon stick add just enough flavor to make the pudding special.
5. The addition of allspice, nutmeg and clove, may be made if you use a half lemon cover and sew it shut. The extraction of the vanilla bean and spices is very important so as not to over-flavor the pudding.
6. Try not to scald the milk. The milk and the ingredients need time to mingle and flavor. The slow process ensures us of this outcome.

Sevasti's Apricot Turnovers

INGREDIENTS

8 ounces apricot gliko (preserves)
1 cup slivered almonds

½ cup light raisins
1 stick of unsalted butter

SPECIAL PASTRY DOUGH
2 tablespoons mastica
1 stick unsalted butter
8 ounces manouri cheese
2 cups flour
2 eggs
Dash of cinnamon and nutmeg

1. Take your butter out from the night before or at least 6 hours before baking.
2. Combine the softened butter with the manouri in a bowl, until a creamy mixture is formed.
3. Lightly beat the eggs and add it to the butter.
4. Add the spices and mastica liqueur and combine with a wooden spoon or blender until smooth.
5. On the clean surface of the table, place the flour making a well in the center of the mound.
6. Place the egg contents in the center and begin to knead them together.
7. Try to incorporate all the dough in the kneading process.
a. If the dough feels a little too dry, add ¼ teaspoon of mastica
b. If it feels too loose, add a little more flour.
8. Work with the dough until it feels elastic and not sticky. Try not to over-knead.
9. Wrap the dough entirely in a plastic wrap and place in the freezer overnight.
10. The next day thaw the dough.
11. Roll out small portions of the dough into circles.
12. Combine the preserves, almonds and light raisins. If the pieces of apricot are large, you may chop them down.
13. Melt the butter.
14. Place 1 tablespoon of the mixture into the center of the circle.
15. Baste the circumference of the circle with the butter.
16. Fold over the circle.
17. Using a fork, gently press the ends together sealing the apricot mixture within.
18. Place a parchment sheet on the cookie sheet and grease.
19. Place the folded turnover on the greased sheet.
20. Baste with butter.
21. Repeat steps 14 to 20 until all the preserve mixture is used.
22. Place the turnovers in the oven and bake at 330°F for about 20 to 30 minutes or until golden.

NOTES:
1. This was a wonderful Symian recipe I received from a great friend of mine, Angela Kyriakakis, belonging to her mother. A small Island tradition with big taste.
2. Do not limit this recipe to apricots. You may use other preserves such as apple, cherry, blueberry, strawberry, etc., all of which are found in Greece.
3. The glyko mentioned in the ingredients above is homemade preserve made in Greek homes with fruits and some vegetables like eggplant and zucchini. The glyko is used for guests being entertained in homes for the first time. A teaspoon containing a portion of the preserve is placed on a dish. It is customary to greet your new guests with this treat in the anticipation that their coming visits will be as sweet as their first. The preserve is also used with toast or other pastries.

I recall my father placing a tablespoon of the preserve in ice water and stirring vigorously, presenting me with fruity, sweetened water.

4. American preserves work just as well. Please check the ingredients and purchase preserves that are as close to natural as possible.

STUFFED BAKED APPLE

INGREDIENTS
6 apples - honey crisps, red or golden delicious, pink lady
1 cup honey
1 tablespoon cinnamon
1 teaspoon allspice and nutmeg
1 cup almond paste
1 tablespoon lavender
½ cup lemon juice
½ cup sliced almonds
1 stick of butter

1. Wash and core the apples, making sure that you do not cut through the bottom of the fruit.
2. Place the cored apples in a bowl with cold water and lemon juice.
3. Knead the almond paste with the sliced almonds and spices.
4. Divide the almond paste into 6 portions.
5. Melt the butter in melting pot with the lavender and honey.
6. Coat the interior of the apple with the butter.
7. Stuff each apple with a segment of the almond paste.
8. Set the apples in the roasting pan.
9. Coat the exterior of the apples with the honey.
10. Bake at 350°F for 40 minutes or until the apples are soft and the peel has a hard gloss color.
11. Serve warm with the syrup from the pan drizzled over each apple.

NOTES:
1. The peel of the apple makes a wonderful container for the fruit. First, it contains the apple fruit itself. Second, it contains the almonds and paste. Third the peel becomes crispy, not burned. It glosses and maintains the flavor of the fruit.
2. The lavender flowers enhance the scent of the fruit.

DAD'S STUFFED FIGS & DATES

INGREDIENTS
1 bag of whole figs or dates (pitted)
¼ pound feta cheese(optional)
1 teaspoon cinnamon
1 teaspoon allspice
¼ cup slivered almonds crushed
¼ cup dark chocolate morsels (optional)
¼ cup dark honey

1. Cut the fig or date on one side exposing the center of the fruit.
2. Crumble feta into a bowl.
3. Add the spices, almonds and chocolate and mix thoroughly.
4. Add the honey and continue to mix.
5. Fill the center of each fruit.
6. Place them on a parchment-covered cookie sheet.
7. Bake at 295°F for 15 minutes.
8. Remove and let cool. Enjoy.

NOTES:
1. On my father's island of Symi, there were no candy stores when he was young. His cookies and candy came from his home. They were made by his grandmother or mother. They were natural and homemade. When he took the time to reminisce, he always remarked how great his "homemade" candy was and he made a point of making it for me and my sister.
2. The feta is optional and is not essential to the recipe.
3. If someone is allergic to nuts, they may be remove and substituted with more feta and honey.
4. Dark chocolate is listed here because of the ease to purchase. Carob grew around my father's house and was incorporated in all his sweets.
5. Sweetriots© makes a wonderful array of dark chocolate nibs (small pieces) that are perfect for this recipe. The flavors of the nibs are wonderful and give you a great selection of flavor.

Printed in Great Britain
by Amazon